THE EXPANSION OF EUROPE

IN THE EIGHTEENTH CENTURY

BLANDFORD HISTORY SERIES
(General Editor R. W. Harris)

PROBLEMS OF HISTORY

HISTORY OF EUROPE SERIES

THE HISTORY OF ENGLAND SERIES

The Expansion of Europe in the Eighteenth Century overseas rivalry discovery and exploitation

GLYNDWR WILLIAMS

Lecturer in History,
Queen Mary College, London

WALKER AND COMPANY

New York

Printed and Bound in Great Britain

Contents

IV

THE COLONIAL EMPIRES IN AN AGE OF REVOLUTION
1763–1815

Acknowledgements

British Museum: Illustrations Nos. 1, 4, 5, 7, 8, 12, 13, 18, 31, 35, 36, 43, 44.

National Maritime Museum: Illustrations Nos. 2, 6, 9, 20, 21, 23, 24, 25, 32, 39, 40.

Hull Museums: Illustration No. 45.
Victoria & Albert Museum: Illustration No. 34.
R. B. Fleming & Co. Ltd.: Africa House, W.C.2. Illustration No. 33.

Radio Times Hulton Picture Library: Illustrations Nos. 3, 10, 11, 14, 15, 16, 17, 19, 26, 27, 28, 30, 37, 38, 41, 42.

No. 46: Photograph by Arthur Strong from cameo by Josiah Wedgwood.

List of Illustrations

LIST OF MAPS

Drawn by A. SPARK

Preface

ONE OF the most noteworthy features of European and American historiography during the last twenty years has been the increasing consciousness among scholars of 'the wider world'. African history, to take one example, has become an important field of study in its own right, not merely a segment of European colonial history. It must be said at the outset then that although the writer hopes he has taken into account some of the most significant recent research in the history of overseas regions the approach adopted in this book is deliberately Europocentric. No attempt has been made to write histories of the indigenous peoples with whom Europeans came into contact; the perspective is European rather than Asian, African or American. The book is a history of European enterprise in the eighteenth century, but enterprise outside the geographical confines of Europe whose bounds are still observed too respectfully by many history text-books. It has been written in the conviction that the overseas activities of European settlers, traders, missionaries, explorers and soldiers have been at least as important in the development of the modern world as the changes within Europe which monopolize the attention of most students at school and university.

Any subject as far-ranging as the expansion of Europe presents harassing problems of order and selection. The arrangement followed is neither wholly chronological nor wholly topical, but a combination of the two. Chapters are grouped into sections to emphasize the main themes of European expansion in the eighteenth century. After an introductory Section I which views the overseas empires at the beginning of the century, Section II, 'Contest for Empire in the West 1700–1763', examines the relentless struggle for dominance in

1

the western hemisphere between France, Spain and Britain. The motives behind imperial expansion are analysed at the beginning of this section, but its main purpose is to trace the gradual establishment of British supremacy in North America and the Caribbean. Section III, 'Widening Horizons 1740–1790', is concerned with European discovery and rivalry in parts of the world comparatively little known and exploited by Europeans before the eighteenth century: in particular India, China and the Pacific. Section IV, 'The Colonial Empires in an Age of Revolution 1763–1815', is centred around the effects of the American and French revolutions, momentous upheavals which in their different ways ushered in the modern period of colonial history. The fortunes of all the imperial powers are followed in some detail, but most attention is paid to the British empire, massively dominant at the end of the Napoleonic Wars despite the earlier setback of the loss of the American colonies.

The bibliography at the end of the volume is more than a guide to further reading; it is an acknowledgement of the writer's debt to the work of scholars from many different countries. More personal thanks are owed to Dr K. N. Chaudhuri, School of Oriental and African Studies, London, Dr Philip Haffenden, University of Southampton, and Dr Peter Marshall, King's College, London. Their scrutiny of parts of the book in typescript revealed various errors and misinterpretations; any which remain are of course the writer's responsibility.

G.W.

January 1966

Mona, Jamaica

I

INTRODUCTION

1

The Rival Empires

BY THE end of the seventeenth century European explorers, traders, settlers and missionaries had reached all quarters of the globe. The barriers of ignorance and fear which had hemmed in medieval Europe had long since disappeared. In a dramatic outburst of energy the maritime nations of Western Europe had taken full advantage of superior technical skills and military resources to dominate vast areas of the world. Great stretches of territory in the Americas had been explored and colonized, the coasts of Africa had been mapped, regular trade routes had been opened to India, China and the Eastern Seas. Despite the considerable gaps which still existed in Europe's knowledge of the wider world, an outline world map of 1700 resembled in most of its essential features one of today's maps.

Among the varied motives which sent Europeans exploring unknown seas and settling distant lands, the most potent was the economic one. Missionary zeal, intellectual curiosity and flight from persecution all played a part; but none was as universal a force as the hope of profit and better standards of living. The determination of individuals, companies and nations to enrich themselves by overseas trade and settlement was the mainspring of European expansion, and deeply affected the economies of the homelands. In Western Europe largely self-sufficient agricultural economies were replaced by far more complex structures, and although local European production and trade remained the dominant material factor, oceanic enterprise provided a vital stimulus. Treasure-fleets carrying silver and gold crossed the Atlantic from America; from the Caribbean islands and the plantation colonies of the mainland came tobacco, sugar, cotton and a wealth of other subtropical crops; East Indiamen brought back precious cargoes of spices, silks, drugs and dyes. Nor was this trade a one-way affair. Outward-bound ships carried European manufactures and supplies for the growing numbers of colonists settled overseas, and for the indigenous populations.

The overseas discoveries enriched and diversified the economic and intellectual life of Europe, but they also introduced new sources of tension and enmity. At the beginning of the seventeenth century only Spain and Portugal possessed overseas empires. In the course of the century Holland, England and France joined them as imperial powers. Given the twin circumstances of unremitting warfare between the nations of Europe, and the relentless competition for trade, conflict overseas could hardly be avoided; and one of the most striking features of European history in the eighteenth century was to be the widening of areas of international tension to include colonial possessions and trade. For much of the century, war between the great powers produced no significant boundary changes in Europe itself; but overseas small groups of rival Europeans were deciding the fate of continents. In terms of world history the activities of these men were infinitely more important than the manœuvring of massed armies on the continent of Europe. International rivalry was both a cause and a consequence of European overseas expansion in the eighteenth century, and warning symptoms of this can already be seen in the developing pattern of European imperialism before 1700.

The Spanish Empire

At the beginning of the eighteenth century Spain still possessed the most extensive empire of any European nation. Mainly acquired during the spectacular half-century of discovery, conquest and settlement which followed Columbus's first voyage in 1492, it was essentially an American empire. The largest Caribbean islands were Spanish: Cuba, Puerto Rico and most of Hispaniola. On the nearby mainland New Spain covered an area roughly corresponding to present-day Mexico, and Spanish garrisons kept a loose hold on Florida. South America was Spanish except for the Brazilian shoulder and part of modern Uruguay (Portuguese), and strips of Dutch and French territory along the Guiana coast. Across the Pacific the Philippines were under Spanish rule, and the great ocean itself was officially regarded as a Spanish lake where other Europeans trespassed at their peril.

Although this expansion owed much to the individual initiative and fortitude of the early *conquistadores*, the territories acquired by Cortés, Pizarro and other adventurers were soon brought firmly under royal control. The Spanish monarch, absolute ruler at home, was determined to maintain full authority over his subjects in the new overseas possessions. These territories were simply treated as part of the royal domain, ruled on the King's behalf by powerful Viceroys. Central America was governed by the Viceroy of New Spain from Mexico City. South America, from the Panama Isthmus to Cape Horn, came under the jurisdiction of the Viceroy of Peru at Lima. The Viceroys were impressive dignitaries who lived in a style many European monarchs would have envied. The scope of their authority ranged over Indian affairs, defence, ecclesiastical matters, and not least the production and shipping home of the silver of Potosí and the gold of New Spain.

Despite the geographical extent and administrative comprehensiveness of the Viceroys' authority, good care was taken to ensure that they did not become 'overmighty subjects' who might be tempted to aim at independence. They were invariably chosen from the Spanish nobility, whose loyalty was unquestioned. Once appointed, their powers were limited by *audiencias*, legal councils whose members served as advisers but who could communicate direct with the sovereign. The Viceroys were also subject to the conscientious, if distant, watch which the Council of the Indies in Madrid kept on the King's overseas possessions, and which was given practical effect by the *residencia*, a review of a Viceroy's administration which was carried out at the end of his term of office.

Lower down the administrative scale was a proliferation of subdivisions, from captaincies-general (areas often the size of a modern South American republic) to municipalities. In an age of slow sea and land communications this elaborate system based on Madrid could not be expected to produce swift decisions. Local initiative was usually frowned upon, a fact well appreciated by the Viceroy who hinted at the secret of his long and pleasantly uneventful term of office with the words: 'Do little, and do that slowly.' When the unprecedented problems and distances with which the Spanish government had to cope are taken into account, then it must be said that the administrative machine for long worked surprisingly well. For all the abuses, scandals and instances of gross inefficiency, there was tighter control over the empire than might have been expected from the size of the areas to be administered. Not until the late seventeenth century, when the vigour and power of the mother country declined in alarming fashion, did the laxity long evident in parts of Spanish colonial administration reach proportions which threatened the future of the whole empire.

Side by side with this governmental structure rose an ecclesiastical one, for Franciscan and Dominican missionary friars had reached the Indies hard on the heels of the early explorers and soldiers, and they in turn had been followed by secular clerics. In the settled areas the familiar system of see and benefice, bishop and priest, was soon established. At one level the Archbishop spoke on equal terms with the Viceroy; at another the local church and priest dominated the life of the surrounding community. Away on the frontiers the friars, soon joined by the Jesuits, spear-headed the advance of European influence. They worked devotedly among the Indian tribes, teaching and training them, and everywhere setting up the little mission stations which often represented the farthest point of Spanish settlement. The Spanish Church in colonial America is open to criticism on a number of issues, but in general its achievement was an impressive one. It accompanied the King's subjects to the New World without doubt or hesitation, and it brought millions of new converts to the Christian faith.

The presence of the Church had an important ameliorating effect on the fate of the large Indian population of Spanish America. Contrary to the assertions of Protestant propagandists of the period, most Indians under Spanish rule were, after the excesses of the *conquistadores*, treated with a degree of moderation. But they never lost their character as a subject people. Their function was to work the huge estates and mines granted by the Crown to the nobility and clergy. For the most part docile and apathetic, the Indians formed a population of exploitation, a serf class, under the ruling caste of Spaniards. Beneath them lay only the Negro slaves brought across the Atlantic to work on the plantations. These enjoyed a measure of legal protection (certainly not granted to slaves in the English plantation colonies), but the large number which ran away to form outlaw communities indicates ill-treatment on a considerable scale. The plentiful supply of land and labour resulted in an economic system of large estates similar in some ways to the English and French plantations in the Caribbean and southern parts of the North American mainland, but totally different from the vigorous farming and trading settlements farther north.

The racial and social composition of the Spanish American colonies produced strains and tensions which official policy increased rather than lessened. Intermarriage and miscegenation between Europeans, Indians and Negroes resulted in a mixed society of stupefying complexity, with subtle but important differences of status existing between hardly distinguishable colour shades. As though the distinctions between mulattoes (mixture of European and Negro), mestizos (European and Indian), and zambos (Indian and Negro) – with all their variations – were not enough, there was a fundamental division among the Spaniards themselves. This was between those born in America, the creoles, and those born in Europe, the *peninsulares*. The best posts in State and Church were normally reserved for Spanish-born whites, and this discrimination led to bitter feelings of hostility and inferiority among the creoles. By the end of the seventeenth century a dangerous gulf had opened between the creoles and the Spanish-born officials who formed the governing class. Both creoles and mestizos resented the social discrimination and political inequality of the Spanish colonial system, and their alienation boded ill for the future of Spanish rule in America.

From an economic point of view the Spanish empire long remained the envy of Europe. The magnificent churches and public buildings of the cities were visible evidence of the wealth accumulating in Spanish hands. From the plantations of Cuba to the grassy pampas of Argentina stretched great tracts of productive land. Exports of sugar, cotton, tobacco, hides and dye-woods probably exceeded in value even the vast quantities of precious metal shipped to Europe. But it was the latter which caught the attention of Europe. 'The wealth of the Indies', as far as the popular imagination was concerned, lay in the holds of the treasure-fleets which crossed the Atlantic year after year. The long-term disadvantages which stemmed from an influx of gold and silver unaccompanied by an equivalent rise in Spain's productive capacity went generally unrecognized; and hopes of finding precious metals spurred other European nations into sending explorers and settlers to the New World.

From the beginning the Spanish government determined to keep the immensely lucrative trade of its overseas empire in Spanish hands. To ensure this, a rigid system of regulations was laid down. In Spain the right to participate in colonial trade was limited to a single trading agency (the *Casa de Contratación*) at Seville, with a branch at Cádiz. In the colonies only a few selected ports were allowed to ship cargoes to Europe. Each year two large convoys under armed escort sailed from Spain, one to Portobelo, the other to Veracruz. The ships carried supplies and manufactures on the outward voyage, and brought home bullion and colonial primary products. No ships were allowed to sail except in the convoys; no ports could be used for trans-Atlantic trade except the designated few; no foreigners were permitted to engage in the trade. In the Philippines the same restrictive system was in force. All trade was conducted by means of official galleons sailing each year between Manila, capital of the Philippines, and Acapulco in New Spain.

This was the official theory. Reality was different, for the disadvantages of the system led to constant evasions. To pay for the convoys, and for the considerable administrative expenses involved, heavy duties were imposed on the goods carried; and although the convoy arrangement introduced a measure of security to the Atlantic crossing it also brought delays, scarcities and high prices. The cramping effect which the regulations had on Spanish colonial enterprise is vividly illustrated by the history of Buenos Aires, today one of the great commercial centres of the western hemisphere. Founded in 1580, it remained because of official Spanish policy a closed port (shut, that is, to all but local shipping) of insignificant size for almost two centuries. The effect of the prohibition on direct trade between Spain and Buenos Aires was that European goods destined for the River Plate region had to follow an absurdly devious route if they were to be imported legally. They were unloaded from the Atlantic convoy at Portobelo, taken across the isthmus to Panama, shipped down the Pacific coast to Callao, and then sent overland by ox-cart or mule-train through Peru, Bolivia, Paraguay and Argentina.

The general result of a system which might well increase the cost of a manufactured article to eight or ten times its European price by the time it reached its colonial destination was the encouragement of smuggling on an international scale. Buenos Aires became a centre for smuggled goods brought direct (and cheaply) from Europe, or obtained from the Portuguese just across the Plate estuary. The Caribbean was a profitable hunting-ground for swarms of illegal traders. Some even made the perilous voyage round Cape Horn to the 'closed' Pacific ports of South America. One estimate of the comparative proportions of legal trade and smuggling in the Spanish American empire in the late seventeenth century puts the latter as high as two-thirds of the whole. So pronounced was the drain of wealth that a favourite theme of cartoonists of the period was the depiction of the Spanish empire as a cow, placidly suckling hungry English, French and Dutch calves.

A policy aimed at monopolizing colonial trade for the mother country was not confined to Spain. The doctrine was one held in common by the colonizing nations of Europe. The difficulty in Spain's case lay not only in the enormous extent of overseas territory to be policed if the trade restrictions were to be enforced, but in the discrepancy between the nation's industrial capacity and the demand of its colonies for cheap manufactures. In comparison with France, England and Holland, Spain was a poor, underdeveloped country. It lacked the natural resources, the highly competitive industries and the energetic merchants which its rivals possessed between them.

The helplessness of the Spanish government in the face of widespread illegal trading was increased by the co-operation between the smugglers and the Spanish colonists (and often even officials). The colonists were eager for European goods, and unwilling to pay inflated prices for the slowly-distributed cargoes of the official convoys. When to this was added the tempting opportunities offered by the Spanish colonies to foreign merchants, then forces in favour of free commercial enterprise were created more powerful than official doctrines of restrictive monopolies, closed ports and artificial trade routes. Those doctrines would have been difficult to put into practice even with a vigorous government and flourishing industries at home; but by the second half of the seventeenth century Spain was in a state of political, economic and moral decline. She no longer had the strength, it seemed, to control an empire acquired in an age when she was the greatest power in Europe; and with the pitiably enfeebled and childless Charles II on the throne the future of that empire became one of the most serious and perplexing problems which faced the statesmen of Europe in the late seventeenth century.

The Portuguese Empire

Portugal also presented by 1700 the spectacle of an imperial power in decline. But whereas Spain had at least preserved the territorial integrity of her empire, even though much of its vitality had gone, the Portuguese empire had shrunk visibly since its days of greatness in the sixteenth century. Then Portugal had laid claim to Brazil, long stretches of the coasts of west and east Africa, Ormuz in the Persian Gulf, Ceylon, Malacca, and several of the Moluccas (the celebrated Spice Islands). She possessed trading posts along the Malabar coast of India, in Japan, and at Macao. On the map these territories had all the appearance of a well-integrated maritime empire. It drew its sustenance only in part from the much publicized spice trade with Europe. The expenses of the Cape route were high, and shipwrecks frequent. Profits were quicker and safer in local Asiatic trade, and Portuguese merchants participated in a lucrative commercial network which extended from East Africa to the China Seas, and dealt in an enormous variety of products. This trading empire of the East was neatly balanced by the large settlement colony of Brazil in the West, with stations across the Atlantic in Africa to supply the American plantations with slaves. The whole was guarded by Portuguese naval strength along the sea-routes, and suffered little in comparison with the great Spanish land empire of the sixteenth century.

The acquisition of this far-flung empire was an extraordinary achievement by a few thousand sailors, soldiers and traders from a small European kingdom with a population of only one million; but the size of the inheritance proved too much for succeeding generations. The central direction of imperial affairs was adversely affected when Philip II of Spain succeeded to the throne of Portugal in 1580, even though the two countries with their empires were officially treated as separate units. Portugal was reluctantly drawn into the struggles of Europe. Spain's enemies now became Portugal's, and could legitimately attack Portuguese colonies and trade. Most dangerous of these enemies were Philip II's rebellious subjects in the Netherlands. The voyages of armed Dutch fleets to the East at the turn of the century revealed that the strength of Portugal's position was largely illusory. Always short of manpower, Portugal was beginning to feel the effect of decades of heavy casualties (mostly from disease) among her venturesome subjects overseas. The use of slave labour, and the official encouragement of mixed marriages to increase the number of permanent settlers, could not compensate for the lack of fighting men. After a long period of easy ascendancy in the Indian Ocean the great Portuguese carracks were under-crewed, or manned by indifferent half-caste or Indian seamen. Native maritime powers had recovered from the first shock of Portuguese intrusion, and were becoming increasingly difficult to hold at bay. The decline in Portuguese strength at sea was bound to weaken her hold over her eastern possessions, for the Portuguese empire was based on seapower. Supremacy at sea was essential; the long line of bases relied on fleets for supplies, reinforcements, and support in case of war.

As rivalry with the Dutch and (to a lesser extent) the English increased, the Portuguese found that they were paying the price for past policies: for religious intolerance, aggressive intervention in local trade, and arrogance towards native states. In company with the Spaniards they had aimed at spiritual as well as temporal conquest; but the destruction of temples and mosques, and the introduction of the Inquisition into the Portuguese possessions in India, stood in sharp contrast to the non-committal religious attitudes of Portugal's Dutch and English rivals. Of more immediate importance as a factor in Portuguese decline was Dutch superiority in material resources and leadership. In a strenuous half-century of conflict the Dutch were able to undersell the Portuguese commercially, and defeat them militarily. The Portuguese had over-extended themselves in the sixteenth century, and in a desperate effort to defend all the scattered bases of their eastern empire they now imperilled the existence of the whole. By the middle decades of the seventeenth century the Portuguese had been driven out of the Moluccas, Malacca and Ceylon by the Dutch; they had been expelled from Japan; Ormuz had been taken by an Anglo-Persian force; and though they still held Goa and some other posts, their position in India had been weakened by the activities of the English East India Company.

The only consolation to the Portuguese for the crumbling of their eastern empire was a sugar boom in Brazil in the first half of the seventeenth century, and a spirited clearing operation mounted in the colony against Dutch invaders. Even there, by the end of the century, soil-exhaustion and the capture by the Dutch of some of the slaving stations in West Africa, had held back Brazilian sugar production in comparison with the fast developing French and English sugar colonies in the Caribbean. Despite the winning back of independence from Spain, the retention of territory in Africa and of a few bases in the East, and the news at the close of the century that gold had been discovered in Brazil, there was no possibility of Portugal again emerging as a great imperial power. A relatively poor and backward nation, Portugal scarcely possessed the resources to develop the colonies it still held. There was neither inclination, financial means nor manpower to acquire further territory. In the forthcoming race for overseas possessions and trade Portugal was to be a non-starter.

The Dutch Empire

One of the most remarkable developments of the seventeenth century was the emergence of the independent Dutch Republic as a great maritime and trading power. The coastal provinces of the Spanish Netherlands had long been commercially-minded and prosperous. Dutch merchants held a respected place in the European trading world, and Dutch fishermen dominated the North Sea fishery. The struggle for independence against Spain inevitably distracted attention from commercial affairs, but as the war slackened in intensity in the last decade of the sixteenth century the Dutch of the rebellious provinces took up with renewed vigour projects of European and overseas trade.

After reports reached Europe of weaknesses in the Portuguese position in the East, Dutch trading fleets were sent to the Indian Ocean and the East Indies in the 1590s. These successful ventures gave notice that the papal-supported Treaty of Tordesillas of 1494, which had divided the globe between Spain and Portugal, no longer had relevance in a world of heretics and businessmen. The volume of Dutch trade to the East increased rapidly, and in 1602 the various groups involved were united into the Dutch East India Company, a powerful national undertaking. Well-financed, with close links with the government, this formidable trading organization possessed the right to establish colonies, to make war and peace, and to negotiate treaties with native princes. It was the representative of the Dutch state in the East, and the establishment and growth of the Company reflected the Dutch attitude to trade. Unlike other imperial powers, the young Dutch nation lived by trade. Its population was small, its natural resources few; all its efforts were directed to the support of its seamen, merchants and bankers.

In the East the Dutch soon began to supplant the fading power of Portugal, and at the same time gradually dislodged the traders of the English East India Company from their footholds in the Moluccas. Efficient and ruthless, the Dutch tightened their grip over the East

Indies from their strategic bases at Batavia and Malacca. They monopolized the spice trade, founded a settlement at Cape Town as a staging post on the route to the East, drove the Portuguese out of Ceylon, set up trading stations in India, opened up a flourishing silk trade with Persia, traded along the coastlands of Asia, touched the coasts of Australia and New Zealand, and established commercial links with China and Japan. (After the expulsion of the Portuguese, the Dutch were the only Europeans allowed to have any contact with the Japanese; and they were confined to the small island of Deshima off Nagasaki.) Dutch captains, it was said, would sail into hell to trade with the devil were it not that their sails might catch fire. Like their Portuguese predecessors, the Dutch did not limit themselves to trade between Europe and the East. They were quick to recognize the opportunities of profit from local Asiatic trade, the 'country trade' as the English were later to call it.

Dutch success in establishing commercial domination in the East soon led to political involvement in the affairs of the region. From their fortified bases in the East Indies the Dutch intervened with increasing frequency in local political disputes in order to protect their trade, particularly in Java. For all their reluctance to become involved in native politics, the Dutch found that they could not simply remain traders. Alliances with local rulers were negotiated, wars were fought, key points were brought under Dutch control, and in some areas protectorates were set up. There was little positive zeal for territorial expansion, but by the end of the seventeenth century the necessity of protecting trade in politically unstable areas had brought the Dutch to the verge of establishing a territorial empire in the East.

The region east of the Cape of Good Hope was only one sphere of Dutch overseas activity in the tropics. In 1621 the Dutch West India Company was founded, but as a plundering rather than an orthodox trading venture. Its fleets mercilessly harried Spanish and Portuguese colonies and shipping; parts of Brazil were occupied for twenty-five years; and on one memorable occasion the annual treasure-fleet bound for Spain was captured. The Company occupied Surinam on the Guiana coast of South America, the island of Curaçao near the Spanish Main, and the two islands of Saint Martin and Saint Eustatius in the Leeward group. On the North American mainland the Dutch held the long coastal strip of New Netherland, with its centre at the mouth of the Hudson River where New York now stands. These were not primarily colonies of settlement. They were bases for privateers, traders and smugglers – strategic points to assist the Dutch to capture the trade flowing from the American empires of other European nations.

For a time the Dutch achieved astonishing success. 'That beats the Dutch' was a phrase used by Englishmen to describe some extra- ordinary feat. Amsterdam became the financial and commercial centre of Europe, its warehouses filled with goods from every part of the world. The local seaborne trade of Europe was dominated by the economical Dutch flyboat, which carried a large cargo yet needed only a small crew. A French estimate in the 1660s calculated that the Dutch mercantile marine was almost twice the size of those of England and France combined. From Russia to the Caribbean, from North America to the East Indies, the Dutch traders swarmed. They did far more than monopolize the trade of their own empire. They supplied the colonies of other European nations with cheap goods, and shipped the goods of those colonies to Europe at low cost. With their well- designed ships, efficient methods of trading, and financial resources which enabled them to offer generous credit terms, the Dutch became the carriers of the world.

By the last quarter of the seventeenth century, however, there were unmistakable signs that the Dutch were losing their predominant position. Their very success brought problems. The example of this small state engrossing so disproportionate a share of Europe's trade led other nations to imitate Dutch techniques. When European powers saw the wealth of their colonies being siphoned off by the ubiquitous Dutch traders they determined to take retaliatory action. The English were the first to move. Trade and Navigation Acts aimed at excluding the Dutch from England's overseas trade were passed. These were followed by open hostilities with the Dutch, and by the annexation in 1664 of New Netherland, for long a centre of Dutch illegal traders in the midst of England's North American colonies. The France of Louis XIV, with Colbert directing her economic life, was quick to follow suit. High tariffs were imposed on imports in an effort to ruin the Dutch, monopolistic trading companies were established to exclude the Dutch from French colonial trade, and wars were fought against the Dutch which were partly commercial in origin.

Dutch reliance on overseas trade and on the industries of other countries made the Republic especially vulnerable to these measures of economic warfare, and even more so to enemy activity along the sea-routes in time of formal hostilities. The three maritime wars with England in the seventeenth century struck heavy blows at Dutch trade, but the damage caused was less serious than the erosive effects of the later wars of 1672–78 and 1688–97. For a nation of only two-and-a-half million inhabitants these wars brought almost insupportable burdens. Fleets had to be kept at sea, large armies maintained in the field to combat the threat of French invasion – and all at a time when trade was dislocated by hostilities. The country emerged from the French wars intact, but with a heavy burden of debt. The Dutch Republic remained a thriving commercial nation and an important colonial power; but by the beginning of the eighteenth century could no longer be considered a first-class power in the sense that France and England were. Both in Europe and overseas, in the commercial as well as the political sphere, the Dutch would clearly have to be content with a more modest place than they had occupied during the first hundred years of their independence.

The English Empire

From unassuming beginnings English colonial enterprise had reached impressive proportions by the end of the seventeenth century. During the early period of Spanish and Portuguese expansion English overseas undertakings had been on a small scale, though Tudor seamen had shown themselves to be among the most venturesome in Europe. Explorers sailed into the icy waters of the Arctic in vain attempts to find a short sea-passage to the Indies which would avoid the southern routes dominated by the Spaniards and Portuguese. English fishermen competed with those of other European nations in exploiting the abundant fisheries of the Newfoundland Banks. Traders sought commercial contacts with the Spanish American colonies in peacetime, and during the long years of war privateers raided Spanish ports and shipping. Drake sailed round the world, and was followed by others seeking to establish trade with the East. Several attempts (all unsuccessful) were made to settle on the North American mainland. Commercial links were forged with Muscovy, the Levant and West Africa.

Yet despite this activity England at the end of the sixteenth century had failed to secure a single permanent foothold outside Europe. Within a generation this state of affairs had dramatically changed.

Peace with Spain in 1604 released capital and energies previously employed in war for peaceful trading and colonizing ventures. Under the first two Stuarts long stretches of the eastern seaboard of North America were settled, safely distant from the Spanish colonies to the south. Virginia, Maryland, Massachusetts, Connecticut and Rhode Island all had their origin in this period. In the Caribbean the 'outer islands' of Saint Kitts, Nevis, Antigua and Barbados were settled – again, well away from the centres of Spanish power. Unlike most of the Dutch and Portuguese overseas possessions these English colonies were from the beginning genuine colonies of settlement. The great reservoir of cheap labour provided by the native populations of south and central America was not to be found farther north, and the communities of newly arrived settlers quickly had to make themselves self-supporting if they were to take root.

The motives of the tens of thousands of emigrants who left England were varied but compelling: land-hunger, the refusal of many Puritans to endure the unsympathetic religious climate of early Stuart England, the perennial desire to make a better living. Colonial promoters and the government were also influenced by a wide range of motives. The conviction that the colonies would produce precious metals, naval stores, spices and other subtropical crops; the desire to find new overseas markets for English manufactures; the fear that England was dangerously over-populated – all were important incentives in favour of colonization. The need to convert the heathen was often mentioned, but this was never the significant force it was in Spain and Portugal. As yet there were few Protestant counterparts of the dedicated Jesuit missionaries.

During the turbulent Civil War period the process of expansion practically halted (though Cromwell's forces captured Jamaica from the Spaniards), but it continued unchecked after the Restoration. The West Indian islands turned to large-scale sugar production based on slave labour. New colonies were established in the Carolinas and Pennsylvania. The Dutch settlements near the Hudson River were seized, and the English colonies of New York and New Jersey emerged in their place. By the end of Charles II's reign English colonies stretched along fifteen hundred miles of coastline from Maine to South Carolina. In the far north the Hudson's Bay Company, granted its charter in 1670, sought to monopolize the fur trade of the region between the Great Lakes and Hudson Bay. Across the Atlantic the Royal African

Company was established in 1672 to exploit a very different kind of trade, the slave trade between West Africa and the plantation colonies of America and the Caribbean.

Nor was overseas enterprise confined to the western hemisphere. The English East India Company was founded in 1600, and after experiencing an uncertain beginning and the humiliation of being driven out of the richest parts of the Moluccas by the Dutch, it settled down to trade in a steady if unspectacular way on the mainland of India. Trading stations were established at Surat on the west coast and at Madras on the east coast. In 1668 the Company acquired the island base of Bombay from Charles II (who had received it from Portugal as part of his Queen's marriage settlement), and later set up a post in Bengal on the site of modern Calcutta. Imports of coffee and Indian cotton fabrics, commodities in which there was little fear of competition from the West Indies, became particularly important. As Indian silks and brocades, Chinese porcelain (our familiar 'china') and tea became fashionable, so the Company prospered. Although rivalry at home and in India checked its development towards the end of the century, and it never had any pretensions in this period of being a great territorial power, the Company quietly built a position of strength which was to stand it in good stead during the struggle with France in the eighteenth century.

To exploit and give coherence to this expanding empire in the east and west, a framework of regulation was soon erected. It was taken for granted in England, as in other countries, that the benefits of colonial trade should be confined to the mother country and her colonies; and during the fierce rivalry with the Dutch in mid-century this conviction was soon expressed in precise, statutory form. Acts of Trade and Navigation prohibited the direct export of certain 'enumerated' colonial products, such as sugar and tobacco, to a foreign country, confined the carrying of goods from Asia, America and Africa to English and colonial ships, and excluded foreign shipping from colonial trade. In return the enumerated products were normally given an effective monopoly of the home market (though a large proportion of them was destined for profitable re-export to the continent of Europe). There was little new in this type of economic regulation. Spain tried to enforce much the same sort of policy. But whereas Spain's inability to meet the demands of her colonies doomed attempts to close the Spanish empire to outsiders, England possessed the industrial and commercial capacity to satisfy her colonies. Although the Acts of Trade were undoubtedly evaded at times, they represented a more effective policy of directing colonial production to the advantage of the mother country than any measures introduced by the Spaniards.

Together with the imposition of commercial regulations went measures designed to keep the colonies politically subordinate. By the end of the century most of the English colonies, though settled as the result of private enterprise rather than state direction, were royal colonies. The administration of a colony normally rested with a Governor, who was appointed in England, an official Council, and (to represent local interests) an elected Assembly. In theory the balance of this arrangement remained unchanged until the American Revolution, but in practice it underwent considerable modification. As the colonies developed, so the Assemblies grew in strength. Taking their inspiration from the constitutional struggles of seventeenth-century England, they made good use of their rights of initiating legislation and controlling finance to wrest power from the Governor and Council. Attempts by the Crown in the 1680s to bring its American empire closer to the centralized French model failed, and by the end of the century English colonists already held a measure of control over their own affairs, and a power to obstruct imperial policy, unknown in other European empires of the period.

Under the Old Colonial System the English colonies flourished. Most valuable, in the eyes of the home government, were the West Indian islands, exporting sugar and other subtropical crops. These colonies were followed, in order of official worthiness, by Newfoundland with its fisheries which supplied southern Europe with vast quantities of salt fish, and the southern mainland colonies with their extensive tobacco and cotton plantations. The New England colonies gave cause for concern rather than pride. They were not only stubbornly independent and notoriously difficult to govern, but they did not fulfil their allotted role as subordinate economic units of the empire. They harboured smugglers; their merchants intervened in the West Indian trade; they persistently attempted to set up their own manufacturing industries; and they produced few primary crops in demand in Britain. In short, they competed with, rather than supplemented, the economy of the mother country.

In general the English colonies at the end of the seventeenth century were prosperous, diversified and for their size populous (about a third of a million inhabitants). They ranged in character from the Quaker-dominated colony of Pennsylvania with its productive farms to the little fishing settlements of Maine, from the slave-based plantation economies of Barbados and Virginia to the sternly Puritan and acquisitive society of Massachusetts. They accepted immigrants from many countries: French Huguenots, Germans, Irish Catholics, Dutch. The birth-rate was rising, and living standards were high. The colonists were politically articulate, and possessed printing presses, newspapers and libraries. They had no large native populations to contend with. The native inhabitants of the Caribbean islands had been practically exterminated. The Indians thinly scattered along the eastern seaboard of North America had been brushed aside, though the watchful tribes hovering on the inland frontiers remained a constant menace. The English colonies were based upon a more solid foundation of genuine settlement and local enterprise than those of any other nation; but there was a flaw in their structure which almost proved fatal.

The very qualities of individualism which helped the colonies' economic and political growth brought serious military weaknesses. On the North American continent, in particular, colonial jealousies and a dogged preoccupation with domestic affairs hampered all efforts at co-operation in the field of defence. Overwhelmingly superior in population though the English colonies were, they were ill-equipped to face the disciplined military forces of the French in North America. This was the more alarming in that events in America and Europe indicated that a bitter struggle between England and France for overseas supremacy lay ahead. By the second half of the seventeenth century it was evident that the movements of French and English expansion in North America were on a collision course. The natural direction of advance for the English colonists was westward, out of the cramped coastal strip, across the mountains, on towards the great central plains, and eventually to the Pacific. Cutting right across the path of this movement was the line of French traders and settlers extending from the Gulf of Mexico in the south to the Saint Lawrence in the north. Farther north still, on Hudson Bay, an undeclared war between English and French fur-traders had already broken out in the 1680s, though the two nations were at peace in Europe. In the Carib-bean, too, the increasing competition between the English and French sugar islands brought rivalry only a degree less intense than in North America.

Even if relations between the English and French governments had remained good, clashes between their subjects overseas would have been difficult to avoid. However, 1689 saw the outbreak of the first of a series of European wars lasting until 1815 in which England and France became national enemies. The causes of the war of 1689–97 are to be found in Europe, which was also the main centre of military operations; but for the first time there was widespread fighting overseas. Englishmen and Frenchmen raided and seized each other's settlements in Hudson Bay, in Newfoundland, on the Saint Lawrence, along the inland frontiers of the North American colonies, in the Caribbean, off the coast of West Africa, and in India. Hostilities were sporadic, often poorly supported from home, and finally indecisive in that all overseas conquests were mutually restored at the Peace of Ryswick in 1697. Nevertheless, they pointed the way to the prolonged struggle for colonial supremacy between England and France in the eighteenth century.

The French Empire

For a nation with great resources and military power, France was a late starter in the overseas expansion of Europe. One result of the internal strife of the sixteenth century, and the preoccupation with continental ambitions, was that French colonial enterprises for long remained unimportant and generally unsuccessful. French fishermen reached the Newfoundland Banks in the early sixteenth century, and stretches of the North American coastline were explored by French seamen searching for a North-west Passage. But although Jacques Cartier discovered the Saint Lawrence River in the 1530s, attempts to found a settlement on its banks failed. Other ventures in central and south America also collapsed, and no permanent colonies were established until the first decade of the seventeenth century, when French settlers arrived at Quebec under Samuel de Champlain, and in Acadia (modern Nova Scotia).

Even then, the growth of the French empire in North America was slow and uncertain. Isolated Acadia was never of great importance, and the little French settlements huddled together along the Saint Lawrence suffered from lack of settlers and investment, from Indian raids, and from the hostility of the English. The spontaneous emigration of tens of thousands of settlers which was building up the English colonies in America at this time had no counterpart in French North America. The Huguenots, who would have made admirable colonists, were rarely allowed to emigrate to the French settlements. Nor did the French display the whole-hearted dedication of their Dutch rivals to oceanic enterprise: the French government provided for its subjects overseas more in the way of officious supervision than material support.

After a number of individual promoters failed to make much headway in Canada, Cardinal Richelieu in 1628 established the Company of New France to administer the North American settlements, and granted it a permanent monopoly of the fur trade. By formally linking trade with colonization the government hoped that the profits from the one would cover the expenses of the other. Instead, the Company concentrated on the more lucrative part of its business, and colonization was neglected. When Louis XIV assumed personal control of French government in 1661 the European population of Canada was only three thousand, a derisory figure for a region stretching from Nova Scotia to the Great Lakes and beyond.

Although Louis XIV's interests were predominantly European, his minister Colbert had far-reaching plans for the growth of French trade and influence, both in Europe and overseas. The unsuccessful Company of New France was abolished, Canada was brought under royal government, and in 1664 its trade was handed over to the newly-created Company of the West Indies. Modelled on the pattern of the Dutch trading corporations (whose success had deeply impressed Colbert), the Company was a more ambitious undertaking than the defunct Company of New France had been. During the ten years of its existence it controlled French trade in the West Indies, South America and West Africa, as well as in North America. Its most profitable field of enterprise lay in the West Indies, where the French had begun to settle in the 1620s at the same time as the English. The efforts of both nations were centred on the islands of the Outer Antilles, which the Spaniards had by-passed in their drive for territory in the western Caribbean and on the American mainland. The two most important French islands were Martinique and Guadeloupe, which in the late seventeenth century developed into sugar producers of enormous value. The western part of Hispaniola was ceded to France by Spain in 1697 and, as Saint Domingue, was in the second half of the eighteenth

c

century to surpass in importance all the other West Indian sugar colonies. The French slaving stations in West Africa formed an integral part of this Atlantic empire, for they assured the Caribbean plantations of an adequate labour supply. The twin of this Atlantic-based trading organization was the Company of the East Indies, also founded in 1664. Its main commercial activities were in India, where it acquired a base at Pondicherry on the east coast; but it was never a flourishing trading concern during the seventeenth century.

Colbert saw a strong New France as an essential condition of his general imperial policy, which aimed at the development of France's colonies, overseas commerce and mercantile marine as parts of a well-integrated trading empire. Success in this direction would buttress his domestic policy, aimed at making France the richest industrial and trading country in Europe. So fresh settlers were sent out to Canada, and with them one of France's finest regiments as evidence of the government's new seriousness about North America. The regular troops soon proved their worth in action against the hostile Iroquois Indians, who for decades had been a name of terror to the French settlers. Now under royal control, the colony of New France was ruled by a Governor and Intendant, with the help or interference of the Bishop of Quebec. It was an autocratic arrangement which worked swiftly and efficiently at times, but also allowed wide scope for clashes of personality. The popular representative element so pronounced in the English colonies was lacking, as it was in the other French colonies. General lines of policy were firmly controlled from Versailles, and the fate of the colony was precariously dependent on the priority which King and ministers thought fit to give France's overseas interests at any particular time.

The first Intendant of New France, Jean Talon, was an able official who lost no time in carrying out Colbert's directives. He encouraged shipbuilding and the production of naval stores, and set up a model farm to stimulate agriculture. He made large grants of land to the *seigneurs* (often retired army officers), who in turn placed settlers on hundred-acre holdings. These plots were usually free of dues for a few years until the land was productive; then the tenants paid rent and performed certain services. As a type of simplified feudal arrangement it was in many ways well suited to pioneer conditions. The Governor did not have the staff necessary to supervise settlers scattered over a vast area, and the *seigneurs* accordingly took over many of the functions of local government.

The French soon expanded away from their Saint Lawrence settlements. The more adventurous left the farms and set off in their canoes, living and fighting among the Indians, and trading for furs. Often ahead even of these hardy *voyageurs* were Jesuit missionaries, courageous and devoted men who, apart from their spiritual activities among the Indians, made important geographical discoveries. By the 1670s the Great Lakes area of Canada had been explored, and in the next decade La Salle journeyed from New France down the Ohio and Mississippi rivers to the Gulf of Mexico. His discoveries opened up exciting possibilities. A French base at the mouth of the Mississippi would serve as a springboard from which attacks could be launched at the rich silver mines of New Spain. To the north a great French empire would straddle the continent from the Gulf of Mexico to the Saint Lawrence, with practically continuous water-communication between the two extremities. But as yet this was only a dream. The French empire in North America was a skeleton, lacking the flesh and blood of population and trade. When Colbert died in 1683 the population of New France was a mere ten thousand; and beaver fur was the only important export. In the last years of the century the colonies were increasingly neglected as the French became involved in the struggle for dominance on the continent of Europe.

The wars in Europe had their echoes overseas. The forces involved were tiny compared with the armies and fleets fighting in Europe, but their clashes were prophetic. By the end of the century France and England had emerged as colonial rivals, especially on the continent of North America. Their empires were very different in character and spirit, but both were essentially expansionist. The French territories in North America were undeveloped as yet, but their potentialities were immense. Added to them were the rich sugar islands of the Caribbean, and possessions in West Africa and India. It was an empire of colonies and trade supported by the enlarged mercantile marine which Colbert had left behind him, and backed by the most redoubtable military forces in Europe. By the end of the seventeenth century the rising imperial power of France offered a strong challenge to the fast-growing English overseas empire.

II

CONTEST FOR EMPIRE
IN THE WEST
1700–1763

INTRODUCTION

THE PERIOD between the outbreak of the War of the Spanish Succession in 1702 and the Peace of Paris in 1763 has a certain purposeful coherence as far as colonial affairs are concerned. The Spanish Succession war was the first major European conflict in which overseas questions played a notably important part, and it set the stage for a half-century of conflict over colonial possessions and trade in the western hemisphere. In the sixteenth and seventeenth centuries the imperial powers of Europe had staked out their claims in America and the Caribbean; by the eighteenth century there was little unannexed territory available within easy reach. As the existing colonies expanded so the chances of contact and friction increased. In North America and the West Indies the colonists of Spain, France and Britain had established themselves within the same geographical areas, and local rivalries were added to existing European enmities to produce a state of tension and hostility. Compared with developments in the later part of the century, when European governments were as concerned about internal unrest in their colonies as about foreign attacks, the overseas rivalry of this period was straightforward and uncomplicated. Colonies were rich enough to be worth fighting for, but not strong enough to rebel against the mother country. Both the value and the subordination of the colonies tended to be taken for granted, and doubts about the permanence, necessity or morality of European rule overseas were rarely heard. No nation questioned the strength of the position achieved by Britain in 1763 after victory in the hardest-fought colonial war Europe had known.

2

Motives and Problems of Empire

Mercantilism

THE POLICIES of European nations in the seventeenth and eighteenth centuries were profoundly influenced by a set of economic beliefs which historians call 'mercantilist'. No simple definition of the term is possible. Mercantilism embraced a multitude of attitudes, theories and delusions. It guided the regulation of domestic industry, international commerce, and colonial trade. Some modern investigators have viewed mercantilism as a system primarily designed to increase the wealth and power of the state; others have seen it as an attempt by commercial interests to use the directive authority of the state for their own ends. But amid the conflicting viewpoints it is possible to detect certain contemporary assumptions about overseas trade and colonies on which there was general agreement. These assumptions have far more than commercial significance. Economic and political rivalry could not be separated, and for the first time economic competition became a major cause of war between the nations of Western Europe.

The most influential of these general concepts can be summed up in the phrase 'the balance of trade'. As early as Elizabeth's reign an English economist had expressed what seemed to him an obvious truth: 'We must always take care that we buy no more of strangers than we sell them, for we should impoverish ourselves and enrich them.' A favourable balance of trade would bring an influx of gold and silver to increase the nation's wealth and its strength. This insistence on the importance of accumulating reserves of gold and silver ('the sinews of war') through a favourable trade balance affected views towards colonial possessions. Colonies were expensive to acquire, administer and defend. Accordingly they were of value only in so far as they

29

brought material benefits to the mother country. Any concept of them as young nations, which one day might become independent, would have been regarded as a whimsical extravagance. Their chief function was simply to supply commodities which the mother country could not produce, and which otherwise would have to be imported from a foreign country, and perhaps paid for in bullion. Self-sufficiency was the ideal aimed at by the European empires of the period, and as late as 1802 a committee set up in the Netherlands to consider Dutch colonial policy reaffirmed its belief that 'the colonies exist for the mother country, not the mother country for the colonies'.

By the late seventeenth century the hope of finding gold and silver in the quantities discovered by the early Spanish adventurers had practically disappeared, and attention was concentrated on more prosaic commodities. Naval stores were indispensable to the maritime nations of Europe, and it was hoped that colonial production of hemp (for ships' cables), tar, masts, planks, and flax (for sails), would lessen the dangerous dependence on the Baltic as a source of supply. The increasing European demand for sugar, cotton, tobacco, ginger and dye-woods could only be met without recourse to the foreigner if a nation possessed plantation colonies in the Caribbean or the warmer parts of America. Spices, silks, coffee and tea were also much in demand, and the maritime nations strove to control the sources of supply.

Possession of the right kind of colonies would do more than allow an uninterrupted flow of these valuable commodities to the mother country for domestic consumption and for re-export. The supplying of the colonies with provisions and manufactures would stimulate home industry. Trade with the colonies would lead to an increase in the number of ships and seamen belonging to the nation, a highly desirable development. Not only financial considerations were at stake. The period was one when war or the threat of war was ever present. Years of peace were intervals in which nations recovered their breath for the next bout of hostilities. If a nation's sources of supply were in foreign hands they might be entirely lost in wartime. The possession of colonies brought security as well as gain to a nation's economy.

Closely linked to this insistence on a favourable balance of trade was the belief that the world's trade was fixed and static. It was taken for granted that one state's commercial gain must be another's loss. States were involved in a continual struggle with each other in the economic sphere. Colbert, perhaps the greatest exponent of mercantilist principles, pointed out to Louis XIV: 'Trade is the cause of a perpetual combat in war and in peace between the nations of Europe.' Given this conviction, to allow benefits which colonies conferred on the mother country to pass by normal, open trade into the hands of another nation was regarded by governments of the period in the same way as trade with an enemy country in wartime would be regarded today. To permit silver from Peru, sugar from Martinique, or spices from the Moluccas to be taken away in foreign vessels and freely sold in foreign lands would have nullified the fundamental motive behind colonial expansion.

In this international struggle for commerce several weapons lay at the disposal of the state. Legislation – the English Trade and Navigation Acts, for example – could be used to exclude foreigners from the closed circle of trade between the imperial power and its colonies. Or, as in France under Colbert, a tariff wall could be set up, designed to keep out foreign imports. Then again, commercial companies could be founded to monopolize the trade of a certain region. Here there were variations of type. In England companies were usually created as a result of mercantile pressure on the government, and therefore tended to have a solid commercial basis but to suffer from lack of official support. In France companies were established as the result of government initiative, and often lacked mercantile backing and private investment. The great Dutch trading companies, on the other hand, were the product of a genuine partnership between the government and merchant classes, and derived much of their strength from this close working alliance.

With commercial rivalry so strenuous, the division between peace and war was sometimes difficult to determine. Europeans frequently fought each other overseas, 'beyond the Line', while their home countries remained at peace. The execution of English traders in the Moluccas by the Dutch in the 1620s, the capture of New Netherland by the English in the 1660s, and the armed clashes between English and French traders in Hudson Bay in the 1680s, are instances of this. These peacetime hostilities were usually on a limited scale, but they took on a new degree of intensity if war broke out in Europe. And war in Europe between countries with rival interests overseas became increasingly common as commercial and colonial considerations became matters of prime concern to the state. The Anglo-Dutch and

Franco-Dutch wars of the seventeenth century are cases in point. In the second half of the century the interaction of events in Europe and overseas began to form a vicious circle. Commercial and colonial rivalries led to an embittering of relations, and sometimes open war, in Europe; this resulted in an intensification of the conflict overseas which in turn made a peaceful settlement in Europe harder to attain.

These factors must not be exaggerated. The dominant figure in the Europe of this period was Louis XIV, and his chief concern was always with the continent rather than with French colonial interests. England and the Dutch Republic were avowed commercial rivals, but joined in alliance between 1689 and 1713. Yet, although the statesmen of Europe had to give priority to considerations nearest home, the commercial interests of their nations ran second only to their political security. In a mercantilist age political and economic considerations had become inextricably bound together.

Seapower and Empire

As European nations acquired colonies and built up their overseas commerce, so seapower became increasingly important. A large mercantile marine was needed to sustain a country's colonies and trade, and an efficient navy to protect them. Colonies, trade and seapower: these were the essential elements of empire. Seapower would decide the fate of the Caribbean islands, virtually defenceless in the face of naval squadrons. The French empire in North America, and the Dutch empire in the East, both depended on seapower to safeguard the ocean life-lines which supplied them. If a country's navy was destroyed, or blockaded in port, then its colonies and seaborne trade lay open to attack by enemy fleets and privateers.

The seventeenth century saw an increasing specialization in naval warfare. The miscellaneous jumble of royal warships, armed merchantmen and privateers which made up a fighting fleet in the previous century disappeared. The bloody naval encounters of the first Anglo-Dutch War in the 1650s showed that merchantmen had no place in the line of battle. Warships became larger and more heavily armed, and soon great three-decked ships of a thousand tons carrying one hundred guns were being built. But seapower involved more than naval strength. An English statesman sensed this when he wrote: 'As trade and commerce enrich, so they fortify our country. The sea is our barrier, ships are our fortresses, and the mariners that trade and commerce alone can furnish are the garrisons to defend them.' Great armed fleets could not be maintained without a flourishing mercantile marine. Navies were manned in time of war by sailors from the ocean-going merchantmen, the fishing fleets, and the coastal carriers and colliers. Warships were built and repaired in dockyards which in peace-time were working on merchant ships. As the navy protected colonies and trade, so they in turn sustained the navy. The three elements of empire were interdependent.

During the seventeenth century England and France emerged as the two leading naval powers. The Spanish navy had been long in decline, and by the end of the century Spain scarcely counted as a naval power. Portugal's few warships were scattered abroad, defending her colonial possessions and the homecoming trade. Successive Anglo-Dutch wars demonstrated the fighting spirit of the fine Dutch navy, but as the Republic became involved in desperate land wars on the continent so its naval strength declined. During the wartime alliance with England between 1689 and 1713 it was England which bore the main burden of naval commitments, and by the close of the wars the Dutch were hard-pressed to put a dozen ships of the line to sea.

With long stretches of Atlantic and Mediterranean coastline, bustling ports at Marseille, Bordeaux, Nantes and Dunkirk, and thousands of seamen, France had all the potentialities of a great sea-power; but the growth of the French navy was a comparatively late development. Although Richelieu made valiant attempts to establish a fighting fleet, it was left to Colbert in the first half of Louis XIV's reign to build a navy which matched that of any other European power. His achievement was a magnificent one, and encompassed all aspects of maritime activity. His general commercial policy led to an expansion of the French mercantile marine: he encouraged shipbuilding by means of state subsidies; dockyards and naval arsenals were built; naval colleges were founded to train officers; an efficient system of recruitment for seamen was introduced. By the time of Colbert's death in 1683 France had a navy capable of challenging the combined English and Dutch fleets.

But French maritime strategy was invariably subordinated to continental ambitions. Once Colbert had gone, the navy no longer had a defender and inspirer close to the King. The battle of La Hogue in 1692, in which the French lost fifteen ships, confirmed French suspicions about the inadvisability of creating huge and expensive fleets. The King's dominant advisers were military men, who argued that sea engagements had little effect on the pattern of war on the continent. The French navy made no further attempt to dispute sea supremacy with the English and Dutch fleets. Ships were sent out individually or in small squadrons to raid enemy commerce, tactics which were profitable to the French and for a time immensely damaging to the allies, but ruinous to any hope of employing the navy as a decisive, war-winning instrument.

England was not distracted by continental ambitions and fears to the extent that the French and Dutch were. England was a maritime rather than a continental power (though governments were sometimes slow to recognize this), an island which needed no large standing army to defend its frontiers. After a period of neglect in the early seventeenth century the navy began to expand under Charles I, and the Commonwealth governments of the mid-century turned it into a formidable fighting force which proved more than a match for the Dutch. Despite some set-backs after the Restoration, of which the most galling was the Dutch sally up the Thames in 1667, the navy expanded steadily in the later Stuart period. The doubling of the mercantile marine in the last forty years of the century provided a firm foundation for English naval power. Careful thought was given to the use of naval forces in war, and strategy was directed to the destruction of the main enemy fleets. Once that was accomplished, England's overseas possessions and trade routes would be secure, the enemy's exposed to attack. This doctrine was not consistently applied. Lack of resources, commitments in Europe, inefficient administration and leadership at times, all affected naval strategy; but by the end of the seventeenth century England stood close to being accepted as the greatest naval power in Europe.

The Missionary Factor

The overseas expansion of the maritime powers of Western Europe cannot be described solely in terms of commercial exploitation and national rivalry. Accompanying it was an extension of the Christian faith which had a dual (and sometimes contradictory) effect. It brought a crusading zeal to the process of expansion, and strengthened the aggressive self-confidence which was so marked a feature of European behaviour overseas. Yet in many areas it helped to soften the harshness of European impact on the indigenous peoples whose lands were invaded and exploited. With a rapidity which matched the achievements of the soldiers and settlers Christianity spread across the oceans to distant lands. Missionary fervour was allied with, rather than opposed to, the commercial motive. As members of da Gama's crew proclaimed on their arrival in India in 1498, they had come to find Christians and spices. Determination to convert the heathen, to combat the forces of Islam, and to discover the legendary Christian Churches of Asia and Africa was an incentive which lived easily alongside more worldly motives.

Until the eighteenth century Roman Catholic missionaries were far more active than Protestant. Catholicism had a well-established missionary tradition which found ample outlet in the empires founded by the Catholic powers of Spain and Portugal. Both the opportunity and need for missionary work were obvious. In contrast, Protestant rulers and Churches showed little interest in overseas missions at a time when Protestantism was fighting for survival in Europe. In Spain and Portugal, Catholicism was virtually unchallenged, and those two countries (together with Italy) provided secure bases for a flow of missionaries overseas. The Catholic missions had their most spectacular successes in America, where the Indian religions were unable to withstand in open combat the organized forces of the monastic orders and the Jesuits. The mission station became a familiar feature of the frontier in Spanish America, and during the colonial period most of the Indians were converted, at least to a nominal Christianity. In Brazil, Catholic missionaries from Portugal worked in more difficult conditions. There were no populous centres as in Peru and Mexico, and for the most part missionaries had to contend with primitive tribes living in remote and inaccessible areas. To the north, French Canada was the scene of some of the most heroic of all missionary labours, although the Indian population was so thinly scattered that rewards measured in numbers of converts were disappointingly small.

Protestant Christianity in the Americas was confined mainly to the European settlements along the north-east seaboard and in the West Indies. Some missionary work was carried out among the Indians, but not with the same intensity and application that the Catholics had shown. All too often the native Indian was regarded as beyond redemption. If the general attitude towards the native population was not one of fear (as it was in the early days of settlement), then it was usually one of contempt. Not until the late eighteenth century did Protestantism appear as a dynamic missionary force which was to swell into the most massive proselytizing effort Europe had produced.

Like trade, Christianity followed the flag; and since European political domination was strongest in the Americas, so Christianity took deeper root there than elsewhere. Africa was still the Dark Continent as far as Europe was concerned. In only a few places had Europeans penetrated inland, and the interior, from the Moslem north to the tiny Dutch Calvinist enclave at the Cape of Good Hope, was pagan – the scene of neither political nor religious endeavour by Europeans. In the eastern hemisphere the political position of the European maritime nations was less firmly established than in the Americas, and the Christian faith was faced with a correspondingly more difficult task. In India, European political power before the eighteenth century was slight; moreover, Christian missions there were in competition with the organized Moslem and Hindu faiths, quite different propositions from the primitive Amerindian religions which had crumbled before the onset of Christianity. Partly because of these factors Christianity made little headway outside the coastal-areas which lay under Portuguese control. In China missionaries fought a brave battle against odds, but the results of their labours appeared insignificant when set against the vast territory and population of the Chinese empire. The Portuguese missionary effort in Japan made a promising start, but the missionaries and their converts were almost exterminated in the savage persecution of the seventeenth century. In general, although Catholic missionaries reached most of the coastal regions of south-east Asia, without the protection of European political strength they gained relatively few converts.

In north-east Asia the Orthodox Christianity of the Russian Empire was also on the move. Missionaries accompanied the soldiers and traders of the Tsar as they marched and fought their way eastward towards the Pacific. These missions were state-directed, and the motives of the Russian government were certainly not exclusively religious. The Spanish experience in America had shown that conversion of a conquered people was one method of keeping them submissive; and the lesson was not lost on the Russians.

Despite set-backs, despite doubts about the sincerity and permanence of the conversions made, the Christian faith by the beginning of the eighteenth century had spread impressively over the world's surface. The previous two centuries had seen the most powerful and sustained missionary effort any religion had mounted, and one which mitigated some of the worse effects of European dominion over native peoples. The balance-sheet of European imperialism in the sixteenth and seventeenth centuries is a sombre one when regarded from the viewpoint of the inhabitants of the Americas. The Caribs of the West Indian islands had practically disappeared. In central and south America the irruption of the European invaders had been accompanied by depopulation and human misery on a colossal scale. In North America rival European groups had cynically used the Indians as their allies in war, and been responsible for the deaths of thousands of them through the introduction of fire-arms, alcohol, and a ruthless land policy. The only steady glow of light in this dismal story of exploitation and oppression is provided by the missionaries. In Spanish America, in particular, they did their utmost to cushion the impact of European rule on the indigenous inhabitants. They urged the Crown to pass protective legislation, denounced the excesses of European settlers at considerable risk to their own position, and strove to instil into the conquerors some regard for the fate of the conquered. Christian humanitarianism had its limits of effectiveness, but it introduced into the process of European overseas expansion a sense of obligation to subject peoples which, however weak it became at times, was never entirely lost.

By the end of the seventeenth century the missionary impulse had noticeably slackened. In part, political factors explained this. Of the Catholic imperial powers, Spain and Portugal had sadly declined, and France was preoccupied with European affairs. The new imperial nations of England and Holland were Protestant, strongly motivated by commercial considerations, and as yet mainly indifferent to missionary work. Nor did Christianity in Europe as a whole possess the same vitality and intensity as it had during the turbulent era of the Reformation and Counter-Reformation. The long continuance of religious conflict and persecution had sapped belief; and this at a time when Christianity was facing in Europe the new challenge presented by scientific advances and rationalist thinkers, and overseas the sophisticated faiths of the Islamic world, India and the Far East. It was a time of religious apathy and disillusionment, when the fashionable ideas of the Enlightenment were hostile to established religion. As far as missionary enterprise was concerned, the eighteenth century marked a pause between two great eras. The Protestant powers of Europe had not yet been swept by the enthusiasm for missions which reached its peak in the nineteenth century; the Catholic powers were no longer as intent on evangelization overseas as they had been in the triumphant years of their imperial vigour.

The Slave Trade

That the compassion extended by organized Christianity to native peoples under European rule had its limitations is revealed by contemporary attitudes towards what seems to us today to have been the vilest and most obvious evil associated with European imperialism – the slave trade. From the time of their first establishment the plantation colonies in America and the Caribbean faced a serious labour shortage. Because of lack of numbers, stamina and inclination, neither white settlers nor the native Indians provided an answer to this problem. But the robust African Negro did, and from the beginning of the sixteenth century slaves were shipped across the Atlantic from West Africa to the mines and plantations of Spanish America. In the seventeenth century, as the outer Caribbean islands were colonized by the English and French, and sugar plantations established there which engulfed large forces of unskilled labourers, the demand for African slaves increased enormously.

The slave coasts of West Africa extended from the Senegal River in the north along three thousand miles of shoreline to Angola in the south. The trade would have been impossible without the co-operation of Africans, who were familiar with slavery as an institution long before Europeans arrived on the scene. (For centuries Africa had formed a great reservoir of slave labour for the Moslem world to the north and east; moreover, domestic slavery was well-established in much of Africa, often in a mild form.) In the actual procuring of the slaves Europeans played a relatively small part, for they rarely ventured far from the coast. There was no large-scale infiltration or conquest of West Africa by Europeans during the slaving era. Lack of unity among the slavers from the competing European nations, the armed strength of the African warrior states, dense tropical forests and deadly diseases all prevented any considerable European penetration before the nineteenth century. Even the slaving companies which built forts or 'factories' on the coast leased the land from local rulers, and their establishments were largely dependent on African goodwill.

Although most of the slaves were prisoners of war or criminals, it would be wrong to think of the slave trade as merely an unorthodox method by which the less desirable elements of African society were removed. As the European demand for slaves grew, so wars were waged, and 'criminals' discovered, simply to provide cargoes for the slave ships. The European slavers encouraged this process by supplying the coastal states with fire-arms and powder. Punitive expeditions struck deep inland as sources of supply near the coast dried up. With this expansion of the trade went an increase in the human misery and ruin which always accompanied it. From the seventeenth to the nineteenth centuries the social and economic organization of the West African states was disrupted by an all-consuming effort to supply cargoes for the European slave ships. Recent research has suggested that African society was more resilient than has sometimes been thought, and that economically the densely populated areas of West Africa could accept the continual drain of manpower. Even so, the trade was a terrible blot upon the European history of the period. The constructive achievements of empire-building which helped to balance the darker aspects of European expansion in other parts of the world had no counterpart in West Africa at this time. In a standard history of Africa this period is simply referred to as 'The Era of Fire-arms and the Slave Trade', a title which indicates the nature of European contact with African society in the seventeenth and eighteenth centuries.

So profitable and wide-flung was the slave trade that no other form of commerce could compete with it, and the older trades in ivory and gold-dust fell away in importance. The demand for slaves never slackened. On the Caribbean plantations the average working life of a slave was calculated at seven years. Mercilessly worked and sometimes brutally ill-treated, the slave population had a higher death-rate than birth-rate; and so replacements were continually needed. The British Caribbean colonies alone (it was officially estimated in 1709) took twenty thousand slaves a year, though many of these were probably re-exported to Spanish America. At times in the second half of the eighteenth century a hundred thousand slaves crossed the Atlantic in a single year, and possibly a total of seven million during the course of the century.

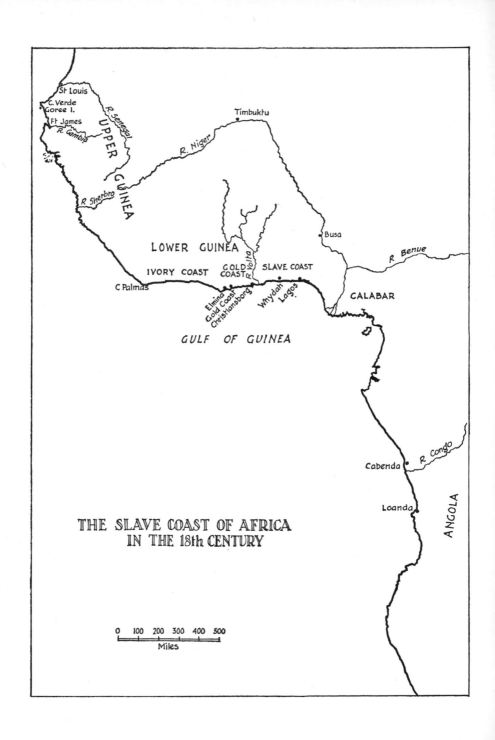

THE SLAVE COAST OF AFRICA
IN THE 18th CENTURY

One does not need to take at face value every word of later abolitionist propaganda to decide that the slave trade was a degrading and repulsive affair, whether its effects are studied in Africa, America or on the notorious 'middle passage' across the Atlantic. It is a measure of the outlook of the age that few voices were raised in protest against the trade until the eighteenth century. Negroes, it was pointed out, had been enslaved by their fellow-Africans before European slavers bought them. The slave trade was regarded as a business, and an essential business at that. Slavery was the foundation on which the economies of the valuable tropical and subtropical colonies of the European nations in the western hemisphere rested. The English and French sugar islands in the Caribbean, the tobacco plantations of Virginia and Maryland, the South American colonies of Spain and Portugal: in varying degree all depended on slave labour. The feeding and clothing of the slaves was an important branch of business in itself. During the century Liverpool developed into one of the greatest ports in the world on the strength of the slave trade. Profits from the trade helped to supply the profits needed for Britain's expanding industries. An English pamphleteer wrote that the slave trade 'may be justly esteemed an inexhaustible fund of wealth and naval power to this kingdom'. He pointed out that the triangular trade between England, West Africa and the plantation colonies brought the mother country an abundance of valuable products, provided an important outlet for English manufactures, and employed a large number of ships and seamen. Frenchmen argued in the same vein, insisting that if France gave up the slave trade she might as well abandon her colonial commerce. Nantes became the French equivalent of Liverpool, with all its great shipowners engaged in the slave trade. To abolish the trade would have wrecked the colonial empires of the day, or so it was thought. Faced with what seemed to be the economic necessity of the African slave trade, all but a handful of people ignored its inhumanity; and the maritime powers of Europe concentrated on seizing as much of it as possible for themselves.

The Spaniards, who had no bases in West Africa, were never able to supply their own colonies with slaves; and despite a system of official contracts illegal slave traders were frequent callers at the Spanish settlements. During the union of the crowns of Spain and Portugal (1580–1640) the Portuguese supplied the Spanish colonies with slaves from their West African possessions; but after 1640 this easy solution disappeared. The official contract to supply slaves to the Spanish colonies, the *Asiento de Negros*, was awarded to various contractors in turn, without much satisfaction being obtained. Meanwhile an illegal trade in slaves flourished, and the official Spanish policy of commercial exclusiveness became harder to enforce than ever.

As the English and French Caribbean islands developed into large-scale sugar producers so the demand for slaves increased at a phenomenal rate. The Dutch were in the best position to meet this demand, with the shipping resources of their West India Company, and newly acquired stations on the Guinea coast. But to allow foreigners – especially foreigners as commercially dangerous as the Dutch – to dominate this vital trade was unthinkable to English and French mercantilists. Instead, the Dutch example was imitated. The English established themselves at the mouth of the Gambia, and in 1672 the Royal African Company was formed to exploit the slave trade. For France, Colbert's West India Company occupied the mouth of the Senegal, and although the company failed, a successor was formed which in 1677 captured the important island base of Gorée (near Cape Verde) from the Dutch.

Despite the obvious importance of the slave trade, profits were often small or non-existent for companies engaged in it. The activities of interlopers, the chicanery of dishonest servants, losses on the 'middle passage' and wartime interruptions all made the trade a peculiarly risky affair. Nevertheless, the conviction that large profits were easily forthcoming was not readily shaken, and rivalry became intense. By the last quarter of the seventeenth century the Dutch position on the slave coasts, so strong in mid-century, was being challenged by both England and France. From 1688 onwards running hostilities took place along the coast between English and French, and (despite their alliance in Europe) English and Dutch. The Treaty of Ryswick in 1697 restored the situation in West Africa to its pre-war footing; but it was clear that the slave trade, and in particular the unresolved question of the disposal of the Spanish *asiento*, had become yet another bone of contention between England and France.

The Spanish Succession
From the moment a sickly four-year-old boy became Charles II of Spain in 1665 the question of the Spanish Succession became of pre-

dominant concern to the statesmen of Europe. As Charles grew to an enfeebled manhood, racked by illness, it became evident that he would die childless; and as his condition veered from critical to desperate in the last years of the century the problem of the succession became of overwhelming and urgent importance. This last of the Spanish Habsburgs ruled over an immense world empire, which in Europe included Spain, large areas of Italy, and the Spanish Netherlands, and overseas some of the richest territories in the Americas. Whoever the new king might be, the balance of power in Europe and overseas would inevitably be affected, and a wrong answer to the problem of the succession might result in a generation of war.

The story of the negotiations between the great powers to find a solution acceptable to all is a complex one, of which only a bare outline can be given here. In brief, three European dynasties had claims to the inheritance of Charles II: the French Bourbons, the Austrian Habsburgs, and the House of Bavaria. France would not consent to Austria gaining the Spanish empire. Likewise, Austria would not tolerate a Bourbon on the throne of Spain, nor would England and the Dutch Republic. The interests of these two countries formed a complicating factor in an already difficult situation. As European powers they could not allow either France or Austria to wreck the continental balance of power by acquiring Spain's European possessions; as maritime powers they could not allow Spain's overseas empire to pass out of Charles II's weak grasp and into the control of Louis XIV. If the Spanish empire fell under French domination English and Dutch merchants would certainly be excluded from their profitable contraband trade with the Spanish colonies, and possibly from their important legal trade with Spain in Europe.

The Bavarian candidate, the Electoral Prince, offered an escape from these difficulties, for under him the Spanish empire would retain its independence from both France and Austria. In 1698, therefore, France, England and the Dutch Republic signed a Partition Treaty agreeing that on Charles II's death the Electoral Prince would succeed to the Spanish throne. He would keep most of the empire except the Italian territories, which were to be divided between France and Austria as compensation for their renunciation of the Spanish throne. Within a few months this carefully negotiated settlement was overturned by the death of the Electoral Prince, and talks began again between Louis XIV and William III, both anxious to keep the peace of

Europe after the long and devastating wars. A second Partition Treaty in 1699 allocated Spain, the Spanish Netherlands and the overseas colonies to the Archduke Charles of Austria, second son of the Emperor. France received only Spain's Italian territories. But neither the Emperor, who stood to benefit most from the arrangement, nor Spain would accept the principle of partition; and shortly before his death in 1700 Charles II made a will bequeathing the whole of his empire to Louis XIV's young grandson, Philip of Anjou.

The dilemma was Louis XIV's. He had to make the agonizing decision of whether to stand by the treaty he had himself negotiated and signed, or to accept the provisions of Charles II's will. He chose the latter course, and the English and French governments acquiesced. Although they were profoundly uneasy about the arrangement, both had war-weary populations to consider, and merely warned Louis XIV that the crowns of France and Spain must under no circumstances be united. Louis did not go as far as that, but took steps which seemed to point in that direction. French troops moved into the Spanish Netherlands, and expelled Dutch forces from the protective line of barrier fortresses they held there under the Treaty of 1697. This ominous move was accompanied by a series of commercial measures in 1701 and 1702 which struck damaging blows at English and Dutch trading interests. The exporting of Spanish wool was confined to French merchants; English and Dutch merchants in Spain were placed under restrictions; French naval vessels patrolled the Spanish American colonies; French pressure forced the Spanish government to concede the coveted *asiento* to a French company.

Opinion in England and Holland quickly changed from a fatalistic acceptance of the situation to indignation and alarm. The military threat was an obvious one, but pamphleteers also stressed the damage to the countries' trade in Spain, the Mediterranean and the Indies, which would result from French domination of the Spanish economy. In September 1701 a counter-stroke was launched – the Grand Alliance between England, Holland and the Emperor – and the next year war was declared. The war aims of the Grand Alliance were political and commercial. The crowns of France and Spain were never to be united. The Spanish empire was to be partitioned, with Philip V (formerly Philip of Anjou) remaining ruler of Spain and her overseas possessions, but with the Italian territories and the Spanish Netherlands passing to Austria. The English and Dutch were to have the same commercial privileges in Philip V's territories as they had possessed in the reign of his predecessor; and the French were to be barred from all trade with Spain's overseas empire. Finally, England and Holland were empowered to capture and retain during the war any Spanish colonial territories.

Despite the commercial and colonial implications of the War of the Spanish Succession the main campaigns were fought on the continent of Europe. There was some agitation in England for attacks on French sugar islands and Spanish treasure-fleets, but throughout the early years of the war British naval resources were steadfastly directed towards the support of Marlborough's continental strategy. In particular, the navy established its dominance in the Mediterranean, where Gibraltar, superbly situated from a strategic point of view, and the island of Minorca with its fine deep-water harbour at Port Mahon, were both captured.

Colonial operations were once again on a comparatively minor scale, and did not form part of any plan of overseas conquest. English and French fleets engaged in destructive raiding activities in the Caribbean; French expeditions plundered Portuguese settlements in Brazil; French privateers from Quebec and from Port Royal in Acadia harassed New England shipping and the fisheries; and brutal border fighting flared up on the North American mainland. The northern English colonies experienced some relief when a combined force of English marines and colonial levies captured Port Royal in 1710; and the next year the most important overseas operation of the war was mounted by the new Tory administration in England, anxious to gain a victory to offset the triumphs of the Whig hero Marlborough on the continent. A seaborne attack was launched at Quebec, capital of New France. The fleet, commanded by Admiral Walker, carried seven regiments of Marlborough's veterans on board, but failed to get within striking distance of Quebec. It lost eight transports through shipwreck, and beat a humiliating retreat. The main significance of this dismal operation was that it had been prepared in England, and had been stopped, not by French forces, but by its commander's ineptitude in face of the natural hazards of the Saint Lawrence navigation. Despite its failure the Walker expedition was a warning to the French in Canada that their position was not unassailable.

These colonial encounters were of little import compared with events in Europe, where England for the first time in her history emerged as a truly great naval and military power. Marlborough struck mighty blows at French armies in the battles of Blenheim, Ramillies and Oudenarde. The French navy ceased to exist as a fighting force. English fleets dominated the Channel, the Narrow Seas and the Mediterranean. Although English commerce suffered severely from French privateers it had more than recovered by the end of the war, whereas French seaborne trade had been practically eliminated. In comparison with her English ally the Dutch Republic made a sorry showing. Dutch troops fought alongside English in the continental campaigns, but on the seas the Dutch fleet had shrunk to a remnant and Dutch commerce had been hard hit.

Behind the English victories lay the new financial strength of the government, vitally important at a time when wars were more costly than ever. While France laboured under an archaic financial system which did little to exploit the productive capacity of the nation and brought the Crown to the verge of bankruptcy, England after the 1688 Revolution produced a rational financial structure capable of supporting great armies and navies without undue strain. The financial arrangements of the Revolution Settlement, and the improved understanding between King and Parliament, resulted in more generous financial grants than any Stuart had ever known. In contrast to the system in France, where the nobility and clergy escaped the most onerous taxes, the weight of taxation in England fell on the wealthiest classes. Furthermore, loans to the government at a fixed interest rate became a secure and popular form of investment. In 1694 the Bank of England was founded, and played its part in financing the War of the Spanish Succession. This political and financial stability after a century of constitutional turmoil was an essential factor in England's defeat and humiliation of Louis XIV, master of Europe for so many years.

After a breakdown of preliminary negotiations in 1708, peace talks were renewed at Utrecht, and the treaties signed there in 1713 are known collectively as the Peace of Utrecht. The most important treaty was that between England and France, and its terms amounted to a partition of the Spanish empire. Philip V retained Spain and her overseas colonies, and renounced all claim to the French throne. The Emperor gained the Spanish Netherlands and most of Spain's Italian possessions. The Dutch were again given the right to garrison barrier fortresses in the new Austrian Netherlands as a guard against future

French aggression. England kept her conquests of Gibraltar and Minorca, and thereby confirmed her new position as a Mediterranean naval power.

It was in the overseas clauses of the peace settlement that England's strength was most clearly shown. France ceded Acadia (renamed Nova Scotia) to England, though without any definition of the inland boundary, and without the island of Cape Breton off the north-east tip of the colony. These were to prove serious omissions. The French handed over the fur-trading posts they had occupied in Hudson Bay to the English Hudson's Bay Company, which now possessed the entire Bay area. France recognized English sovereignty over Newfoundland, though French fishermen were given the right to dry fish along a specified stretch of the coast, another reservation which promised trouble for the future. In the Caribbean the island of Saint Kitts, formerly divided between English and French settlers, became an English possession. Finally, Spain granted the *asiento* for thirty years to the English South Sea Company, together with the right to send one ship each year to trade at Portobelo. This latter concession was the first official departure from the Spanish doctrine of commercial exclusion in the overseas empire.

The terms of the peace settlement did more than indicate the ascendancy of England in an exhausted Europe. The retention of important naval and commercial bases showed the determination of the English government, spurred by an influential and vociferous mercantile section, and by the manufacturing interests, to secure and expand the nation's trade overseas. In Admiral Mahan's words, England had 'become a sea power in the purest sense of the word, not only in fact, but also in her own consciousness', and this development was bound to affect the course of European overseas expansion and rivalry in the eighteenth century.

Areas of Tension: North America and the Caribbean 1713–1748

The Maritime Powers after the Utrecht Settlement

THE TREATY of Utrecht marked an important stage in the gradual establishment of Britain's commercial and maritime ascendancy over other European nations. From the British point of view the War of the Spanish Succession had been both successful and profitable. Enemy overseas commerce had almost disappeared from the oceans. The resources of the Dutch – wartime ally but peacetime competitor – had been strained by exhausting continental campaigns. The peace settlement had brought an impressive list of gains, among them valuable strategic bases. A few years after the Treaty a member of Parliament linked the country's flourishing economic condition with the favourable terms of the Utrecht settlement:

> The advantages from this peace appear in the addition made to our wealth; in the great quantities of bullion lately coined in our mint; by the vast increase in our shipping employed since the peace in the fisheries and in merchandise; and by the remarkable growth of the customs upon imports, and of our manufactures.

The Dutch position contrasted sharply with this confident British combination of riches and power. Wealth was still present, but not in the proportion that had made the Dutch Republic the predominant commercial and financial power of Europe in the seventeenth century. Amsterdam remained one of the great financial centres of Europe, and the Dutch carrying trade was still greater than that of any other nation; but in other spheres the superior resources of the British and French were making themselves felt. In the new era of open warfare for colonial possessions and overseas trade the Dutch suffered severe handicaps. A population of only two-and-a-half million could not support indefinitely both a first-class fleet and army. The ever-present danger of French invasion compelled the Dutch to maintain an army at crippling expense, and the navy deteriorated. During wartime the Dutch might find profit as a neutral carrier of goods, but only if the belligerent nations were agreeable. A nation as vulnerable as Holland was, by land and sea, to military and economic pressure, could no longer be a serious rival in the struggle for supremacy overseas.

Under its Bourbon king, Philip V, his energetic wife, Elizabeth Farnese, and a succession of capable ministers, Spain was making a spirited recovery from its financial and economic collapse at the end of the seventeenth century. After decades of incompetent government, ministers of the calibre of Alberoni and Patiño brought new life and purpose to the administration. They put the national finances on a sounder footing, encouraged industry and commerce, and restored the navy as a fighting force. Deprived by the Utrecht settlement of territory in Italy and the Low Countries, Spain still possessed overseas an empire of vast size; but it remained to be seen whether the reforms at home would enable Spain to exploit her colonies more efficiently than hitherto. A Ministry of the Indies was established in 1714 to direct colonial policy, replacing the old Council of the Indies, and in 1717 a step in the direction of a more realistic commercial system was taken when the *Casa de Contratación* was removed from the cramped riverside port of Seville to the more spacious harbour of Cádiz. On the other hand it was not a reassuring portent that the main efforts of the Spanish Crown after Utrecht were directed towards Italy. The Italian ambitions of Philip V and Elizabeth Farnese soon led to war and a senseless dispersal of Spain's limited resources. The most significant episode in the brief bout of hostilities in which Spain found herself engaged was the destruction of the new Spanish fleet by the British off Cape Passaro in 1718. This was convincing evidence that Spain alone could not seriously challenge Britain's supremacy at sea. Only one country could hope to do that – France.

Even after the defeats and humiliations of the War of the Spanish Succession France remained the most powerful single country in Europe. France had been defeated only because Louis XIV's ambitious policies had raised against him a coalition of all Europe. With a population approaching twenty million, France far outnumbered any other European country (the population of neither England nor Spain at the beginning of the century reached six million). To support this population France had fertile lands and active industries at home, and overseas an empire little diminished by the Utrecht settlement, and capable of considerable development. The country's recovery from the wars was rapid, and during the administration of that astute statesman, Cardinal Fleury (1726–43), the French economy expanded steadily. Fleury saw the necessity for economical financial management at home, the encouragement of domestic industry, and a cautious foreign policy. He was also aware of the value of France's overseas possessions and trade, and of the great importance of seapower in this respect. Under his guiding hand the French navy gradually recovered from its destruction during the long wars of Louis XIV's reign, and by 1739 it could boast fifty ships of the line (still numerically inferior to the British navy with its eighty heavy ships, but the French vessels were generally of better quality). France's greatest handicap in any struggle with Britain was her geographical position. Unlike Britain, she could rarely concentrate wholeheartedly on overseas warfare, and could never devote resources to the navy at the expense of the army. Security of France's land-frontiers was always the first consideration of French statesmen. Until 1778 France invariably found herself in that least enviable of strategic postures in hostilities with Britain – a war on two fronts.

Britain and France in North America

In Europe Britain and France were linked from 1716 to 1731 by an alliance of mutual self-interest; but this temporary diplomatic understanding was not reflected overseas, least of all on the North American continent. There the British colonies, after a century of settlement, extended along the coast from Nova Scotia and Maine in the north to the Carolinas far away to the south. In the period between the Utrecht settlement and the outbreak of the Seven Years War in 1756 the population of those colonies was to rise spectacularly from less than four hundred thousand to one-and-a-half million. The colonists were prosperous and energetic, their wealth based on agriculture, fisheries and trade. Although the colonies were still predominantly rural, in some parts of the settled coastal strip relatively sophisticated urban communities had developed. Philadelphia in this period became the second largest city in the British empire, ahead of Bristol and Liverpool. Above all it was a restless society, and the most marked feature of the colonial scene in the first half of the eighteenth century was the westward movement towards and across the barrier of the Appalachians, which hemmed in the English colonies on the Atlantic coastal plain. This was an expansionist movement in which private enterprise was more prominent than state planning, where the imperial government followed rather than led. It was the beginning of a march which was to end only at the Pacific, and it was bound to bring the English colonists into conflict with the French.

Geography, if nothing else, dictated that the French settlements in North America would be of a different character from the English. Instead of finding themselves on an oceanic coast from which access into the interior was generally difficult, the French traders and settlers were able to follow the route prospected by Jacques Cartier and Samuel Champlain. They entered the continent by way of the Saint Lawrence and the Great Lakes, waters which encouraged them to penetrate deep into the interior. French explorers and fur-traders pushed west and south, leaving only a thin trail of settlements behind them, mainly along the banks of the Saint Lawrence. In the second half of the seventeenth century La Salle, after sailing down the Ohio and Mississippi rivers, took possession of the vast Mississippi basin for France, and at the end of the century forts were being built along the Gulf coast near the mouth of the river. The French now commanded the mouths of both the Saint Lawrence and the Mississippi, vital entry points at the ends of a long line stretching across the North American continent. If that line could be strengthened, the English colonists would be stopped from expanding westward out of their Atlantic settlements. If it could be tightened, the English might be driven into the sea.

Strategically the French held most of the vantage points, but the very rapidity of their advance brought grave weaknesses. Enterprising and courageous Frenchmen had explored thousands of miles of territory, towards the Rocky Mountains in one direction, down the Mississippi to the Gulf of Mexico in another. But they did not occupy the vast regions they traversed. Nor could they, when the total population of New France as late as 1740 was only fifty thousand. The French made few settlements except those required for the fur trade, and since the extermination of the beaver made it imperative to keep moving to fresh trapping grounds, these were rarely permanent. The English colonists in contrast moved inland as inexorably as an incoming tide, building roads as they advanced, clearing and settling the land. Although their progress was slower and less impressive on the map than that of the French, there was a solidity about it which the French could not match. They were militarily inefficient compared with their rivals; but behind them lay the British navy, a powerful weapon when it is remembered that New France was dependent for supplies, munitions and reinforcements on ships from Europe.

After the Treaty of Utrecht the consolidation by the French of their lines of expansion in North America began to take on an even more menacing appearance to the English than the early journeys of the swift-moving French explorers and traders. The all-important entrance of the Saint Lawrence was guarded by the building in the 1720s of the great fortress of Louisbourg on Cape Breton Island, jutting out into the Gulf of Saint Lawrence opposite Newfoundland. In the same region the French tried to nullify the effects of the cession of Acadia to Britain by seeking (with considerable success) to retain the loyalty of the predominantly French population. To the north-west the French fur-traders thrust ever deeper among the Indian tribes in an effort to offset the advantage the Hudson's Bay Company possessed by being able to bring ocean-going vessels through Hudson Strait each summer to the shores of the Bay. The westward expansion continued, led now by La Vérendrye and his sons, who opened up the Lake Winnipeg and Lake Manitoba areas, and then pushed on towards the Missouri in search of furs and a route to the Pacific. Finally, away to the south, the French followed up the exploits of La Salle by founding New Orleans in 1718. At this time Louisiana, as the Mississippi basin was called, represented little more than a name on the map; but a remarkable financier and speculator, John Law, saw in it the centre of a great French empire.

John Law and Louisiana

Law was a much-travelled Scotsman who during the course of an adventurous life had made a close study of European state finances. He was convinced that France suffered from an archaic financial system which ignored the advantages of paper money and a well-organized credit system. Although it possessed greater natural resources than either Britain or Holland it lagged far behind those countries as far as national finance and overseas trade were concerned. Some of Law's ideas were basically sound, and there was a measure of truth in his famous dictum: 'Wealth depends on commerce, and commerce depends on circulation.' In France, now governed by an old acquaintance the Regent Philip of Orleans, Law pressed for an opportunity to put into operation a programme which, he claimed, would make it the greatest commercial nation in Europe; and in 1716 the Regent gave him permission to found a private bank whose notes could be used to pay government taxes. The next year Law obtained a further concession. He was granted a twenty-five-year monopoly of trade and government in the almost totally undeveloped region of Louisiana, on condition that he sent out to the colony at least 6,000 white and 3,000 coloured settlers. To exploit this grant, Law founded the *Compagnie d'Occident*, which in the course of the next two years absorbed all other branches of French overseas trade, including those with Africa, India and China. In 1719 it was re-named the *Compagnie des Indes*.

The potentialities of the new company were enormous, but they were essentially of a long-term nature. French trade to many of the regions included in the company's grant was of a sickly character, and would need decades of patient nursing to rival that of the English and Dutch. But Law was a man in a hurry; he moved at a pace dictated by the feverish enthusiasm of French investors for company shares as well as by his own sanguine temperament. To attract investors Law's agents had issued grossly misleading reports in which Louisiana appeared as a region of untold wealth, an El Dorado where diamonds and lumps of gold lay waiting to be picked up. Share prices began to rise, slowly at first, and then with staggering rapidity. Fortunes were made in a matter of days, even hours (it was now that the term 'millionaire' was first used). By the middle of 1719, 500-*livre* shares were changing hands at 15,000 *livres* in the crowded thoroughfare of the Rue de Quinquempoix in Paris. Riding on the crest of this boom, Law was given the right to collect all government taxes, and to issue paper currency; and at the beginning of 1720 he was appointed Controller-General of France, with power over the entire economy of the country.

A financial edifice erected in so short a time was bound to have weaknesses, and one of the most serious was that there was nothing in the economic development of Louisiana to justify the extravagant rise in share prices. The enthusiasm of investors for Mississippi shares (Law's Company of the Indies was invariably called the Mississippi Company) was not accompanied by any eagerness among Frenchmen to make their home in Louisiana. Efforts to encourage voluntary emigration failed, and regulations were introduced allowing the transportation of vagabonds, prostitutes and unemployed. The death-rate among these wretched people was high, both on the voyage and in the colony, and those who survived rarely made good settlers. New Orleans, one day to become one of the great cities of North America, remained an unhealthy huddle of wooden shacks, and the region's trade was tiny in relation to the inflated price of the company's shares in Paris. As realization of this spread, and as the conservative financiers of Paris mustered their forces in opposition to Law, the first cracks in Law's position appeared. In the spring of 1720 share prices began to fall; and by the end of the year Law's 'system' had collapsed, and the financier had fled the country.

The attempt to give a powerful financial impetus to France's overseas trade and empire had failed (as had Law's associated plans for financial reform within France). Speculation as wild as that seen in 1719 was no substitute for the steady investment of capital, business skill and manpower which had built up the commercial empires of the English and Dutch. In America, Louisiana settled down to a quiet, almost stagnant existence after the few years of excitement which accompanied Law's wondrous schemes. At no time did it achieve the standard of growth of most of the English colonies in North America during this period; and the history of Louisiana reveals the defects of the French colonial system in the eighteenth century. The insistence that non-Catholics did not make eligible settlers kept out not only the French Huguenots but also the industrious Germans, Dutch and Scots who were doing much to build up the English colonies. The restrictive effects of centralization were quickly apparent. All important decisions were taken in France, and put into effect by government officials in the colony. There the division of responsibility between the Governor and the Intendant led to disputes which at times paralysed the administration. The system was an authoritarian one, with no provision for participation by settler representatives. Communications with home were slow, the quality of officials willing to go out to the colony was poor, and in general the system led to inefficiency, fraud and the discouragement of that individual enterprise so vital to a pioneering venture. The few inhabitants could not produce a revenue even remotely approaching the cost of administering this immense region, and it soon became painfully clear to the French government that in

Louisiana it had acquired a ruinously expensive overseas possession.

If not of great commercial worth at this time, Louisiana remained of considerable strategic importance. It was a wedge thrust between the Spanish settlements in Florida and Texas, and during the short European war of 1719, in which France and Spain were on opposite sides, fighting broke out in the region. Controlling as it did the great waterway of the Mississippi, Louisiana served as a base for the extension of French influence far into the interior. Expeditions were sent into the Missouri and Arkansas country to explore, trade and keep pace with the reported expansion of Spanish influence from New Spain northward along the eastern slopes of the Rockies. Fortified posts were built along the Mississippi, and others established across country in a north-easterly direction to link up with the French settlements south of the Great Lakes. In the region of the Lakes themselves the French were also busy erecting forts, some of them of stone (as at Fort Niagara). These activities brought the French into contact with the first English traders and settlers advancing from the east: with Carolinians in the Mississippi valley; with New Yorkers near Lake Ontario; and with Pennsylvanians and Virginians in the most sensitive and vital region of all, the Illinois country between the Mississippi and Ohio rivers. This was the linchpin of the French position in the interior. Its importance stemmed from its strategic position, and from the corn crops the fertile soil of the region produced. These helped to sustain French troops in the area, and were to become increasingly important as the contest approached for control of the interior, and considerable bodies of troops began to operate in the Ohio valley.

Farther north, British efforts to turn Acadia into a military base which would guard the New England colonies were hampered by the refusal of the French inhabitants to renounce their allegiance to France. At the opposite end of the line of English settlements the new colony of Georgia, founded in 1733, was intended to perform the same function of a buffer-colony, this time protecting the rich plantation colonies of the south. But here also there was friction, for the new settlements lay hard against the Spanish military colony of Florida, and skirmishes along the undefined boundary were frequent.

The twenty-five years after the Treaty of Utrecht, then, saw a dangerous increase of tension in North America as the subjects of France, England and Spain approached and touched upon one another's territories. But the size of the area over which the small

E

groups of traders, settlers and soldiers were moving, the difficulty of communications, and the distance from the centres of power in Europe, all made any full-scale trial of strength between the imperial powers of Europe in the North American continent unlikely at this time. A direct confrontation was much more probable in a region easier of access, wealthier, and linked more closely with mercantile interests in Europe – the Caribbean.

The South Sea Bubble and Anglo-Spanish Disputes

Nowhere was the commercial rivalry of European powers overseas more clearly demonstrated than in the Caribbean. For long the wealth produced in, or passing through, the region had fired the imagination of European statesmen, merchants and privateers. Across the narrow isthmus of Panama passed the silver of Peru to await shipment to Spain on the treasure-fleet from Portobelo. Farther north, Mexican silver was loaded onto another fleet sailing from Veracruz. Together with the precious metals were carried indigo, cotton, dye-woods and cochineal, commodities for which there was a ready market in Europe. In the Caribbean itself the sugar islands were accounted the most valuable of all colonies in relation to their size, and the competition between them had become ruthlessly intense by the early eighteenth century. In the struggle for overseas trade and dominion between the maritime nations of Europe the Caribbean was a focal point. It was the scene as well as the cause of war; for in all the major European conflicts from 1739 onwards the region saw large-scale hostilities as well as the incessant sniping activities of privateers. Later in the century an English observer noted of the region: 'Thither the combatants repair, as to the arena.'

The crucial issue of the early years of the century, the fate of Spain's immense colonial empire, had been settled in 1713 by the simple expedient of leaving Spain's overseas territories in the possession of Philip V. But the 'equilibrium' of the Utrecht settlement was a precariously-balanced one as far as Spanish America was concerned. Officially at least, the traditional Spanish policy of commercial exclusion was still observed. Spain would supply her colonies with the European merchandise they required, and in return would absorb all the precious metals and crops they produced. As we have seen, this attitude was one adopted by all the main colonial powers, but in Spain's case it was hopelessly inconsistent with her resources. It was an ideal rendered difficult in the first place by the heavy duties Spain herself inflicted on her colonial trade. A Spanish Minister of Finance admitted:

> With such high duties and such restrictive freights, and other notable hindrances, it may be said that we have shut the door of the Indies upon the manufactures of Spain, and invited all the other nations to supply those goods to the Spanish dominions, since every port in fourteen thousand leagues of coast is open to them, and those provinces must be supplied from somewhere.

The natural result of official Spanish policy was the encouragement of smugglers from all nations, and in the struggle for trade and concessions in the Spanish empire after 1713 the English appeared to hold an advantage. At Utrecht they had prised open a small but possibly significant chink in the wall the Spanish government was trying to maintain around its American empire. During the War of the Spanish Succession a French company had held the grant to supply slaves to Spanish America, the *asiento*. Then, by the Treaty of Utrecht, the concession was transferred for thirty years to the English South Sea Company. It was permitted to bring in 4,800 slaves a year, and to keep factors at seven of the most important Spanish American ports. The Company was also given the right to send one ship of not more than 500 tons (raised in 1716 to 650 tons) with a cargo of trading goods to the Spanish American trade fairs each year. Although greeted with the most extravagant hopes in England – it was described on one occasion as 'the feather and flower of our trade' – the *asiento* concession was not nearly as lucrative as had been imagined. In the first place, the misnamed 'annual voyage' proved to be an erratic business. Subjected to various restrictions, interrupted by short wars between England and Spain in 1719 and 1727, and always dependent on Spanish goodwill, this particular concession led to only eight voyages during the entire period of the grant. Nor were profits readily forthcoming from the supply of slaves, for the Company found itself undersold by illicit traders who supplied slaves of inferior quality at cheaper rates.

Illusions in England about the potentialities of trade to Spanish America were dramatically spotlighted by the South Sea Bubble of 1720, the English equivalent of Law's grandiose Mississippi project. By 1717 the South Sea Company, whose ostensible commercial basis when founded in 1711 had been the anticipated *asiento* concession and the development of trade with Spanish America, was essentially a finance company. It aimed at taking over part of the National Debt, and in negotiations with the government between 1717 and 1720 succeeded in doing this. It then had the task of persuading holders of high-interest-bearing government bonds, which made up much of the National Debt at this time, to convert them into South Sea Company stock at a lower interest rate. The bait the Company used was the immense capital now at its disposal (for it was authorized to create £1 of new stock for every £1 of the National Debt it took over, regardless of the price at which that stock actually sold) and the profits still hopefully expected from the *asiento* and the monopoly of British trade with Spanish America which the Company possessed.

Clever propaganda and a large measure of credulity on the part of the investing public led to a rush to buy stock which pushed share prices at one stage to 1050, and resulted in scenes of frenzied buying and selling which rivalled those in Paris at the height of the Mississippi mania a few months earlier. Indeed, although there was an element of deliberate fraud in the South Sea Company's financial confidence trick which was not present in Law's projects, there were close similarities between the two schemes. Pamphlets issued in London to persuade investors to buy South Sea Company stock described Law's Mississippi schemes in glowing language, and stressed 'the almost incredible advantages thereby accruing to the French King and a great number of his subjects'. The bubble was pricked in England as quickly as in France, and although the financial consequences were not quite as serious they produced a political crisis of first-class magnitude. Again, as in France, one of the most important long-term consequences of the spectacular financial losses of 1720 was the severe damage caused to the confidence of investors in distant overseas enterprises.

The fanciful hopes with which the South Sea Company was launched, and which helped to inflate the bubble of 1720, typified the exaggerated views held in Europe of the wealth and resources of Spanish America. In reality, despite the eye-catching amount of bullion brought home on the treasure-fleets, the market there for European goods was a limited and mainly static one at this time. But disappointing though the South Sea Company's trade was, it roused Spanish suspicions that it was serving as a cloak for smuggling on a grand scale. A Spanish report described how the Company was ingeniously abusing its concession in 1735:

> Whilst the English were permitted to send an annual ship, called *navio de permisio*, she used to bring to the [Portobelo] fair a very large cargo on her own account, never failing to touch first at Jamaica, so that her loading alone was more than half of all those brought by the galleons. For besides that her burthen so far exceeded five hundred Spanish tons that it was even more than nine hundred, she had no provisions, water, or other things which fill a great part of the hold. She indeed took them in at Jamaica, from whence she was attended by five or six smaller vessels loaded with goods, which when they arrived near Portobelo were put on board her, and the provisions removed into tenders. By which artifice that single ship was made to carry more than five or six of the largest galleons; and this nation having a free trade, and selling cheaper than the Spaniards, that indulgence was of infinite detriment to the commerce of Spain.

More irritating still to the Spanish government were the private traders engaged in smuggling, particularly the British vessels working from their base at Jamaica in the heart of the Spanish Caribbean. The Spanish authorities had justifiable grievances. The British government was more nonchalant than other European governments in supervising the activities of its subjects. It made no move to follow the French example in instructing traders to give bond that they would not engage in illicit trade. For its part, the Spanish government was faced with a situation in which foreign vessels were sailing hither and thither in the Caribbean, ostensibly trading with their own colonies, but often smuggling goods into the Spanish colonies. The only answer to this problem, maintained Spanish officials, was to stop and search any foreign vessel in the Caribbean which appeared near Spanish shores. If found to be carrying contraband (that is, any Spanish colonial product), it would be seized.

The British vehemently contested this Spanish claim to intercept and perhaps confiscate any foreign vessel not on a direct route to or from one of its own colonies. Not only was the inference that the Caribbean was a Spanish lake in which the ships of other nations could not sail without permission objectionable in principle; there were certain practical difficulties. A British vessel might well have Spanish produce on board which had been obtained legitimately (through the

South Sea Company, for example). Moreover, the system of prevailing winds in the Caribbean made the Spanish insistence that all foreign vessels sighted near Spanish colonies were suspect absurdly unrealistic. Merchantmen bound from England to Jamaica passed near the southern coast of Puerto Rico, and on the homeward voyage very close to Cuban shores.

Unfortunately for the cause of peace, the Spanish government could not afford to keep enough official squadrons at sea to enforce the rules it had laid down. Instead, colonial governors had to rely on private coastguard vessels, often manned by crews of ruffians, the notorious *guardacostas*. These were paid on a commission basis, and their attitude was hardly distinguishable from that of privateers in time of war. They were more interested in taking prizes than in preserving Spain's trade monopoly. Vessels were seized on dubious evidence, cargoes were confiscated, and crews ill-treated and imprisoned.

Despite the increasing frequency of incidents between their nationals in the Caribbean, neither the Spanish nor the British government was eager for war. In England Walpole was still firmly in control, and insistent, as always, on the virtues of a negotiated settlement. Spain had drifted away from her French ally after the latter made a separate peace in the War of the Polish Succession in 1735, and was in no position to wage war with so redoubtable an adversary as Britain. But governments cannot always control the actions of their subjects, and in 1737 no fewer than twelve British vessels disappeared in the Caribbean. In answer to British protests that this was the work of *guardacostas* the Spanish government adopted a conciliatory attitude and began investigations. While these pursued a laboriously slow course, public opinion was becoming inflamed in England. In part, this was the work of the parliamentary opposition to Walpole, which at last saw a chance to overthrow the most powerful politician of the age. By irresponsibly stirring up a public agitation with exaggerated accounts of Spanish cruelties the opposition hoped to discredit Walpole and force him from office. The first part of its task was not difficult. The old hatred of Spain was not far submerged. Pamphlets, newspapers and cartoons extolled the glorious days of Drake and Cromwell, and reminded readers of the horrors of the Spanish Inquisition. Petitions from the great trading cities calling for forceful action poured into Parliament. Characteristic of the emotional attitudes struck was the criticism of Walpole's calm stand by an alderman of the City of London: 'Seventy of our brave sailors are now in chains in Spain. Our countrymen in chains and slaves to the Spaniards! Is this not enough to arouse all the vengeance of national resentment?' A merchant skipper, Captain Jenkins, arrived at the House of Commons with a bottle containing his ear (lopped off, he claimed, by *guardacostas* in 1731) to add a dramatic note to the uproar.

In the midst of all this excitement urgent negotiations were taking place between the British and Spanish governments. In the autumn of 1738 it was agreed, as a preliminary to a general settlement of differences, that Spain would pay £95,000 compensation for damage received by British merchants in the Caribbean; and a convention to this effect (the Convention of Pardo) was signed in January 1739. Both sides had made concessions. The British government had cut its claim for compensation from £140,00 to £95,000; the Spanish government, though financially in dire straits, pledged speedy payment. Unhappily the whole transaction depended on the South Sea Company paying the sum of £68,000 which it owed the Spanish Crown as a quarter-share of the proceeds from its 'annual ship' to the Caribbean. This the Company refused to pay until it had been given satisfaction for the losses it had suffered during the hostilities in 1719 and 1727, when Spanish officials had seized its property in America. On this obstacle the negotiations foundered, and the chances of an international settlement were wrecked by the selfishness of a private trading company with a none too reputable history. The Spanish government in retaliation suspended the *asiento*. Given the height of feeling in England, and the regard paid to the *asiento*, this intemperate action made war certain. Open hostilities started in the summer of 1739, when British squadrons were ordered to intercept the galleons, and Edward Vernon was sent to the Caribbean to harry Spanish shipping. In October war was formally declared.

Substantial sections of the nation had obviously been spoiling for war. Their motives were mainly discreditable, springing from greed, ambition and boredom; but beneath the unedifying froth of the agitation for war lay some serious considerations. As a great commercial power Britain now held certain interests in the New World which had to be protected. The humiliating restrictions which she had been forced to accept in earlier times could no longer be tolerated. The arrogance which often accompanied this new determination was

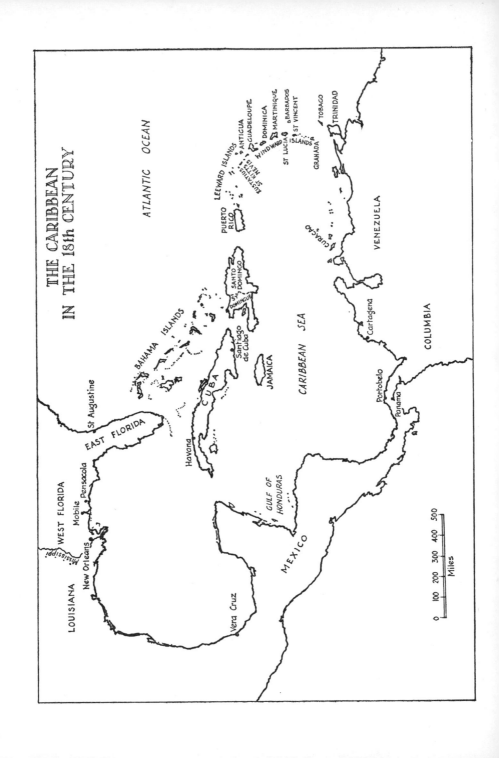

THE CARIBBEAN
IN THE 18th CENTURY

ATLANTIC OCEAN

LEEWARD ISLANDS
ANTIGUA
GUADELOUPE
DOMINICA
MARTINIQUE
ST LUCIA
ST VINCENT
BARBADOS
GRANADA
TOBAGO
TRINIDAD
WINDWARD ISLANDS
STATIUS
ST KITTS
NEVIS
PUERTO RICO

SANTO DOMINGO
ST DOMINGUE

BAHAMA ISLANDS

Santiago de Cuba

CUBA

JAMAICA

CARIBBEAN SEA

CURAÇAO

VENEZUELA

Cartagena

COLUMBIA

Portobelo

Panama

St Augustine

EAST FLORIDA

Havana

GULF OF HONDURAS

WEST FLORIDA
Pensacola
Mobile

LOUISIANA
New Orleans
Mississippi

MEXICO

Vera Cruz

0 100 200 300 400 500
Miles

reflected in the words of a member of the parliamentary opposition: 'The grievances of England admit but of one remedy, and a very short and simple one: that our ships shall not be searched on any pretence. This alone can go to the root of our grievances; all less than this is trifling, hurtful, and fatal to our commerce.' In short, England must demand rights which she herself would never consider granting to the traders of other nations.

Then again, amid the light-hearted clamour for war could be glimpsed an anxiety about Britain's commercial position. France, it was felt, had recovered with unexpected rapidity from the wars of Louis XIV, and her trade and industry were expanding at an alarming rate. War with Spain would probably involve war with France as well, and provide an opportunity to increase Britain's trade at the expense of the enemy. A belligerent pamphleteer summed up this argument when he wrote: 'We should not only distress our enemy to the last degree, but by ruining their commerce, and destroying their colonies, which they could hardly prevent whilst we are so much their superiors by sea, we should in a great measure retrieve our own, and make them flourish again as formerly.'

Whatever the arguments advanced at the time in favour of war, the events leading to the Anglo-Spanish conflict of 1739 (the War of Jenkins's Ear, as it is usually named) make depressing reading. National honour on both sides became all too easily identified with the interests of smugglers and desperadoes. The real significance of the war was that it was the first major conflict between European powers fought because of overseas disputes. The convention that colonial issues should not be allowed to complicate European diplomacy was fading fast. Colonies were regarded as integral parts of the national economy, and overseas commerce of sufficient importance to justify open war.

The War of Jenkins's Ear

The general shape of the war was clearly mapped from the beginning. Spain, with its sprawling, vulnerable empire, would be forced onto the defensive. Britain, with a government spurred on by a bellicose public opinion, would take the offensive. Spain possessed an army far greater in size than Britain's, but she could muster only forty ships of the line. This was about half the number Britain could put in service, and Spanish naval weakness eliminated any possibility of an invasion of

England. Although operations might be launched against Gibraltar and Minorca, the chief Spanish weapon was likely to be commerce-raiding. The small size of Britain's regular army just as effectively ruled out any prospect of large-scale British landings in Spain. But British naval strength made attacks on Spain's overseas trade and her colonial possessions an alluring possibility. The refusal to accept Spain's right of search, so contentious an issue in the long months of negotiation before the outbreak of war, faded into the background. Legalistic haggling about maritime rights was replaced by more exciting discussions about the dismemberment of the Spanish empire. Some of Spain's colonies could be taken by direct assault; in others subversion of the creole or Indian inhabitants would lead to their breakaway from Spanish rule, with plentiful opportunities for British traders. The feeling of the country was expressed in unmistakable fashion in the parliamentary debates of November 1739. Speaker after speaker urged the government to attack Spanish America, 'where', as one member put it, 'we can make them feel most sensibly the weight of our resentment: it is by conquests in that part of the world where we can most effectually secure or enlarge our navigation, and it is there where they can least resist us.'

No scheme was too madcap to be laid before the government for consideration, and the files of leading ministers bulged with plans for assaults on all parts of the Spanish empire. But if the choice of objectives seemed unlimited, British resources were not. The navy was more impressive on paper than on the high seas. Its ships had deteriorated during the years of peace; it had seen little fighting for a generation; its organization and many of its senior officers were of doubtful quality. It had to protect home waters, control the Mediterranean and defend Britain's commerce before it could spare forces to attack Spain's overseas empire. Confronted with these problems, the government, with Walpole at its head unconvinced of the wisdom or necessity of the war, delayed taking decisions. Meanwhile, reinforcements were being sent from Spain to the Caribbean. Finally, at the end of 1739, the government determined to send a powerful expedition to the West Indies under the command of Lord Cathcart. There Admiral Vernon in November had secured an unexpected success when he captured Portobelo with a mere half-dozen ships; and popular reaction in Britain made it essential to follow up this minor victory. At the same time, a smaller expedition under Commodore

Anson was to be sent round Cape Horn into the Pacific to raid Spanish possessions and trade, and (it was hoped) encourage the Spanish colonists to revolt.

A complication remained. What would be the attitude of the French government to any substantial British conquests in the Caribbean? Fleury had hinted broadly enough that France would not stand by to watch the balance established by the Utrecht settlement blatantly upset. His warning was ignored, and preparations for Cathcart's expedition continued. That Fleury was in earnest, even to the point of open war against Britain, was shown by his decision to send a fleet to the West Indies in 1740 under the Marquis d'Antin with instructions to attack either Vernon or the expedition on its way out from England to join him. This done, d'Antin was to seize Jamaica. Further orders envisaged d'Antin joining the fleet of the Spanish admiral, Torres, which had sailed for the Caribbean a few weeks earlier.

When reports of d'Antin's departure (though not of his full instructions) reached England extra ships were added to the expedition sailing to join Vernon, and secret orders given to it in turn to attack d'Antin. When the rendezvous with Vernon was made the British fleet would number thirty-five ships of the line, and would be opposed by a possible total of forty enemy ships if the French and Spanish fleets joined each other as ordered. Never before had such formidable fighting forces been seen in Caribbean waters, although two of the nations involved were officially still at peace. The French and British governments passed the winter of 1740–1 nervously waiting for reports of a great battle in the Caribbean. But the news never came. Sickness among the French crews, storm damage to Torres's ships, the failure of the French and Spanish admirals to agree on united action, erroneous information given to Vernon by his scouting cruisers about the position of the enemy – all added up to a tale of misfortune and mismanagement which reduced the anticipated clash of these mighty fleets to a brief skirmish between a few French and English men-of-war. D'Antin's fleet ignominiously returned to France (by now embroiled in the War of the Austrian Succession), England and France remained at peace for another three years, and Vernon was left free to attack Cartagena.

The ambitious British operations planned for 1741 got off to a bad start. Lord Cathcart died almost as soon as he reached the Caribbean, and Brigadier-General Wentworth, who had never seen active service, took over command of the land forces. At first relations between him and Vernon, still in command of the fleet, were good; but soon after the expedition arrived at Cartagena in March 1741 and the first landings were made, differences of opinion began to appear. Vernon, with his earlier West Indian experience, knew that disease was the most dangerous enemy of raw troops, and he favoured swift, sharp assaults on the Spanish positions. Wentworth, regardless of the weakness of the fortifications confronting him, moved with ponderous deliberation as if engaged in the slow-motion siege operations of the Low Countries rather than in surroundings where tropical fevers, dysentery and scurvy weakened his forces daily. He insisted on prolonged bombardments, the establishment of defensive camps, and formal daylight assaults which ended in disastrous losses. Vernon expressed his feelings about the capabilities of Wentworth and his officers in biting remarks about 'the slow proceedings of our Gentlemen of Parade, who having been so long trained to nothing but Reviews, can't so readily shake off the rust of idleness'. Before the end of the Cartagena operations there was only a pretence at co-operation between the two commanders, and in May 1741 the reduction of the troops through sickness and battle from 8,000 to only 3,500 effectives caused the abandonment of the assault.

With these reduced forces an attack on the strong fortifications of Havana, the centre of Spanish power in the Caribbean, was out of the question; but an attempt upon Santiago at the eastern end of Cuba seemed feasible. Santiago was an important privateer base, and if the capture of Cuba was planned at a later date its possession would give the British a helpful foothold on the island. The fleet arrived at its objective in July, and a Council of War decided that the troops should land some distance from the strongly defended harbour, and march to attack the town from the land side. To Vernon's despair the story of the Cartagena campaign was repeated. Despite the feebleness of Spanish resistance Wentworth refused to advance. The troops died by the hundreds in their unhealthy camp, Vernon's letters to Wentworth became increasingly irate, and finally in November the attempt was given up.

There was one more fiasco to come. The Council of War decided to attack Panama, but on this occasion the troops were not even landed. On arrival off Portobelo on the opposite side of the isthmus in March

1742 Wentworth decided that the project was impracticable because of the imminence of the rainy season and the limited number of assault troops – factors perfectly well known before the expedition left Jamaica. Little wonder that the testy Vernon wrote home of his lamentable colleague that his opinions were 'more changeable than the moon'. By the end of 1742 both Vernon and Wentworth had sailed for home. Their recall marked the end of the optimistic policy, adopted three years earlier, of large-scale combined operations in the Caribbean aimed at the capture of important Spanish possessions. Commerce-raiding replaced grand plans of territorial conquest. At home Walpole had resigned, and the new ministry was determined to give direct military assistance to Austria in the continental war, a policy which left little room for ambitious expeditions overseas.

Anglo-French Hostilities

The outbreak of war between Britain and France in 1744 again directed attention to the Caribbean. With fierce rivalry already existing between the British and French sugar islands it looked as though the eastern Caribbean would quickly become the scene of merciless raiding and destruction by both sides. For half a century the French islands, with their great stretches of fertile soil, had gradually been asserting their competitive supremacy over the smaller British islands. The three most important French colonies in the Caribbean were the envy of other European nations. Saint Domingue (the western part of Hispaniola, acquired by France in 1697) was rapidly becoming the most valuable tropical colony, for its size, in the world. Already it supported 30,000 Frenchmen, 100,000 slaves, and exported vast quantities of sugar, cotton, coffee and indigo. Guadeloupe, largest of the Leeward Islands, probably produced more sugar than all the British West Indian islands put together. Martinique, though not as important a sugar producer as Saint Domingue or Guadeloupe, was the administrative centre of the French West Indies, and a great commercial entrepôt visited by hundreds of merchantmen each year. Its fine harbour made it an important naval base and a haunt of privateers.

To many of the English planters war offered a chance to redress the balance. They were not interested in acquiring the French islands; that would merely reduce the price of their own sugar. Instead, as a pamphleteer insisted in 1745: 'By a well-managed descent upon their sugar islands we should at once ruin them, and promote the welfare of our own for many years. This might be done by only destroying their sugar-works, and carrying off their slaves.' The West Indian islands were particularly vulnerable to this sort of destructive raiding expedition. The smallness of the white population, especially in the British islands, resulted in the local militia being few in number, as well as generally ill-trained and of low quality. The planters were understandably reluctant to arm their slaves. Fortifications were often tumbledown and without cannon. The few regiments of regular troops stationed in the islands were invariably under strength and badly equipped.

Fortunately for the islands, external factors saved them from marauding forces for the time being: their turn was to come in the Seven Years War. Neither government could spare the forces necessary for large-scale offensive operations in the Caribbean. The French and British armies were engaged in continental campaigns, and navies were fully occupied in home waters and in the Mediterranean. What few aggressive projects overseas the British government considered from 1744 onwards were directed at the French in North America, where there was considerable enthusiasm among the British colonists for the capture of French bases. In the Caribbean both sides confined themselves to efforts aimed at disrupting the enemy's trade and starving his colonists through the weapons of blockade and interception. In this sort of warfare the advantage lay with the British. The powerful West India lobby in London was continually prodding the government to send more naval vessels to the Caribbean for commerce protection. British squadrons were kept permanently at Jamaica and the Leeward Islands. Naval dockyards at Jamaica and Antigua enabled the ships to be repaired, provisioned and kept on station for two or three years.

The French, on the other hand, had no dockyard facilities in the Caribbean, and ships from Europe could serve only for short spells of duty, rarely more than six months at a time. As the dominant naval power, Britain could afford to scatter her vessels in colonial waters for local defence, and still keep enough heavy ships in European waters to repel any concentration of French and Spanish forces. Nevertheless there was a certain inflexibility about the system which benefited the numerically inferior enemy. The French normally collected their ships together each winter in their home ports, and sent them where they thought fit the next spring – a procedure which involved the British Admiralty each year in a worrying game of guesswork about the destination of the main French fleets. To this extent the rigid station system, the result of political pressure as much as of any strategic consideration, restricted the British freedom of concentration and manœuvre.

With the French islands left unprotected for long periods, the French government tried to safeguard the trade of its Caribbean colonies by means of a convoy system. Both sides used convoys, but since the British navy generally controlled the Caribbean and European waters it was the French application of the system which was given the more searching test. The French merchants had to pay the cost of the naval vessels acting as escorts to the West Indian convoys, in theory four warships to a convoy. The system quickly ran into the perennial difficulties attendant upon it: delays in getting the ships to the place of rendezvous, irregularity of sailings, problems of shepherding a large number of merchantmen (sometimes as many as 250). Imperfect though the system was, the skill and courage of the French commanders undoubtedly kept losses lower than they would have been if merchant ships had to sail without escort, prey to warship or privateer; but by 1747 British dominance in European waters made the passage of the huge, scattered convoys increasingly perilous. Losses mounted at an alarming rate, and the French Caribbean islands endured a period of scarcity and hardship before peace came in 1748.

In North America formal operations during the war were confined to an assault on the massive French fortress of Louisbourg on Cape Breton Island. Louisbourg was an obvious objective: obvious, whether one looked at the stronghold in the broad context of the Anglo-French struggle for domination in North America (as did Governor Shirley of Massachusetts), or whether one had suffered from the attentions of Louisbourg privateers, as had many New England merchants and fishermen. Towards the end of 1744 Shirley received reports that Louisbourg was weakly garrisoned, and he persuaded the Massachusetts Assembly to fit out an expedition to seize the fortress without waiting for help from England. Land forces could be found in the colony, but naval support was essential, and this Massachusetts could not provide. The enterprising Commodore Warren, in command of the Leeward Islands squadron far away in the Caribbean, came to the rescue with three warships. These escorted the little New England vessels carrying 4,000 volunteers to Louisbourg, and were later reinforced by ships from England. Warren's force arrived at a most inopportune moment for the French garrison, for it captured twenty French vessels on their way in to Louisbourg with provisions and ammunition.

Attempts to take the fortress by storm failed, and the attackers settled down to besiege it. A steady battering fire was directed at the fortifications, no food reached the beleaguered defenders, and before a final assault could be launched the dispirited garrison surrendered. It had been defeated not so much by the efforts of the brave but raw Massachusetts levies as by the hopelessness of its position once Warren's squadron established command of the sea approaches, and cut off all possibility of aid. Warren's local supremacy at sea was supported on the other side of the Atlantic, where French reinforcements intended for Louisbourg were blockaded by British squadrons off Brest.

An impressive list of advantages could be drawn up from this single victory: the gaining of the most important French harbour in North America; the destruction of a valuable French fishery; the relief afforded to the New Englanders; the demoralization of France's Indian allies; and finally the opening of the Saint Lawrence for an attack on Quebec. After some hesitation the British government in 1746 decided to take advantage of this unexpected colonial success by sending an expedition from England up the Saint Lawrence to Quebec, at the same time as colonial troops were advancing on Montreal overland. The whole plan collapsed when contrary winds held up the sailing of the expedition from Portsmouth, and it was diverted to Brittany where it failed miserably to attain its objective. A strong French expedition which slipped the blockade in 1746 and sailed with the intention of re-taking Louisbourg and raiding the New England coast met an even more melancholy fate. Its ships were shattered by storm, the men were stricken by disease, and it returned to France with 8,000 dead. With these misfortunes on both sides, the momentum went out of the North American operations. Plans were discussed, but little was accomplished before peace came in the autumn of 1748.

The Treaty of Aix-la-Chapelle

The situation at the time of the peace negotiations of 1748 clearly reflected the strength and weakness of the two great powers which were to contest overseas supremacy throughout the eighteenth century. On the continent of Europe France was triumphant. Her armies had captured Flanders, and now lay poised for a campaign which might overrun the Dutch Republic. But at sea Britain was supreme. Naval victories by Anson and Hawke in 1747 had smashed the French navy; and successful commerce-raiding and a tightening blockade were throttling French overseas trade. Lacking adequate naval protection, French colonies lay exposed to attack in the Caribbean, North America and India.

Continuation of the war would have involved a desperate race to see which side could win further victories – France in Europe, or Britain overseas – and at the same time stave off disaster in the other theatre. The gamble was one which neither side was prepared to take, and early in 1748 serious peace negotiations began. To persuade France to relinquish her hold on the conquered Austrian Netherlands, Britain and her allies could offer only one territorial compensation – Louisbourg. Despite the fortress's strategic importance the British government did not hesitate to sacrifice it in order to gain security nearer home. Louisbourg was returned to France, which in turn gave up the territory it had conquered in the Low Countries, and Madras in India. Over four of the islands at dispute in the Caribbean – Dominica, Saint Lucia, Saint Vincent and Tobago – an uneasy compromise was reached. They were to be 'neutral islands', settled neither by British nor French colonists. As far as Britain and France were concerned, little had been settled by the war. It had made chances of amity and co-operation between the subjects of the two nations in North America, the Caribbean and India slimmer than ever; but had done nothing to indicate which side would emerge the victor. Although Britain's supremacy at sea had been confirmed, French military strength on the continent seemed sufficient to win back by a simple process of barter any overseas possessions she might lose.

Equally uncertain was the question of future relations between Britain and Spain. Large-scale hostilities between the two countries had died away after Vernon's failures in the Caribbean, and the merging of the Anglo-Spanish conflict into the War of the Austrian Succession. But the original causes of friction remained: the *asiento* concession, contraband trade and the right of search, and the vexed question of the small British logwood-cutting settlements which had

F

stealthily appeared in the Bay of Honduras in Central America. Towards the end of the war prospects of an agreement seemed good. Philip V of Spain died in 1746, and was succeeded by the unambitious Ferdinand VI, who left foreign affairs to Carvajal, a realistic statesman who could see the advantages of an alliance with so strong a naval power as Britain. But an attempt to make a separate peace in 1747 failed, and in the web of negotiations which led to the Treaty of Aix-la-Chapelle the only Anglo-Spanish dispute to be settled was the *asiento* issue. A compromise was reached, and it was agreed to let the concession run for another four years, although by the terms of the original agreement (as interpreted by Spain) it should have expired in 1744. Apart from this the Treaty settled little in the disputed area of Anglo-Spanish maritime and colonial differences.

The main theme of the Aix-la-Chapelle settlement was a general return to the *status quo*. This was hardly a satisfactory result for nations which had expended their manpower and resources in the war. Apart from Prussia, which retained Silesia, all the great powers had reason to feel aggrieved. Britain had given up her sole conquest, and had reached no agreement with Spain about the issues which had led to war in 1739. France had suffered heavy losses to her navy and overseas commerce, and had restored the territory she had seized in the Low Countries and India. Austria failed to regain Silesia. Spain was no nearer to recovering Gibraltar and Minorca. The Treaty of Aix-la-Chapelle was only a truce, in Carlyle's words 'a mere end of fighting because your powder is run out'; and eight years later general war broke out once more.

4

Climax of the Contest:
The Seven Years War 1756–1763

THE STRUGGLE between Britain and France for overseas supremacy had not held a prominent place in the War of the Austrian Succession. Operations in North America, the Caribbean and India had been of a comparatively minor nature. But the years after the Treaty of Aix-la-Chapelle brought a new urgency and ruthlessness to the colonial rivalry between the two great powers. In India a policy of territorial expansion by the French under Dupleix menaced the British trading settlements (see Chapter 5); in the Caribbean the French showed no inclination to evacuate the 'neutral islands' in the Windward group; and in North America frontier fighting threatened to swell into open war. It was there, above all, that the pace of developments made it most difficult for the British and French governments to remain aloof from the actions of their subjects. By 1754 tension had reached breaking-point, and undeclared but bitter warfare was waged for two years before the formal outbreak of hostilities in May 1756. As far as Britain and France were concerned, the tremendous world conflict we know as the Seven Years War could more accurately have been termed the Nine Years War, and before its close the political fate of much of North America had been settled.

Frontier Clashes in North America

The storm centre of conflict between British and French colonists in North America during the years immediately after the Aix-la-Chapelle settlement was the Ohio valley. Its fertile lands had long attracted the attention of Virginians, and after the signing of peace in 1748 freed the colonists from the irksome necessity of standing in defence along their formal frontiers, land companies were formed to settle the region (where British traders had been active for some years). Most impressive of these organizations was the Ohio Company, founded in 1748, which was given a grant by the Crown of half a million acres. The funds at the disposal of the company, and its support both in Britain and Virginia, made it a formidable undertaking; but its challenge was met by the Governor of New France, Galissonière.

Galissonière was well aware of feeling in France that Canada and Louisiana were useless colonies whose possession imposed an intolerable strain upon French finances. By many they were regarded as examples of the parasitic type of colony referred to by Montesquieu when he wrote: 'An empire may be compared to a tree the branches of which, if permitted to grow beyond a certain point, absorb all the sap from the trunk.' Other critics pointed out that the distances involved made co-operation between Quebec and New Orleans difficult, and that the life-lines of both colonies could be cut by a sea power commanding the Gulf of Mexico and the entrance of the Saint Lawrence. In a vigorous reply to these criticisms Galissonière asserted that Canada was not only a country of great potential resources, but that it formed the main obstacle blocking the way to British domination of North America and the Caribbean. In his view, which was accepted by the French government, Canada should be strengthened as a barrier against British ambitions in the New World.

Galissonière's actions in North America were in keeping with his words. In 1749 he sent soldiers into the Ohio valley to claim it for France. By a mixture of tactful handling and displays of force, the Indian tribes of the region were won over to the French side, and many of the British traders deserted the valley. In an area where European forces were thin on the ground Indian alliances were of the utmost value, poor fighters though the Indian warriors often were in open battle. The powerful Six Nations of the Iroquois Confederation were formally in alliance with Britain, but they showed a marked suspicion of Virginian plans for settlement on their hunting grounds in the Ohio valley, and refused to stand in the way of French penetration of the region. As always, traders were preferable to settlers in Indian eyes. The first French thrusts were followed by the forcible expulsion of the remaining British traders, the building of forts, and the arrival of strong groups of French troops.

These advances by the French into territory granted to the Ohio Company by the British Crown were clearly taking the affair out of the category of a boundary dispute which could be confined to the colonists involved, and into that of a first-class international crisis. The President of the Board of Trade was not being unduly alarmist when he told the British government that, unless the French were stopped,

> they will be in possession of near two-thirds of the very best unsettled land on this side of the Mississippi and Saint Lawrence, while Great Britain will not only lose near one-half of the territory to which it is indisputably entitled, but in case of a future rupture will find it extremely difficult to keep the other half.

The first clash of arms came in 1754, when French troops who had forced Virginian frontiersmen to abandon a fort they were building at the junction of the Ohio and Allegheny rivers were confronted by a smaller force of British colonials under the command of a young officer, George Washington. After a preliminary skirmish Washington's little force was defeated, and withdrew. The war was still unofficial, but after this incident there could be no doubt of its reality. The defeat revealed to the British government what had been clear to discerning colonists for some time: the dangerously weak military position of the colonies. Prosperous Virginia, with a population of close on a quarter of a million, could muster only six hundred men for the defence of its frontier at this moment. Other colonies, Pennsylvania for one, refused to make any attempt to raise troops. Inter-colonial jealousies, reluctance by colonial assemblies to incur extraordinary expenditure, pacifist objections to the use of force, the unpopularity of militia service: all these factors hindered the defence of the colonies. At Albany in June 1754 delegates from seven of the colonies agreed to Benjamin Franklin's proposal to establish a council which would operate a common defence policy; but the colonies refused to accept the recommendations of their representatives, and the plan came to nothing.

Now fully conscious of the gravity of the situation, the British government decided to take firm action. In this it was stiffened by the pugnacious attitude of the French in India and the Caribbean. Two regiments were to be sent to North America commanded by Major-General Braddock, the first British regulars ever to serve in America. Two further regiments were to be raised in America, colonial levies were to be recruited, and with these forces Braddock was to push back intruders, area by area, wherever they had encroached on territory claimed by Britain. The first priority was to expel the French from the scene of their recent triumph, Fort Duquesne (on the site of modern Pittsburgh) in the Ohio valley. In the summer of 1755 Braddock took his army, with its heavy artillery, from the settled parts of Virginia through difficult, mountainous country to within striking distance of the fort. The march was a triumph of endurance and tenacity, and speaks well for Braddock's often-criticized military capacity; but it ended in utter disaster. The garrison at Fort Duquesne had been strengthened on news of Braddock's arrival in Virginia, and when his army drew near the fort it was ambushed with an appalling thoroughness. British regulars and colonial militia were caught in a deadly cross-fire, Braddock himself was mortally wounded, panic-stricken men fired at each other in the confusion, and out of a force of about 1,500 men almost 1,000 were killed or wounded.

News of the catastrophe brought terror and despondency to the British colonists, especially those in the exposed frontier settlements. French forces had defeated with humiliating ease, first Washington's little colonial army, and now Braddock's regiments. The defeat made the failure of the British navy to prevent French reinforcements of picked troops from reaching America (the first regular battalions to be sent out for almost a century) even more disturbing than it had seemed at first. Reports of the impending dispatch of these reinforcements had placed the British government in a dilemma in the spring of 1755. If the convoy was allowed to reach America, the military balance there would tilt even further in France's favour; if it was destroyed as it left port, a European war would certainly break out. Finally, a compromise course of action was adopted, which, it was hoped, might block the French reinforcements and yet avoid war in Europe. Admiral Boscawen was ordered to intercept the French convoy, but to do so as it approached the Gulf of Saint Lawrence, not near European coasts. The convention that limited warfare 'beyond the Line' need not embroil European nations in general hostilities was weaker than it had been in the seventeenth century, but so convenient a doctrine still commanded a certain degree of acceptance.

In the event the gamble failed. Boscawen managed to capture only two of the French ships on their outward voyage, and that after fierce fighting. The others slipped past in fog, ice and gales. This meagre haul was not worth the risk taken. A British minister wrote ruefully, 'What we have done is either too little or too much' – too little in that the French regiments and supplies had reached their destination, too much in that Boscawen's attack had given the French an excuse for an immediate declaration of war. The diplomatic situation and French unreadiness avoided this for the time being; but the fighting of 1755, and the support sent to North America by the governments in Europe, showed that the warfare between Britain and France overseas was official in all but name.

The trend of events during the rest of 1755 and the early months of 1756 did little to lighten the gloom on the British side. The only relief from constant French pressure came in the north, where in 1755 the French were driven from Fort Beauséjour, a strong-point commanding the narrow neck of the Acadian peninsula. Though by European standards an unimpressive timber and earthwork fortification, Beauséjour was a key link in a chain stretching from the heart of French Canada to its eastern citadel of Louisbourg. Without it, the French threat to New England was reduced, and Louisbourg was reduced to an isolated outpost whose only communication with other French settlements was by sea. At the same time the awkward problem of the fifteen thousand French inhabitants of Acadia, formally under British sovereignty since the Treaty of Utrecht, was solved by their expulsion. Harsh though this action was, it was one which the Acadians had brought on themselves. Understandably perhaps, they had steadfastly refused to change their allegiance, and had remained active supporters of the French cause. Years of experience had shown that there would be no tranquillity or security in the peninsula while they remained.

But this weakening of the French position in the north-east was exceptional; elsewhere the tide was flowing strongly in favour of the French. Attempts by British colonial forces to mount attacks on French strongholds south of the Great Lakes failed. Further French reinforcements reached Canada, and with them a new and energetic commander in the Marquis de Montcalm. In 1756 Montcalm showed his capabilities by capturing the important British trading centre of Oswego on Lake Ontario, together with its supporting forts. As news of defeat and disaster reached them from every side the British colonists would have found it difficult to recognize the modern analyses given of the Anglo-French struggle in North America, with their insistence on the fundamental weakness of the French position.

Grave weaknesses there were, it is true, and in the long term they were to be decisive. Indeed, it was appreciation of these weaknesses by the French which helped to throw them onto the offensive in a bold attempt to turn back the steadily advancing British. But this general trend was not easy to discern in the mid 'fifties. For years British colonists had seen the French grip tightening on their western frontiers, had experienced the ceaseless raiding of Indian tribes in alliance with the French, had been slowly pushed back from the approaches to the Appalachians. Any complacency which knowledge of superior numbers and wealth might have given them soon disappeared in the early fighting. Half-trained colonial levies were no match for French professional troops, fine soldiers from the greatest military nation in Europe – nor, it appeared, were British regulars. Measured against the all-out war effort and unified control of the French in Canada, the British colonies presented a sorry spectacle. Colonies squabbled among themselves. Authority was divided between the British commander-in-chief, colonial governors, and colonial assemblies. To raise levies was a difficult task, and to keep them in existence harder still. One colonial governor explained to a new British commander-in-chief: 'The people in these colonies are quite unused to war and martial discipline.' Faced with an apparently invincible combination of highly-trained French regular troops, Canadian militia adept at backwoods warfare, and ferocious Indian allies, colonial morale sagged. As the frontier areas were hastily evacuated, defeatist feelings spread among the colonies. Help from Britain on a scale far larger than had been previously envisaged was clearly necessary if the French were to be overcome.

The Struggle for Dominance in North America

Britain finally declared war on France in May 1756, and three months later this contest merged into the Seven Years War, which began when Frederick II of Prussia invaded Saxony at the end of August. Further operation sin North America now had to be viewed in the light of the general European situation. It was fortunate for the hard-pressed British colonies that at home William Pitt had at last come into office. For long Pitt had been a voice in the political wilderness, pointing unheeded at the menace of France's rising commercial and maritime strength. As early as the War of Jenkins's Ear he had declared: 'When trade is at stake it is your last entrenchment: you must defend it or perish.' Now, brought into office after a series of military disasters, Pitt saw clearly that the best form of defence for Britain's great empire of trade and settlement was attack.

There were no limited objectives in Pitt's planning. His one desire was the destruction of the power of France, Britain's rival in every sphere of overseas activity. While strong British forces would be sent to North America and the Caribbean, blockading squadrons would keep French reinforcements helplessly bottled up in their home ports. On the oceans France's seaborne commerce would be harried and destroyed. In Europe generous help would be given to Britain's new and formidable ally, Frederick II. This was an integral part of Pitt's strategy, intended to avoid committing British armies to the continent, and yet to prevent France from gaining territory which, as in 1748, could be regained only by restoring colonial conquests. To the direction of this strategy Pitt brought the attributes of a great war leader: boundless energy, supreme self-confidence ('I am sure I can save this country', he once said, 'and nobody else can'), and the ability in a moment of national disillusionment to rally support from all sections of the country.

In Pitt's comprehensive war plan, based on Britain's anticipated command of the sea and her superior financial resources, America was given high priority. It was there that the immediate threat was greatest. Furthermore, the conquest of Canada, which was Pitt's ultimate aim, promised much. It would gain the Canadian fisheries and fur trade for Britain, and give the British colonies security in which to develop and expand. In Pitt's estimation of the North American situation in 1756 the most effective single stroke that could be made to reverse the critical trend of events would be an attack on Louisbourg, the key to the Saint Lawrence. With Louisbourg gone, Quebec would be in danger, and the French would be thrown back on the defensive.

First the British had to endure further losses, and the situation was not helped by Pitt's temporary removal from office between April and June 1757. In that year Montcalm overwhelmed Fort William Henry on Lake George, an advance British post pointing at the heart of New France; and the massacre of many of the garrison by Indians stressed the horrors of colonial warfare in which Indian allies were used. Nor did Pitt's planned counter-stroke of an attack on Louisbourg materialize. Forces were assembled, but the presence in the harbour

at Louisbourg of seventeen great ships of the line with accompanying frigates – the most powerful naval force yet seen in North
American waters – made an attack on the fortress too dangerous a
risk.

The year 1757, then, had been another year of success for the French
in North America, and they planned to follow it by further attacks in
1758 on the colony of New York. But Pitt, back in office, and mortified
by 'the last inactive and unhappy campaign', was gathering forces for
an effort which was to eclipse French aggressive projects. He made
the autocrat's mistake of trying to direct operations in detail from
London, but his grasp of overall strategy was firm, and he never lost
sight of the importance of seapower. The western squadron of the
home fleet was to blockade the French ports and stop relief forces
sailing for America, where British forces were to be employed in a
triple thrust. Louisbourg was to be taken by an amphibious operation
as a prelude to an attack on Quebec: one army was to move on Fort
Duquesne in the Ohio valley; and another was to advance on Montreal
by way of the Lake Champlain route. In America the British commander-in-chief Lord Loudoun had gradually gathered together the
supporting services essential to North American campaigning: boats
for the rivers, light sloops and armed scows for the lakes, wagons and
sledges for land transport, heavy mortars for siege work. With these
went groups of experts in the specialized techniques of warfare in the
interior: boatmen, carpenters, gunners, engineers, and the indispensable rangers for scouting and skirmishing.

The attack on Louisbourg under Amherst's command was a
complete success. In style it was far nearer to a conventional European
siege operation than a typical American encounter. While in home
waters the British navy prevented French fleets leaving for Louisbourg
with reinforcements and supplies, at Cape Breton Island Amherst's
men were settling down to their task of besieging the strongest fortress
in North America. Heavy guns battered all parts of the town day after
day. Red-hot shot and great bombs were lobbed into the town, and
sent the buildings up in flames. At the end of July 1758, seven weeks
after the British forces had landed, Louisbourg capitulated, and the
next year its fortifications were demolished. The way into the Saint
Lawrence was now clear of French forces.

The attack on Fort Duquesne also went according to plan under
Forbes. His progress towards the fort, slow but methodical, his army

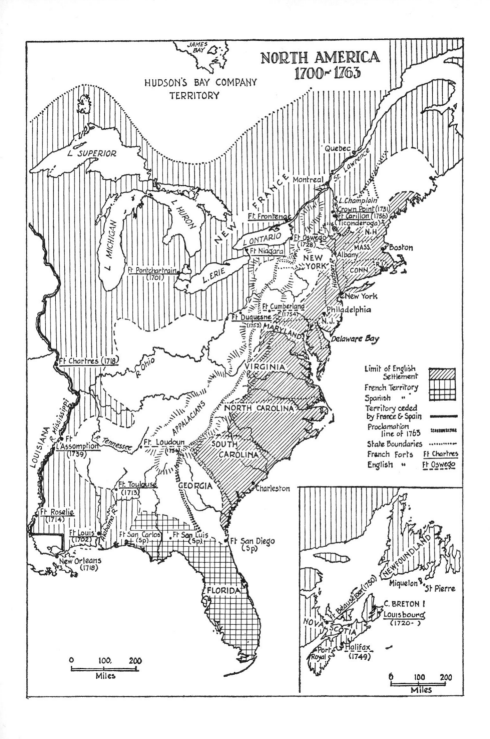

NORTH AMERICA
1700~1763

HUDSON'S BAY COMPANY
TERRITORY

JAMES BAY

L. SUPERIOR

L. MICHIGAN

L. HURON

NEW FRANCE

Quebec

St. Lawrence

Montreal

Ft. Frontenac

L. ONTARIO

Ft. Oswego
(1728)

Ft. Niagara

L. ERIE

Ft. Pontchartrain
(1701)

L. Champlain
Crown Point (1731)
Ft. Carillon (1756)
(Ticonderoga)
N.H.
MASS.
Albany   Boston
NEW
YORK
CONN.
New York
Philadelphia
N.J.
Delaware Bay

Ft. Cumberland
(1754)
Ft. Duquesne
(1753)
MARYLAND

Ft. Chartres (1718)

R. Ohio

VIRGINIA

APPALACIANS

NORTH CAROLINA

LOUISIANA

R. Mississippi

Ft.
L'Assomption
(1739)

R. Tennessee

Ft. Loudoun
(1756)

SOUTH
CAROLINA

Ft. Toulouse
(1713)

GEORGIA

Charleston

Ft. Roselie
(1714)

Ft. Louis
(1702)

Alabama R.

Ft. San Carlos
(Sp)

Ft. San Luis
(Sp)

Ft. San Diego
(Sp)

New Orleans
(1718)

FLORIDA

Limit of English
Settlement
French Territory
Spanish   "
Territory ceded
by France & Spain
Proclamation
line of 1763
State Boundaries
French Forts   Ft. Chartres
English   "   Ft. Oswego

0   100   200
Miles

NEWFOUNDLAND

Miquelon   St. Pierre

Ft. Beauséjour (1750)

C. BRETON I.
Louisbourg
(1720-)

NOVA SCOTIA

Port Royal

Halifax
(1749)

0   100   200
Miles

building a road dotted with defensive posts as it marched through the wilderness, showed the resources the British now had to hand. As the advancing army drew near, the French could do nothing but blow up the fort and retreat. But triumph at Duquesne (re-named Fort Pitt by Forbes) was more than offset by the disaster which overtook the main army at Ticonderoga as it struck northward towards Montreal under Abercromby. Bad generalship sent the British assault forces on that most deadly of tasks – a frontal assault unsupported by artillery against an entrenched enemy. This egregious piece of folly was committed even though the French defences were dominated by an overlooking hill. A few cannon placed there would quickly have driven the French from their prepared positions, tactics which (as a captain present that day put it) 'must have occurred to any blockhead who was not absolutely so far sunk in idiocy as to be obliged to wear a bib and bells'. The criticism was justified: more than 1,500 attackers fell that day in courageous but fruitless attempts to take the French defences by storm, and the army withdrew.

In marked contrast to this example of military ineptitude was the British siege and capture of Fort Frontenac earlier in the year without the loss of a single man. This unspectacular but important engagement weakened the French position on Lake Ontario, and knocked away a defensive bulwark from the upper Saint Lawrence region. Despite the stand at Ticonderoga French defences had been smashed at three points: Louisbourg, Duquesne and Frontenac. The tide had turned, and it was difficult to see how New France could hold out against the forces poised against it unless it received substantial help from the mother country. Here, once again, seapower played a decisive part. The British navy was at the peak of its strength. Reforms under First Lord of the Admiralty George Anson had turned it into an efficient fighting instrument which allowed Pitt to maintain supremacy in home waters and so prevent French relief expeditions from sailing overseas, and at the same time to set in motion attacks on the French West Indies and prepare a final assault on Canada.

In 1759 the crumbling defences of New France were again to be attacked by land and sea. The capable Amherst replaced Abercromby, and was instructed by Pitt to send forces to seize Fort Niagara, a move which would cut off Canada from Louisiana. Amherst himself was to take an army and try once more the Lake Champlain approach. To the north-east the young Brigadier-General James Wolfe, who had distinguished himself at Louisbourg the previous year, was to command an assault up the Saint Lawrence to Quebec.

Faced with the coming ordeal, New France was showing signs of alarming weakness. In order to resist the simultaneous thrust of superior British forces at widely separated points its limited military and economic resources were stretched to the utmost. New France was unable to exist without regular supplies from Europe, and the food situation was becoming critical as fewer ships slipped through the British blockade, as Forbes's troops overran the fertile Ohio country, and as all able-bodied men were called from the farms for military service. There was no hope of help on a massive scale from France. The French government bluntly told the Governor-General of New France that 'the continuance of war in Europe, the too great risks of the sea, and the necessity of concentrating His Majesty's naval forces, do not permit of hazarding part of them to bring you assistance'. Only four ships were to be sent to Canada by the government in 1759 (together with a few private vessels), and there was no guarantee that these would arrive. As always, the position in Europe dominated the thinking of the French government, and the planned invasion of England was absorbing French attention and resources at this moment. It would not be just to say that New France was to be abandoned to its fate, but its plight was certainly low on the French government's list of priorities.

Realization of the position was bound to have a dispiriting effect on morale in Canada. The Indian allies of the French were melting away as successive defeats and withdrawals destroyed the illusion of French invincibility. The government at Quebec was distracted by personal rivalries at the highest level. The Marquis de Vaudreuil, Governor-General and therefore commander-in-chief of the Canadian regulars and militia, was involved in angry differences of opinion with the commander of the French regular troops, the Marquis de Montcalm. This bickering could only weaken New France at the moment of its greatest danger.

The Fall of New France

Early in June 1759 a great British armada commanded by Vice-Admiral Saunders entered the Saint Lawrence: two hundred transports and warships (including twenty-two ships of the line), carrying on board an army of 8,500 troops under Wolfe. Most of the soldiers were regulars, highly-trained and disciplined fighting troops with experience of American conditions. It was probably the finest army that had seen service in America. Wolfe himself was only thirty-two, but had considerable experience, and despite his unmilitary appearance was a courageous, even reckless soldier. In choosing him for this crucial operation Pitt had taken a calculated risk; Wolfe had never commanded a force in the field, and his strategic abilities were largely unknown.

About Wolfe's naval counterpart, Charles Saunders, there were no doubts. He was a vastly experienced officer, and his abilities were shown by the superb way he nursed his ships up the unknown waters of the Saint Lawrence without a single loss. For too long Wolfe's name stood in solitary glory as the hero of the Quebec campaign, to the neglect of the less colourful but essential role played by Saunders and his ships. This was a point on which the French needed no reminder. The abandonment of Walker's attempt on Quebec in 1711, when several ships were wrecked hundreds of miles from the city, had persuaded the French of the impossibility of a large hostile force making its way upriver without charts. Accordingly, little effort was made to harass Saunders's ships as they felt their way through the shoals, rocks and treacherous currents of the uncharted river in a magnificent piece of seamanship; and the defenders of Quebec received with consternation reports of the fleet's steady progress.

At the end of June Wolfe's force sighted its objective: the famous fortress standing on the cliffs rising almost sheer out of the waters of the Saint Lawrence. The problem presented to Wolfe as he encamped his men on the opposite bank, and set up his cannon to bombard the city, was a perplexing one. Cliffs, water or fortifications protected the city on all sides. For weeks Wolfe and his officers pondered the problem of how to get their forces across the river and to grips with the French. One attempt, made near the Montmorency Falls a few miles below Quebec, ended in a bloody repulse. At the end of August Wolfe was pointing out in despair that 'my antagonist has wisely shut himself in inaccessible entrenchments, so that I can't get at him without spilling a torrent of blood, and that perhaps to little purpose'.

Wolfe adopted and then discarded at least half a dozen plans of assault before drawing up in early September (perilously near the end of the campaigning season) a final and successful one. This envisaged a night landing at the Anse au Foulon (later known as Wolfe's Cove), one-and-a-half miles above Quebec, where a narrow path ran up the side of the cliff from the shore. Modern investigations have thrown doubt upon some of the romantic stories associated with the attack; but the drama of the occasion, as Wolfe's boats drifted silently downstream past the French defences, remains. By good fortune, skilful seamanship and French slackness, the first assault troops got ashore almost unchallenged, and overwhelmed the picket defending the clifftop. By 6 a.m. an army of 4,500 redcoats was drawn up in line of battle on the Plains of Abraham outside the Quebec fortifications, a depressing sight for the French. Montcalm, without waiting for reinforcements to reach him, moved out to give battle. His haste was the more surprising since, although the size of the two armies was about the same, in quality they were very different. Wolfe's army consisted of veteran regulars, whereas a large proportion of Montcalm's forces was made up of Canadian militia. In a battle fought on a formal European pattern there could only be one result. The advancing French line broke before the accurate musket fire of the British infantry, and fled in disorder. Both Wolfe and Montcalm were mortally wounded, but the day belonged to the British. The defeated French army withdrew to Montreal, Quebec surrendered, and the end of New France was in sight.

While Wolfe was taking Quebec, to the south Amherst was operating in a less dramatic but nevertheless effective fashion. In July Fort Niagara fell to British forces, a surrender which further weakened the French position on Lake Ontario. To the east the capture of Ticonderoga and Crown Point gave Amherst command of Lake Champlain. By the end of the year the French had fallen back into last-ditch defensive positions guarding Montreal and the nearby Saint Lawrence settlements. With Quebec gone, the jaws of the pincers were closing remorselessly on the remnants of New France.

For a few brief weeks in the spring of 1760 French hopes flickered to life again. During the winter the British garrison in Quebec suffered cruelly from disease and cold, and in the spring French forces returned to besiege the city. After another battle on the Plains of Abraham the British were driven back inside the walls of Quebec, and both sides waited for help to arrive upriver from Europe. The fate of the battered city was still in the balance, but in May a British frigate arrived, the outrider of a squadron bringing reinforcements and supplies. As an example of the decisive importance of seapower in colonial campaigns this episode can scarcely be bettered. The French raised the siege, and retreated once more to Montreal. There in September 1760 they surrendered to Amherst, who had just completed his advance from the south. The conquest of New France was complete. It remained to be seen whether it would be made permanent at the peace settlement.

Conquest of the French West Indies

Pitt's main overseas objective in the Seven Years War was to guarantee the security of the British North American colonies by conquering Canada. Until the end of 1758 British efforts were directed to this end. But with the fall of Louisbourg and Fort Duquesne in that year the balance on the North American continent tipped decisively in Britain's favour, and Pitt felt free to devote some of his attention to the Caribbean. Given the superiority of British resources at this time, expeditions against the French West Indies made good sense, whether looked at from a strategic or commercial point of view. Capture of the enormously rich sugar islands would strike a blow at France far more damaging in the short term than any achievements of British arms in North America, and the threat of this might well prevent France sending assistance to her beleaguered colonists in Canada.

Moreover, the islands were being used as bases for French privateers, which were bringing into their harbours hundreds of British prizes each year. For once the British West Indian planters, normally opposed to projects which might bring the French islands into the British colonial system and thus force down the price of sugar, were in favour of Caribbean conquests. Ceaseless harrying of trade by French ships, and the danger of French raids on their vulnerable plantations, had brought home to the planters the advantages of having the more important French islands in British hands. And if, as was expected, the islands were used as bargaining counters at the peace negotiations in order to retain Louisbourg and regain Minorca, then no permanent damage would be done to the commercial position of the British sugar colonies.

As a preliminary to direct attacks on the French West Indies a small expedition was sent early in 1758 to West Africa, which captured French slaving and trading stations on the Senegal river. Late in the year a more powerful expedition seized the island of Gorée and a French post on the Gambia river. These were far more harmful blows to French commerce than might appear at first sight. The loss of all the

French posts in West Africa was bound to have a crippling effect on the French Caribbean islands, which received regular shiploads of slaves from those stations. However, the main assault planned in 1758 was directed against Martinique, largest of the French islands, and a nest of privateers. In November a force of six thousand troops with a strong naval escort sailed from England for the island. The first soldiers to land in their special flat-bottomed boats met such dogged resistance in trying to advance across a terrain of steep hills and ravines, covered by tropical forest or high cane-brakes, that a Council of War decided that the expedition's resources were too limited to take and hold the island. Instead, the force sailed north to Guadeloupe.

Again, this was no easy prize. The climate as usual proved the deadliest enemy, and the number of fit soldiers was soon reduced to about half the number that had sailed from England. A West Indian planter had told Pitt in 1758: 'Whatever is attempted in that climate must be done *uno impetu*; a general must fight his men off directly, and not give them time to die of drink or disease.' The defenders of Guadeloupe, local militia and slaves, plus a few regular troops, were not impressive in numbers or quality, but at least they had the advantage of being acclimatized. The island surrendered in May 1759 after three months of fighting, which caused considerable casualties and damage to property. French resistance had probably been stiffened by the planters' fear of their dire fate if the British were successful; but the articles of capitulation drawn up by the victorious commanders were remarkably generous. The islanders were to be allowed to remain neutral for the duration of the war; they were still to be governed by French laws and customs; in general they were to have freedom of trade within the British empire; and no British planters were to settle on the island before the signing of a peace treaty. Under these favourable terms, with British and American ships bringing in provisions and slaves, and with the British market open to receive the island's sugar, the French plantations flourished. To many British planters the whole affair seemed a betrayal of their interests. In some quarters at least it had been assumed that the conquest of Guadeloupe would be followed either by the destruction of the plantations, or by the eviction of the French owners and their replacement by British planters. Instead, Guadeloupe sugar grown by French planters was flooding the British market and bringing down prices.

G

Unenthusiastic though some of the British planters may have been about further conquests, Pitt still had his eyes fixed on the original objective of the 1759 expedition. He could prepare a second expedition to Martinique secure in the knowledge that the French government was powerless to intervene. French land forces were tied down in campaigns against Prussia and Hanover; more important, the British naval victories of 1759 off Lagos and in Quiberon Bay had destroyed the French navy as an effective fighting force. Pitt himself resigned in October 1761, but the planned expedition went on, and at the beginning of 1762 a huge British fleet arrived off Martinique. Monckton, a fine soldier who had fought under Wolfe at Quebec, was in charge of the troops, almost 14,000 strong; in command of the fleet was one of England's finest sailors, Rear-Admiral Rodney. A superbly directed amphibious operation put the army ashore without loss, and after initial resistance of some stubbornness by French troops fighting in difficult, hilly country the superior numbers and armament of the British forces began to tell. The badly organized island militia and the outnumbered French regulars were in danger of being overwhelmed, and talk by the Governor-General, de la Touche, of a fight to the death came to nothing in the face of opposition by the merchants and planters of the islands to such suicidal notions. In February 1762 the French forces surrendered on terms very similar to those offered to Guadeloupe.

The fall of Martinique had a catastrophic effect on France's already precarious position in the Caribbean. Dominica, one of the 'neutral islands', had already been captured in 1761 by a British force waiting for the main assault on Martinique. In February and March 1762 Saint Lucia, Saint Vincent (both 'neutral islands') and Grenada were also taken. French power in the Caribbean had been broken, but there was no certainty about the permanence of the British conquests. The soldiers and sailors had won their victories; it was for the diplomats of Europe to decide what the fruits of those victories should be.

The Spanish Empire under Attack

The early part of the Seven Years War saw Britain and Spain on reasonably amicable terms. Although the Treaty of Aix-la-Chapelle had done little to settle the issues at dispute between the two nations in the Caribbean, there was a significant change in atmosphere after the war. Both sides could see the advantages of an understanding with the other; and in 1750 a commercial treaty was signed which regulated the conditions of Anglo-Spanish trade in Europe, and abolished the irritant of the *asiento* concession in return for a cash payment from Spain. This prosaic but effective piece of negotiation typified the new effort at understanding between the two governments, and although clashes in the Caribbean between British traders and the *guardacostas* still occurred, the home governments were careful not to magnify these incidents into issues of national prestige. Attacks by Spanish warships on British logwood cutters in the Bay of Honduras and on the Mosquito shores were disowned after protests from London, and the minister responsible was dismissed. On the outbreak of war in 1756 confidential military information was sent by the British government to the Spanish foreign minister, Don Ricardo Wall ('our friend Wall' to the British government), and Spanish suspicions were aroused by French rather than British war aims.

By mid-1757 the situation had changed. The old differences over Gibraltar and the logwood settlements remained; and to them were added those disputes over maritime trade which were almost inevitable between neutral and belligerent trading powers in time of war. Then in 1759 Ferdinand VI, pitiably enfeebled in body and mind, died, and was succeeded by his vigorous half-brother the King of Naples, who became Charles III of Spain. Wall continued in office, but his influence was weakened. The King was determined to direct his own foreign policy, and this was strongly pro-French. One of Charles III's first actions after his accession was to warn the British government that Spain would not stand by idly and watch Britain wreck the overseas equilibrium established by the Utrecht settlement. Already outraged by the evidence presented to him of British smuggling activities within the Spanish colonial empire, Charles viewed with alarm the fall of French colonies to British attacks. The surrender of Quebec, he told the French ambassador, 'made his blood run cold'. The Duc de Choiseul at the head of the French government assiduously played on the King's fears, pointing out that if the British conquered France's overseas possessions and then turned on Spain, they would be masters of Europe. In face of the threat of overwhelming British domination the two nations moved closer together, and in August 1761 the Bourbon rulers of France and Spain signed a secret Family Compact which provided for the entry of Spain into the war unless peace was made between Britain and France within nine months. A passage from one of the drafts drawn up by the Spanish negotiators reveals Charles III's fears of British overseas aggression. It referred to

> the intention the British court has formed and follows of reigning despotically on all the seas, and taking for itself all those dominions and ports of the East and West Indies which serve as rungs in a ladder for navigation . . . of aspiring to a position where no one shall have trade other than that which it pleases the British nation to allow to them.

The strain which rumours of the Family Compact placed on already tense Anglo-Spanish relations soon proved intolerable, and war was declared in January 1762, three months after Pitt had resigned from office because of the Cabinet's refusal to support his demand for a preventive war against Spain. Charles III's policy which led to war was not far from being suicidal. His vision of an alliance between a rejuvenated France and a fresh Spain against an enemy nearing exhaustion after years of incessant warfare was an illusion. France was past rejuvenation in this war: her fleets had been destroyed, her finances wrecked, and her most profitable colonies conquered. Spain did not have the military, naval or financial resources to make an impression on the battle-hardened British armies and fleets, ably led, and backed by the wealth of the greatest commercial power in the world. The grandiose strategic plans by which Charles III hoped to defeat Britain merely confirm the unreality of his war aims. Bourbon forces were to be launched at important points in Britain's commercial and strategic system: at Gibraltar, Jamaica, Portugal and the West African slaving stations. In conjunction with these assaults a plan was to be put into operation to exclude British goods from as many countries in Europe as possible, and so bring Britain to her knees.

No part of this plan had the slightest chance of success. Spain was soon too concerned about defence to think of launching offensive operations overseas. Even the campaign against Portugal's weak and poorly-armed forces was mishandled, and ended in a miserable fiasco when British forces reached the scene. Nor was the attempt to anticipate Napoleon's Continental System of half a century later any more effective. So far from preventing British goods from entering other countries in Europe, the Spanish government proved unable to keep them out of Spain itself.

In Britain, meanwhile, plans were being laid for two expeditions which were to strike crippling blows at Spain. One was to be directed against Havana, the centre of Spain's Caribbean possessions, the other against Manila, a key point in Spain's Pacific empire. The projects were copies of those planned at the beginning of the War of Jenkins's Ear, but the execution was very different. Years of experience under Pitt of sending powerful expeditions overseas helped to get the Havana expedition away on time, even though Pitt's guiding hand had been removed. There was little of the uncertainty and delay that had afflicted the Caribbean expeditions of the earlier war. Objective, route and assault plan were all laid down beforehand in precise terms.

The land forces for the Havana expedition were commanded by the Earl of Albemarle, who had served as Cumberland's aide-de-camp but had never held military command before. The fleet, happily, was under Pocock, who had already proved his worth in Indian waters. It was characteristic of the imaginative planning that had distinguished the British war effort of the previous three years that the fleet was sent through the little-known Old Bahama Channel to attack Havana from the east, rather than by the normal approach of the Yucatán Channel. The Spanish garrison was taken by surprise, although this advantage was thrown away by Albemarle's insistence on conducting formal siege operations against the outlying castle of Morro, when Pocock's command of the sea would have allowed a direct attack on the city of Havana. Commanded by the veteran Don Luis Vicente de Velasco, the Spaniards recovered from their early panic and put up a dogged resistance. At last the castle was stormed, and in mid-August 1762 Havana surrendered. Casualties were far higher than necessary: well over a third of the attacking force died, mostly from disease. Even so, the capture of Havana was a notable triumph, and losses were small in comparison with those suffered in the bloody and often profitless European campaigns of the war. The great citadel of the Spanish Indies had fallen for the first time in its history, a morale-sapping blow to Spain. Into British hands came an immense amount of booty: nearly a hundred merchantmen, nine ships of the line, a dozen smaller warships, and merchandise worth £750,000. Rarely have dreams of glory and conquest so quickly turned to ashes as those of Charles III. Within a few months of the declaration of hostilities Spain was fighting a desperate defensive war to save her overseas empire.

The attack on Manila was a revival of a plan first mooted in 1739, but never put into effect. Lieutenant-Colonel Draper, an officer who had served in India, and had amassed a great deal of information about Manila's defences during a visit to China, was sent to Madras with orders to put together a force strong enough to attack Manila. His efforts to collect men and material produced a force alarmingly small for the job in hand: less than a thousand regular troops, together with some native soldiers. But the fact that the expedition was prepared in India and not in Europe made secrecy easier, and Draper had the advantage of complete surprise. Indeed, the appearance in Manila Bay of his fifteen ships in September 1762 was the first indication that the Spaniards had that their country was at war with Britain. Within a fortnight a series of courageous assaults by the British forces broke Spanish resistance. By the end of October the Philippines had surrendered, and acknowledged George III as their sovereign until the fate of the islands was decided at the peace negotiations.

The Peace of Paris

The first tentative feelers for peace had been put out as early as 1759, when the Duc de Choiseul became French foreign minister and obtained a close view of the inefficiency of the French war effort. He realized that a continuation of the struggle might result in so crushing a defeat for France that she would take a generation to recover, and he was convinced that it was better to negotiate reasonable terms than to be forced into accepting a dictated peace at a later stage. His pessimistic views were probably shared by Frederick II on the opposing side, who was in a desperate plight; but Britain, Austria and Russia thought differently. They refused to talk peace while some of their most important war aims remained unfulfilled. Not until 1761 did negotiations begin in earnest, and they were soon interrupted by the entry of Spain into the war. However, the Spanish disasters of 1762, Pitt's resignation and his replacement by the less belligerent Bute, the withdrawal of Russia from the war, and renewed French pressure for a settlement, helped to bring the negotiations to a successful close in November 1762. In February 1763 the definitive Treaty of Paris was signed between Britain, France and Spain, and in the same month Austria and Prussia signed the Treaty of Hubertusburg.

The latter simply restored the *status quo* in central Europe, but the Treaty of Paris was a far more complex affair. In Britain it was also highly controversial. One veteran minister referred to 'the most glorious war and most honourable peace this nation ever saw', but to Pitt the Treaty 'obscured all the glories of war, surrendered the dearest interests of the nation, and sacrificed the public faith by an abandonment of our allies'. The final allegation need not be taken too seriously in so far as it referred to the government's refusal to continue subsidizing Frederick II after the coalition against him had disintegrated. This may have been bad diplomacy by a government which was soon to find itself isolated in Europe, but it was not bad faith. More pertinent was Pitt's accusation that important conquests had been surrendered without adequate compensation. France had been given back the sugar islands of Guadeloupe and Martinique, the smaller but strategically important Saint Lucia, Gorée in West Africa, Belle-Île-en-Mer in the Bay of Biscay, and the trading factories in India. She also kept certain fishing rights in the Gulf of Saint Lawrence and the little islands there of Saint Pierre and Miquelon for use as fishing stations. Havana had been restored to Spain, and since the news of the capture of Manila had been received too late to be considered in the peace negotiations the Philippines were returned without any territorial compensation.

Even so, Britain's list of gains was an imposing one: Canada, Grenada, the long-disputed 'neutral islands' of Saint Vincent, Dominica and Tobago, Senegal in West Africa, Florida (from Spain), and the restoration of Minorca. While in office Pitt had appreciated the impossibility of keeping all the British conquests. In 1759, that glorious year of victories, he had observed that 'peace will be as hard to make as war'. In this the harassed Bute would have agreed with him. Bute's attitude was dominated by two considerations. His political position was far from strong, and he wanted to conclude negotiations as soon as possible before some unlucky accident of war could give his political opponents a chance to overthrow him. But, domestic politics apart, it was also his sincere desire to negotiate a permanent peace rather than a temporary truce as the Treaty of Aix-la-Chapelle had proved to be. He hoped to avoid the usual tedious haggling and bargaining of diplomatic negotiations, and frankly told Choiseul that 'instead of going the ordinary way of forming pretensions much stronger than one could wish to conclude, I have traced the plan of an equitable peace such as the French could accept with honour'. These were creditable sentiments, but they were also potentially dangerous ones.

Bute and Pitt considered the peace negotiations from diametrically opposed viewpoints. Bute and some of his colleagues were alarmed by the prospect of an over-mighty Britain, an imperial colossus that would draw the united hostility of a fearful and envious Europe. They preferred to show moderation at the peace conference, and to work for a future in which the friendship of France and Spain might become a reality. Pitt's attitude was sterner and less hopeful. He foresaw that the victorious war was a prelude to new dangers. To Pitt the Family Compact, rather than British power, was the greatest menace to the peace of Europe, and he would have conducted the peace negotiations on the assumption that the Bourbon powers were planning a war of revenge. Bute had returned Saint Lucia to France on the ground that it was essential to the security of Martinique; Pitt would have tried to keep it for that precise reason. In West Africa Pitt would have demanded Gorée as well as Senegal in an attempt to undermine the French West Indian plantations. He would also have insisted upon exclusive rights to the Newfoundland fisheries in order to deny French sailors a traditional (if much overrated) training ground.

On the thorniest single issue of the negotiations – whether Britain should keep Canada or Guadeloupe – Pitt's views are not at all clear. That the question should be discussed at all throws an illuminating light on eighteenth-century mercantilist values; but the issue was not as simple as it might appear to modern eyes. On the one hand was a vast expanse of wilderness, threaded by only a few lines of settlement ('this wretched country, covered with snow and ice eight months out of twelve, and inhabited by savages, bears and beavers', Voltaire had described it); on the other an immensely rich Caribbean sugar island. From a short-term economic point of view there was only one answer. In 1761 the exports of conquered Guadeloupe totalled £600,000, Canada's a mere £14,000. The financial discrepancy did not end there, for Canada would need an expensive army to hold it in submission. Moreover, the removal of the French threat from North America might weaken the loyalty of Britain's colonists. A pamphleteer expressed this feeling when he wrote: 'A neighbour that keeps us in some awe is not always the worst of neighbours.'

Yet the decision was made to keep Canada, and despite a lively pamphlet war on the subject there is little evidence that either leading ministers, or Pitt, ever seriously considered retaining Guadeloupe in preference to Canada. The Anglo-French conflict had started in

North America, and the primary war aim of the British government had been victory there. Even the wealthiest sugar island could not counterbalance the advantages that came with the banishing of French power from North America. To have handed back Canada would have made nonsense of the British war effort. The government only wavered in its determination when Martinique was captured early in 1762, since it was not easy to see how both Guadeloupe and Martinique could be returned to France without a public outcry, or what France could possibly offer as satisfactory compensation.

Choiseul produced a solution to this dilemma when he offered to cede to Britain all French territory in North America east of the Mississippi. With Canada gone, and with it the vision of an enormous French empire dominating the North American continent, there seemed little point in France retaining Louisiana in the south. The arrangement also had obvious advantages from the British point of view. Bute could now claim that he had secured the whole of the continent as far as the left bank of the Mississippi except Spanish Florida – an extension of territory clear to the least geographically-minded of George III's subjects. The political map of North America was still further simplified when Spain gave up Florida to Britain as part payment for the recovery of Havana, and received Louisiana west of the Mississippi (including New Orleans) in compensation from her French ally. There was an attractive neatness about this final arrangement, and members of the Bute administration were able to make a reasoned defence of it, pointing out that domination in North America assured Britain of a strong and prosperous empire.

As far as the general shape of the settlement was concerned, the chief British negotiator, the Duke of Bedford, spoke good sense when he criticized Pitt's violent insistence that if the war had been fought to a finish, and the harshest possible peace terms imposed, France would have been destroyed as a commercial and maritime power. This, Bedford rightly thought, was 'fighting against nature'. The true validity of Pitt's stand lies in the fact that he was acutely aware of the probability of a Bourbon war of revenge, regardless of the precise terms of the peace settlement, and saw the need to extract further concessions to make the British empire commercially more prosperous and strategically more secure. And on this issue Pitt was right, and the administration wrong. Choiseul's secret correspondence shows that during the peace negotiations he was already thinking in terms of a new war by France and Spain against Britain. Within two months of the signing of the Treaty of Paris a French officer was ordered to survey the British coastline to find suitable landing-places for an invasion fleet, and in France Choiseul began the task of rebuilding the army and navy. That the assumption on which Bute made peace was an erroneous one was shown twenty years later, when the Bourbon powers in alliance with the rebellious American colonies finally wrecked the first British empire.

In neither France nor Spain was there much room for dispute over the terms of the treaty. Charles III resented the lack of attention paid by Choiseul to Spanish interests, but, set against the catastrophic course of the short war, Spain's territorial losses were slight. The acquisition of western Louisiana at least gave Spain a buffer colony between the British and her rich silver mines in New Spain. It is true that issues in dispute between Britain and Spain were settled in favour of the victorious power, but this was only to be expected. Spain was forced to recognize the rights of the logwood-cutters in Honduras, and to renew the Anglo-Spanish commercial treaties. British predominance in the valuable Spanish market accordingly remained untouched, to the intense irritation of both Spain and France.

In France the peace terms were accepted as being as good as could be expected after so disastrous a war, and French historians have paid tribute to Choiseul's adroit handling of the negotiations. Several colonies had been lost, but the largest of these – Canada – was reckoned to be of little material value. Much more important was that the heart of France's overseas empire remained intact. Some outlying dependencies had gone, and dreams of immense territorial empires in North America and India which only ten years before seemed to have substance were shattered. But the lucrative West Indian sugar islands, the essential slaving station of Gorée, the fisheries, and the Indian trading establishments, remained; and these were enough to assure France of a future as a prominent maritime trading power.

For Britain the Treaty marked a further stage in the nation's growth as the dominant imperial power of Europe. The Utrecht settlement half a century earlier had pointed the way and had established Britain as the leading sea power in Europe. The achievement in the Seven Years War was greater, both from the point of view of victories won and territories gained. This is not to say that the British supremacy of 1763 was necessarily permanent. Elevated positions are usually vulnerable ones; past achievements quickly fade unless a new generation is ready to follow them up vigorously; new problems and personalities can soon change the situation. The foundations had been laid for the greatest European overseas empire the world had ever known. Power, wealth and will-power all seemed to be present; but the dangers were as great as the opportunities. The Bourbon powers had been defeated, not crushed. The immensity of the post-1763 empire brought its own problems in the years after the Peace of Paris. One phase of the contest for empire between Britain, France and Spain had ended, and ended decisively in Britain's favour; but a new phase was about to begin.

III

WIDENING HORIZONS
1740–1790

Introduction

THE EXTENSION of European trade and power overseas during the eighteenth century was accompanied by a surge of interest at home in the distant lands visited by the explorers, traders and missionaries. Travel books, ranging from the highly imaginative to the solidly factual, became one of the most popular forms of literature. The adventures of fictional heroes were often played out against an exotic background: Defoe's *Robinson Crusoe* is perhaps the most notable example. Some authors adopted the literary device of writing about far-off regions as a cover for attacks on their own countries. Swift set that most effective of satires, *Gulliver's Travels*, in the unknown stretches of the Pacific, and Voltaire's *Alzire* was given a Peruvian background. Other writers expressed themselves through the opinions of supposed visitors visiting Europe for the first time, and reporting home on what they saw: Montesquieu's *Lettres Persanes* and the Marquis d'Argens's *Lettres Chinoises* are fine examples of the use of this type of satirical vehicle.

The demand for serious factual works on overseas countries was met in part by the production of massive collections of voyages and travels. This is the classic period of such collections, ranging in size from the multi-volumed compilations which graced the libraries of nobles and wealthy merchants to the low-priced abridgements which found a more popular sale. The circumnavigations and other discovery voyages of the second half of the century were invariably followed by the publication of detailed accounts. These in turn would be abridged, serialized in newspapers and periodicals, and supplemented by unofficial and sometimes racier accounts. Swift translation into other European languages was accepted practice. Du Halde's four-volume pioneer work of 1735, *Description géographique, historique, chronologique et physique de l'Empire de la Chine*, appeared in English the next year. When Padre Burriel's *Noticia de la California* was published in Madrid in 1757 to give a rare glimpse of the Spanish colonial empire north of Mexico, it was translated into English, French and Dutch. The *Relación Histórica del Viage a la América Meridional* by Jorge Juan and Antonio de Ulloa was published in Madrid in 1757, and appeared in English translation before the year was out. If no voyage had been made to a part of the globe in which interest was growing, then the difficulty could be made good by the publication of apocryphal accounts. The search for a North-west Passage in the eighteenth century was certainly stimulated by the publicity given to accounts of voyages allegedly made through the passage by Lorenzo Maldonado in 1588, Juan de Fuca in 1592, and Bartholomew de Fonte in 1640.

Maps rivalled books as a means of arousing interest in distant regions. Beautifully engraved and coloured maps had a wide sale, and were important as a means of illustrating the geographical theories of the day as well as representing known geographical data. The same distinction must be made between the factual and the fictional as in literature. Some maps were drawn by conscientious cartographers who preferred to leave a region blank rather than fill it with doubtful detail; but to others an empty space was an admission of failure. The Pacific in particular was a happy hunting-ground for speculative cartographers. Straits, islands, even continents were shown without any convincing evidence of their existence. One day they might prove to be imaginary, but for the moment they gave the map an appeal (and a sale) that could not be matched by the work of less inspired cartographers. Paris was the great centre of cartography in the eighteenth century, and the maps produced by Guillaume de l'Isle, J. N. Bellin, Philippe Buache, Robert de Vaugondy and other renowned French geographers found a ready sale throughout western Europe. Between France, Holland and England there was a free interchange of published maps, and their merits were keenly debated in the learned societies, and in the periodicals which reached the general reading public.

This growing output of descriptive material about the wider world was bound to have an effect on European thought. Although the idea of the 'noble savage' can be traced back at least to Montaigne's writings, it was during the eighteenth century that it became a cult. Occasionally an Iroquois or a Polynesian would be brought back to Europe, to become an object of public curiosity, and to gratify the wish of the *philosophes* to see from the comfort of their studies a representative of the primitive peoples they had acclaimed as being

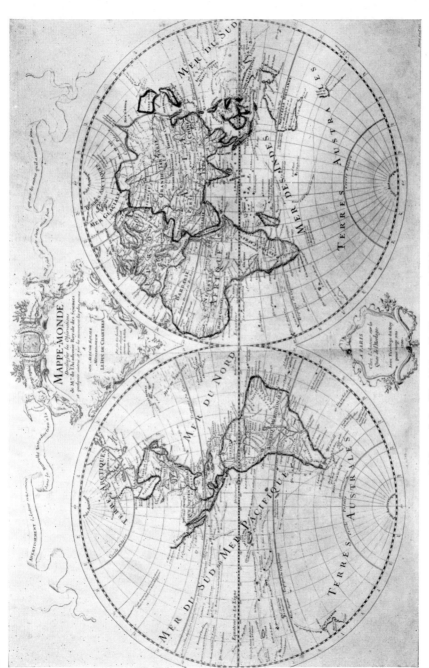

1 Map of the World by Guillaume de l'Isle, 1700

2 The *Royal Sovereign*: line-of-battle ship, 1703

3 JOHN LAW

4 Mississippi Mania: the Rue Quinquempoix, Paris, 1720

5 British sailors in a Spanish gaol: anti-Spanish print, 1737
(*Cavendish, Raleigh and Blake are depicted in the clouds*)

6 Vernon's attack on Portobelo, 1739

7 Fort Beauséjour, 1755

8 The Price of War: Quebec after the siege, 1761

9 The Spoils of War: the captured Spanish fleet at Havana, 1762

10 Marquis de Montcalm

11 James Wolfe

12 The Peace of Paris: Bute under attack, 1763

13 Fort St. George, Madras, 1754

14 Joseph Dupleix

15 Robert Clive

16 Clive at Plassey, 1757: the patriotic myth

17 WARREN HASTINGS

18 'Blood on Thunder fording the Red Sea': Gillroy's attack on Warren Hastings, 1788 (*Thurlow was Lord Chancellor at the time of Hastings' impeachment*)

19 The Emperor Ch'ien Lung receives George Macartney at Jehol, 1793

20 LOUIS-ANTOINE DE BOUGAINVILLE

21 JAMES COOK

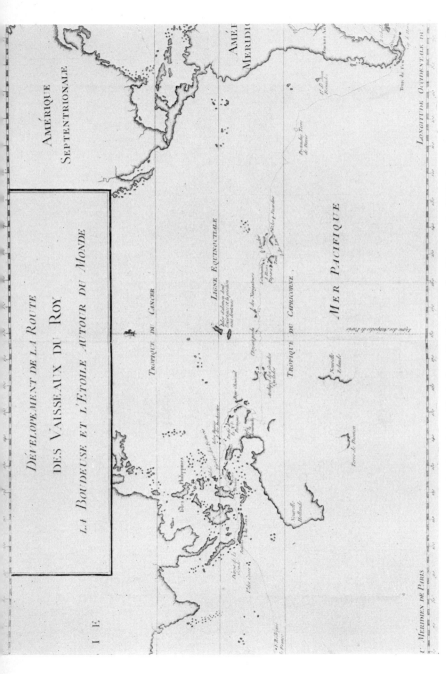

22 The South Pacific before Cook: Bougainville's track, 1767–8

23 Harrison's fourth marine timekeeper, 1759

24 Cook's ships at Tahiti, 1773

A VIEW of SNUG CORNER COVE, in PRINCE WILLIAM's SOUND.

25 In search of the North-west Passage: Cook on the Alaskan coast, 1778

26 Port Jackson and Sydney Cove, New South Wales, *c.* 1792

27 BENJAMIN FRANKLIN

28 GEORGE WASHINGTON

29 Philadelphia in the mid-eighteenth century

30 Cornwallis surrenders to Washington at Yorktown, 1781

(*An imaginative reconstruction by a contemporary artist, who ignored the fact that Cornwallis was not present in person at the surrender. Standing between Washington and Cornwallis are two Frenchmen, the Duc de Lauzun and the young Lafayette.*)

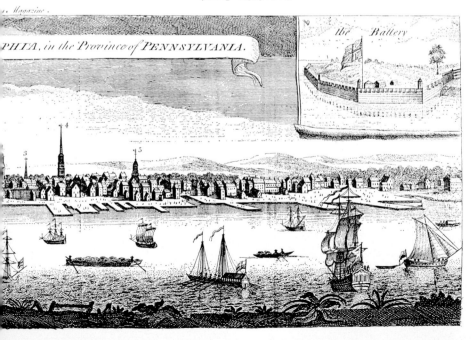

31 The Dutch settlement at Capetown, 1784

32 and **33** (*Left*) The *Princess Royal*: a typical East Indiaman. (*Right*) Indian sepoy *c.* 1805: backbone of the British army in India

34 Tipu Sultan, the 'Tiger of Mysore'
(*Life-sized model made by a French mechanic for the violently anti-British
rulers of Mysore, showing the 'Tiger' attacking an Englishman. Inside the model
a clockwork mechanism moves the beast's head and produces a tiger's snarl.*)

35 Calcutta at the time of Wellesley

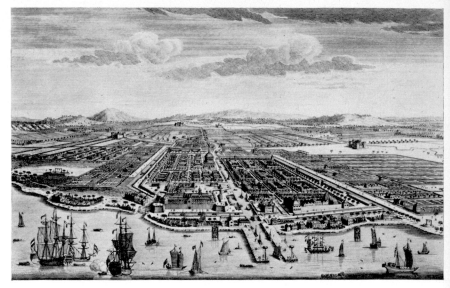

36 Batavia in the mid-eighteenth century

37 HERMAN DAENDELS

38 STAMFORD RAFFLES

39 Battle in line ahead: the French and British fleets off Negapatam, 1782

40 Breaking the line: the Battle of the Nile, 1798. (*The leading British ship has just rounded the head of the anchored French line.*)

41 Simon Bolivar   **42** Toussaint l'Ouverture

43 Lima in the eighteenth century

44 Map of Africa by Le Roche, 1747

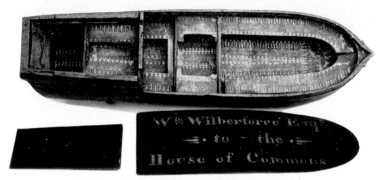

45 A slave-ship

(This model was made for Wilberforce so that he could demonstrate the way in which slaves were packed into the hold of an Atlantic slaver.)

46 The Wedgwood anti-slavery cameo, designed by Hackwood

innocent of the vices and corruptions of western civilization. The supposedly idyllic existence of these remote peoples was a reassurance to the rationalist thinkers of the day that the 'state of nature' which figured so prominently in their writings had historical as well as theoretical justification. As knowledge of the Pacific grew with the explorations of the post-1763 period, so did public interest in the vast ocean and its lands. Museums displayed specimens and trophies brought back by the voyagers; pantomimes and plays were written with Pacific themes; accounts, views and maps had a wide sale; and in England James Cook became a new type of national hero.

But even the noble savage and the Pacific must yield pride of place to China as a source of fascination to Europe. Lack of first-hand knowledge about the Manchu Empire, and the difficulty of gaining admittance into China, seemed to increase rather than diminish curiosity about a fortunate country which was thought to be prosperous and powerful, governed on enlightened lines, and sensibly possessed of a deistic form of worship. Diderot, Quesnay and Voltaire were only a few of the writers who praised this land where superstition, bigotry and corruption were apparently unknown. No part of the authorized account of Anson's voyage around the world in 1740–4 aroused more controversy than the section on the expedition's stay at Canton, where the author expressed some forthright opinions on the knavery of the Chinese. Nor was interest confined to literary circles: the enthusiasm for Chinese arts, crafts and fashions which appeared in the sixteenth century as the first Portuguese cargoes reached Europe rose to a peak in the eighteenth century. Formal gardens were designed in Chinese fashion, and dotted with Chinese pavilions and pagodas. Some even had Chinese junks floating on their ornamental lakes. Furniture and ornaments were painstakingly lacquered by European craftsmen imitating Chinese techniques. Once the secrets of porcelain had been mastered in Europe, 'china' reached a vast new market. Many great houses had a 'Chinese room', decorated with Chinese-style wallpapers, and furnished with chairs, tables and sidepieces embellished with dragons and lacquer work. Black China tea became the national drink of England, and popular throughout northern Europe. By the second half of the eighteenth century a reaction had set in against certain aspects of this craze (although Chinese decorative influence was never entirely to disappear, as a glance at any willow-pattern set of modern china will show). As

European trade increased at Canton so did traders' irritation at their treatment (see Chapter 6), and disillusioning reports reached home about some customs of Chinese society less admirable than those praised so ecstatically by the *philosophes*.

Fashions came and went, but serious interest in the wider world steadily increased. Year by year fresh knowledge of the distant parts of the globe reached Europe; and with knowledge came a new degree of tolerance and understanding. The casual and brutal superiority which the early *conquistadores* showed toward the native populations was rarer now. Among the men of the eighteenth century there was not the same conviction of the superiority of European customs and institutions. Towards the end of the century influential men questioned the morality of ruling and exploiting native peoples; missionary work began to expand once more; the slave trade ran into fierce attack; and in India the growing British empire of trade and dominion came under critical scrutiny at the same time as a new European interest in Indian learning developed (the Asiatic Society of Bengal was founded in 1784). It was against a background of increased interest, speculation and debate about the eastern world in particular that European expansion from the mid-century onwards took place. Until then, and despite the earlier activities of the Portuguese and Dutch, the lands and oceans of the East had remained realms of mystery – fascinating to philosophers, tempting to merchants. Here the maritime nations of Europe were breaking new ground while their rivalries in the western hemisphere continued unabated. And in the quest for new areas of exploitation it was the British, late starters but strong finishers in the race for territory and trade in the Americas, who were the pace-setters.

5

The Clash of Trading Empires in India 1744–1763

FIGHTING BETWEEN the British and French in the War of the Austrian Succession was not confined to the western hemisphere. For the first time India was the scene of formal hostilities between the two belligerent European powers. The spreading of the Anglo-French conflict to regions so remote from Europe indicated the growing intensity of colonial rivalry between the two nations, but it had a wider significance. It marked the beginning of European intervention in the internal affairs of India which was to lead in time to the establishment of British dominion throughout the subcontinent.

Early European Traders in India

The first Europeans to reach India by way of the Cape were the Portuguese at the end of the fifteenth century, but the maritime empire they established in the East dwindled to insignificant size as they were followed and overtaken by the Dutch, English and French. Rivalry in the seventeenth century between the Dutch and English East India companies ended in victory for the Dutch, but the English humiliation had long-term benefits not apparent at the time. Gradually thrust out of the Spice Islands, the English concentrated more vigorously on India, and whereas the Dutch were to find that the trade in cloves, nutmegs and other spices was difficult to expand, the English on the Indian mainland opened a trade in commodities for which there appeared to be an inexhaustible demand in Europe. These included silks and cottons, saltpetre (for gunpowder), indigo (for blue dye) and coffee. The only serious drawback to the trade was that India in this period was not a receptive market for European manufactures. British exports of cloth and metals amounted in value to only one-third of the cost of imports from India, and the balance had to be made up largely by bullion shipments. The China trade in tea which developed rapidly during the eighteenth century suffered from the same difficulty.

After the amalgamation of the two rival East India companies in England in 1708 into the United East India Company the British established their position as the strongest European power along the coastline of India. The solidity of the Company's trading position was shown by the regular payment of annual dividends of 8–10 per cent. In India the native settlements around the Company's main centres of trade at Madras (Fort Saint George), Bombay and Calcutta (Fort William) were growing from year to year, and one day were to become the three greatest cities in India. Linked to these three 'dependencies' were smaller Company trading centres, but territorial acquisition was far from the minds of most Company directors in the first half of the eighteenth century. Trade was the objective, and had developed satisfactorily without any attempt at territorial aggrandizement. Such an attempt, indeed, would have seemed lunatic. The British inhabitants of the settlements numbered only a few hundred, and their armed strength appeared derisory in comparison with that of the local Indian rulers, who could put armies of tens of thousands into the field. The political and military weaknesses of the Indian states, and the turn of events in the north, where the Moghul Empire which had dominated India since the sixteenth century was slowly disintegrating, were as yet not realized.

Several other European powers formed trading companies in the first half of the eighteenth century in efforts to tap the riches of India: the Ostend Company in 1723, and a few years later Danish and Swedish companies. The main interest of the Ostend Company is the example its short career affords of the unscrupulous intensity of the competition for international trade, and of the importance of political support for overseas trading ventures. After the Treaty of Utrecht Belgian merchants found themselves at a severe disadvantage compared with their European rivals. Not only was Antwerp lost as an international port, but their new overlord, the Austrian Emperor, possessed no colonies with which they could trade. With the western colonies of their European competitors closed to them, Belgian traders turned to the East. In neither China nor India were there formal European colonies and monopoly rights of the type established in America and the Caribbean; and so in 1723 the *Société Impériale et*

Royale des Indes, the Ostend Company, was founded. Working from the port of Ostend the Company made several profitable voyages to China, and planned to set up establishments in India. Unfortunately for these hopes, maritime affairs came low on the Emperor's list of priorities. The British, Dutch and French were all disturbed by the activities of this new rival – especially when it began to receive Spanish help – and put pressure on the Emperor to abolish the Company. In 1731 the Emperor sacrificed the Company as part of an agreement reached with Britain in the Treaty of Vienna. A successful company had been eliminated by diplomatic pressure ruthlessly exerted by its foreign competitors.

By the 1730s neither the Belgians, Danes nor Swedes presented a serious threat to the British traders in India. The Dutch in Bengal and elsewhere were, as always, competitors to be reckoned with, but in India – as in North America and the Caribbean – the main rival was France. The French were latecomers on the scene, for their first real effort in the East had not been launched until the establishment by Colbert in 1664 of the *Compagnie des Indes Orientales*. Despite state support, and the acquisition in 1674 of Pondicherry on the Coromandel coast south of Madras, the French company led a faltering existence for more than half a century. The reluctance of French merchants and capitalists to invest in so distant an enterprise, lack of initiative in the management of the Company, and above all the constant warfare of the last half of Louis XIV's reign, all militated against the healthy growth of this government-sponsored trading organization. After 1706 it stopped sending its own ships to the East, and instead granted licences to private traders; and in 1719 it was lucky to escape disaster when it became involved in John Law's grandiose schemes.

After the collapse of Law's system the Company was gradually reorganized on a more solid footing, and between 1728 and 1740 the value of its exports from India increased almost tenfold. In India the Company's main centre of power was at its fortified settlement of Pondicherry, and it possessed smaller posts in Bengal and along the Malabar coast. It also occupied the islands of Mauritius and Réunion (then known as Île de France and Bourbon) in the southern Indian Ocean. The former base was of particular importance. Sometimes referred to as the 'Gibraltar of the East', it was splendidly situated athwart the main trade routes between Europe and India, and its dockyards at Port Louis were capable of repairing and refitting warships. When Joseph Dupleix, energetic and ambitious, moved from Chandernagor in Bengal to become Governor at Pondicherry in 1742, the Company's future looked bright. Yet, in comparison with its long-established English rival, it displayed serious weaknesses. Its trade was still only half that of the East India Company, and despite heavy state investment its influence at home was not as consistent as that of the powerful East India interest in London. In some ways the close supervision of its activities by the government hindered the Company's development as a commercial undertaking. Then again, although in France the Company possessed a fine port and dockyard at L'Orient in Brittany, it had no harbour facilities in India to match those of the British company at Bombay. Finally, France's heavy continental commitments made it doubtful whether in time of war the Company would receive sufficient naval support from home to protect its trade if hostilities spread to Indian waters.

The War of the Austrian Succession

Until the War of the Austrian Succession the rivalry between the British and French companies in India was essentially commercial. There was no suggestion of a race for territory. The situation was patently different from that in North America and the West Indies, where Europeans had conquered and settled, as well as traded. In those regions the native populations were relatively few in number, and ill-organized to resist European intrusion. India, in contrast, was a land of ancient civilizations, with a population of tens of millions. Its rulers held court amid magnificent surroundings, and commanded massed armies. The tiny European settlements dotted along the coast existed on sufferance. One of the chief officials of the East India Company expressed what seemed to be no more than the realities of the situation when he humbly referred to himself in relation to the Emperor at Delhi as 'the smallest particle of sand, John Russell of the East India Company, with his forehead at command rubbed on the ground'.

Few men appreciated the importance of the news from the north, where in 1739 the invading Persians dealt a shattering blow to the Moghul Empire when they defeated the imperial army and sacked Delhi. As the authority of the once mighty Empire weakened and dissolved, the land was ravaged by war. In addition to the Persian and Afghan invaders sweeping down from the North-West Frontier,

Marathas from the west swept across the Deccan (the great central plateau of India) and even threatened the fertile lands of Bengal in the east. Within the old confines of the Empire the subahdars and nawabs governing the provinces were breaking away from the enfeebled grasp of Delhi, and setting up independent states. In several of these, disputed successions and civil wars had led to a complete breakdown of government, and it was at a time of near-anarchy in much of the interior that in September 1744 reports reached the European trading settlements on the coast that Britain and France were at war in Europe.

News of the outbreak of war brought a worrying problem for the British and French companies. Should they fight, or ought they to follow earlier precedent and observe a neutrality which would leave them free to trade in peace? The position was a difficult one. Both companies were aware of the harmful effect open warfare might have on their commerce and poorly defended settlements. On the other hand, if naval support was forthcoming from Europe, national hostilities would present both opportunity and excuse for destroying the rival's commerce. Since Britain was the stronger naval power this argument carried more weight with the East India Company. Proposals by the directors of the *Compagnie des Indes* for a mutual neutrality were rejected (though not without some misgivings), and shortly after the declaration of war a small British naval squadron was sent to the Indian Ocean under the command of Commodore Barnett.

The French had no regular naval ships in eastern waters, but the balance of advantage among the tiny forces involved was soon altered. Barnett died and was succeeded by a less enterprising commander in Peyton, who was shaken by the unexpected arrival on the Indian coast of a squadron of converted French East Indiamen under La Bourdonnais, Governor of Mauritius and Réunion, and a fine seaman. After two indecisive encounters between the British and French squadrons Peyton timidly withdrew from the Coromandel coast, leaving the French free to besiege Madras. Barnett had summed up the weak state of the Madras defences when he wrote home shortly before his death: 'If I was Governor, I should never sleep sound in a French war if there were five hundred Europeans in Pondicherry.' His point was proved when in September 1746 the garrison surrendered to La Bourdonnais after only token resistance.

Fortunately for the British company, quarrels between La Bourdonnais and Dupleix, together with the destruction of part of the French fleet in a storm, sapped French strength. An attempt by Dupleix to follow up the victory at Madras by capturing nearby Fort Saint David was forestalled by the timely arrival of British naval reinforcements. These were soon joined by a strong naval force sent from England under the command of Admiral Boscawen which tried to take Pondicherry, and was thwarted more by its own incompetence than by any efforts of the defenders. News of peace in Europe put an end to this game of 'tit for tat' along the Coromandel coast, and by the Treaty of Aix-la-Chapelle in 1748 Britain recovered Madras at the price of returning to the French the North American fortress of Louisbourg.

One of the most noteworthy features of the fighting in this comparatively minor theatre of war was the steady increase in the strength of the forces involved. Boscawen's fleet in the last year of the war consisted of six large naval vessels, more than a dozen Indiamen, twelve hundred troops and eight hundred marines; and was the most powerful force yet sent by Britain into eastern waters. The East India Company might wish to limit hostilities in order to avoid retaliatory measures against its trade, but in this age of colonial rivalry considerations of national prestige were reaching into every quarter of the globe.

Equally important for the future was the changing relationship between the European belligerents and the Indian rulers with whom they were in immediate contact. On the outbreak of war Dupleix at Pondicherry astutely countered the anticipated British superiority at sea by persuading the local Indian ruler, the Nawab of the Carnatic (the region inland from the European settlements on the Coromandel coast), to issue orders forbidding the British and French to engage in hostilities within his domains. Dupleix had little intention of honouring this ordinance save when it suited his purposes, and when the French obtained temporary command of the sea in 1746 he had no hesitation in attacking Madras. The outraged Nawab sent an army towards Madras to exact obedience from the French, but it was twice routed by a much smaller force composed mainly of French soldiers in the employ of the *Compagnie des Indes*. These engagements dramatically demonstrated the effect that advances in European military techniques and armaments were to have on the battlefields of India. European infantry, armed with musket and bayonet, and supported by quick-firing field guns, were clearly more than a match for native armies vastly superior in numbers. On a few previous occasions European companies had been involved in local military operations aimed at protecting their trade; but now the way lay open for a more purposeful intervention in Indian affairs.

The Career of Dupleix

Britain and France were officially at peace once more, but the peace was no more real in southern India than in North America. To Dupleix the important development of 1748 was not the signing of a treaty far away at Aix-la-Chapelle but the deaths of the two most powerful Muslim rulers in southern India: the Subahdar of the Deccan, and his vassal (in theory at least) the Nawab of the Carnatic. The succession in the Carnatic was disputed between two claimants, Chanda Sahib and Muhammad Ali. Dupleix saw in the resultant confusion the opportunity to increase French influence, and decided to put his forces at Chanda Sahib's service. It was soon evident that these troops, few in number but well-equipped, were tipping the balance in favour of the French-supported candidate.

At this point the affair took on a wider significance when the new Subahdar of the Deccan intervened, and advanced with an army into the Carnatic. French intrigues undermined his position, and in December 1750 he was killed and his nephew recognized as Subahdar. The new ruler quickly showed his appreciation of French help. When he arrived at Pondicherry he ostentatiously took Dupleix on the throne beside him, and then appointed him ruler of the eastern Carnatic, south of the Kistna river. The French had already received grants of land from Chanda Sahib, some of it near the British settlements, and now even more valuable prizes seemed to lie within Dupleix's reach: territorial domination of the eastern seaboard of India, decisive influence in the Carnatic and the Deccan, and possibly the chance to establish a permanent French protectorate over the two states.

The menace of the novel policy being pursued by Dupleix needed no emphasis to the East India Company officials along the Coromandel coast. Almost daily they heard reports of Dupleix's triumphs, and at Madras had visible evidence of French encirclement. Even so, the policy of the Company directors in London remained one of strict non-intervention in Indian politics. Admiral Boscawen, with his fleet and all but five hundred of his soldiers, was recalled to Europe after the cessation of formal hostilities; and news of armed interference by the Company's servants in yet another disputed succession, in the province of Tanjore, was greeted with angry surprise in London. While the directors of the *Compagnie des Indes* heaped praises upon Dupleix for enterprises which (he was told) brought glory to the French nation and profit to the Company, the British directors were fiercely critical of any forward movement by their servants in India. But this traditional objection to political intervention, on the ground that it was both dangerous and expensive, could not be long maintained in the face of Dupleix's successes, which threatened to turn the Carnatic and the Deccan into French puppet states.

The arrival of a new Governor, Thomas Saunders, at Madras in 1750 heralded a new and more positive phase of British policy. Saunders, an austere, taciturn figure described by one contemporary as 'the man on earth I should dread as an enemy', played Dupleix at his own game – a more momentous move than either could have realized at the time. Diplomatic activity at the Indian courts was backed by military support for Muhammad Ali, who from his mountain fortress at Trichinopoly was disputing the claim of the French candidate in the Carnatic. The story of the next three years is one of sieges and battles, marches and counter-marches, in which a few hundred Europeans at the head of armies of native sepoys performed remarkable feats of heroism and endurance. In the sphere of negotiation nobody on the British side could match the subtle Dupleix, but the French Governor had few pretensions to military skill, and his only capable commander, the Marquis de Bussy, had been sent north with French troops to the Deccan. There he achieved striking successes, but the weakening effect of this division of French forces was painfully obvious in the Carnatic where mediocre French commanders proved unable to withstand the British forces directed by the experienced Stringer Lawrence (a retired army officer) and the young Robert Clive, now at the beginning of a brilliant career.

The turning-point in the struggle for the Carnatic came in 1752 when a French-led army which was supporting Chanda Sahib was surrounded and forced to surrender, and Chanda Sahib was executed. Dupleix's efforts to retrieve the situation only made matters worse, for in an unsuccessful attempt to storm Muhammad Ali's citadel at Trichinopoly more than four hundred French soldiers were killed, wounded or taken prisoner – a crippling blow in a campaign where the number of Europeans involved was always small. These disasters sealed Dupleix's fate in France. There the government, anxious not to become entangled in war with Britain at that moment, and the economy-conscious directors of the *Compagnie des Indes*, had been receiving with concern reports of Dupleix's latest activities. It was true that farther north, away from British centres of influence, Dupleix could point to considerable successes in the Deccan. French forces under Bussy had established Salabat Jang at Hyderabad as Subahdar of the Deccan, and supported his authority against internal rivals and invading Maratha armies alike. Salabat Jang's dependence upon Bussy and his soldiers was reflected in the concessions he made to the French. The provinces of Arcot, Trichinopoly and Madura in the Carnatic (all nominally subject to the Subahdar) were granted to the French free of tribute; and, north of the Coromandel coast, territory in the Northern Circars was ceded to Bussy which gave the French control of the rich delta regions of the Kistna and Godavari rivers. Unhappily for Dupleix, the first concession was more apparent than real as long as a nawab in alliance with the British controlled the Carnatic, and it was the dismal news from that region rather than the more promising trend of events in the Deccan which made most impression in France.

The case against Dupleix looked at from France was a damaging one. The continual campaigning in the Carnatic had grievously injured French commerce there, and that British trade had also been hard hit was little consolation. Dupleix's aggressive schemes – or what was known of them – were countenanced only as long as they were commercially beneficial. When they hindered rather than stimulated trade, led to the loss of hundreds of French lives, and threatened to become a drain on French resources, then it was felt that the time had come to put a stop to the activities of a Governor who appeared to be turning into a reckless adventurer. In 1754 Dupleix was recalled, and his successor negotiated a provisional treaty with the British. This made various territorial recommendations, but its main purpose was to restore conditions in which both companies could pursue their commercial interests. The immediate balance of advantage probably lay with the French, who retained for the time being the additional territory along the Coromandel coast which they had acquired during Dupleix's governorship, and whose strong position in the Deccan was left untouched. But the general situation in the south, compared with

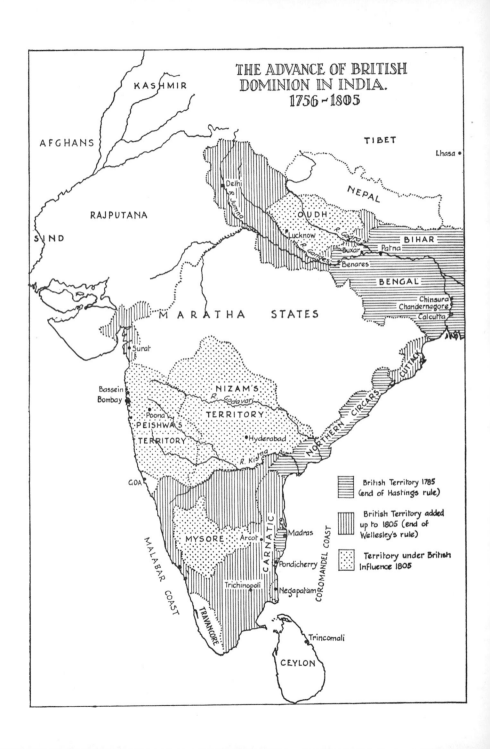

THE ADVANCE OF BRITISH
DOMINION IN INDIA.
1756~1805

KASHMIR

AFGHANS

TIBET

Lhasa

Delhi

NEPAL

RAJPUTANA

OUDH

SIND

Lucknow

BIHAR

Buxar

Patna

Benares

BENGAL

MARATHA STATES

Chinsura
Chandernagore
Calcutta

Surat

Bassein
Bombay

NIZAM'S

R. Godavari

TERRITORY

CUTTACK

Poona

PEISHWA'S

NORTHERN CIRCARS

TERRITORY

Hyderabad

R. Kistna

GOA

British Territory 1785
(end of Hastings rule)

British Territory added
up to 1805 (end of
Wellesley's rule)

Territory under British
Influence 1805

MALABAR COAST

MYSORE

Arcot

CARNATIC

Madras

COROMANDEL COAST

Pondicherry

Trichinopoli

Negapatam

TRAVANCORE

Trincomali

CEYLON

that four years earlier, represented a victory for the British. Dupleix's great effort to win control of the Carnatic had failed, and the new awareness by the British of the French threat made it unlikely that Dupleix's successors could equal the spectacular advances he had made in the years immediately after 1748.

Dupleix returned to France dismissed and disgraced, but the influence of his policy remained. His historical importance lies in the fact that he was the first European in a position of authority to appreciate that the political condition of India in the mid-eighteenth century made it possible for a European power to build up a territorial empire there. There was no national unity, no national leader; only a destructive struggle for power and wealth between the leaders of competing religions, races and factions – Hindus, Moslems, Marathas, Persians, Afghans. In such an environment the effect of disciplined, well-armed European soldiers and sepoys would be out of all proportion to their numbers. The degree of deliberation and foresight behind the ambitious plans which unfolded in the years 1748–1754 is not easy to assess. Historians once saw in Dupleix's career from 1742 onwards evidence of a carefully considered plan for French territorial dominion in India, sketched out (some claimed) during his eleven years in Bengal before he moved to Pondicherry. His failure was blamed on a short-sighted government at home which refused to support him. A more convincing interpretation based on recent research is that throughout the 1740s Dupleix, like the British, was concerned primarily with commercial expansion. It was while in pursuit of this that he became inextricably involved in political and military activities; for to achieve commercial supremacy over the British Dupleix needed more financial support than was forthcoming from the Company in France, and he turned to the possibility of obtaining revenue locally. Regular funds could be collected from the Indian states only through the exercise of some form of political control. The shape which this might take was suggested to Dupleix by events after 1748 when the disputed successions in the Carnatic and Deccan, set against the general background of political confusion in India, offered the opportunity for decisive intervention. Once committed to this policy, clashes with politically and militarily weak Indian states made it difficult to call a halt. Nor was Dupleix the man to be content with partial success. His imaginative plans expanded from month to month as circumstances encouraged his inclinations; and soon political ambitions began to overshadow commercial objectives.

The main weakness of Dupleix's system was that neither the Carnatic nor the Deccan was a rich enough area to provide an adequate base upon which French power could be established. The contrast between the limited financial and military resources at Dupleix's disposal and the far-reaching scope of his schemes provides the fundamental explanation of his failure. Neither the French government nor the *Compagnie des Indes* was primarily responsible for this. Admittedly, Dupleix did not receive generous support from home, but it must be remembered that he was constantly stressing in his letters to France that his system would be financially self-supporting. Furthermore, there was an understandable reluctance in France to send money to a country where Dupleix and his subordinates were reported to be accumulating vast private fortunes. As far as military aid was concerned, Dupleix was sent more soldiers than his British opponents received. It was better British leadership in the field, not numerical superiority, which was the decisive military factor. After 1750 Dupleix was playing a lone hand, and when he ran into difficulties a government which had never officially recognized his schemes disowned him.

Dupleix's importance is not diminished by his failure. His role was that of a pathfinder. With the help of Bussy in the Deccan he showed that it was possible for a determined European power with small but efficient military forces to establish political control over large areas of India. It was the French example which Clive was soon to follow in Bengal, and which pointed the way to eventual European domination of India.

Clive in Bengal

The signing of the provisional treaty between the British and French at Madras in 1754 brought an uneasy peace to the Carnatic. Although bickering continued, open war was avoided. British attention shifted first to the Deccan, where it was hoped that Clive might be able to make some impression on the strong French position, and then suddenly to Bengal. In 1756 the startling news reached Madras that Calcutta – the most important of the East India Company settlements in India – had been captured by the new Nawab of Bengal, Siraj-ud-daula.

During the ten years of sporadic warfare in the Carnatic the European trading companies in Bengal had been ordered by the Nawab, Alivardi Khan, to observe a strict neutrality; and they had continued to trade peacefully and profitably in the richest province in India. The fertile valley of the Ganges was the heartland of India, and Bengal commanded its eastern entrance. The province was agriculturally self-sufficient; before the industrial revolution in Western Europe, it was one of the world's leading centres of textile manufactures, and enjoyed a flourishing inland and foreign trade. From Bengal were exported the products of the Ganges valley: exquisite silks and cottons, saltpetre and opium. Calcutta, until 1690 a collection of huts on a swampy site one hundred miles upstream on the Hooghly river (the western branch of the Ganges), was developing under the British into a key centre, and was soon to become a great hub of civil and military administration. Already by mid-century the British had taken full advantage of the Imperial *firman* of 1717 which gave them important commercial privileges, and held a dominant position in the economic life of Bengal.

However, the European political position in Bengal was far weaker than in the south, where Madras and Pondicherry had become independent settlements controlling considerable military forces; and although the main establishments of the European trading companies at Chinsura (Dutch), Chandernagor (French) and Calcutta lay within twenty-five miles of each other, no hostilities took place. Disturbances in Bengal came rather from the raiding Marathas in the western part of the province. This comparatively tranquil state of affairs ended abruptly when Alivardi Khan died in 1756, and was succeeded by Siraj-ud-daula, who already possessed an unenviable reputation for cruelty and viciousness. The old Nawab had once compared the European traders in Bengal to bees, 'of whose honey you may reap the benefit, but if you disturb the hive they will sting you to death'. The headstrong young ruler who succeeded him disregarded this prophetic advice. Alarming reports of European dominance in the Deccan and the Carnatic made him apprehensive for his own position, and he determined to restrict the activities of the British and French companies in Bengal. When the British refused to accept his proposed limitations on their defences Siraj-ud-daula marched on Calcutta. The Company fortifications there were lamentably weak, the defence of the citadel of Fort William (described by one Briton as 'a building which many an old house in this country exceeds in its defences') was scandalously mishandled, and the Nawab's army overwhelmed the few hundred defenders. The British surrender was followed by the notorious incident of the Black Hole of Calcutta, when according to the generally accepted account only 23 persons out of 146 shut up for the night in the fort's tiny, airless guardroom survived. (Several Indian historians have queried this figure, which certainly does not rest upon the most reliable of evidence.) The tragedy, more widely publicized in the nineteenth century than at the time, seems to have been the result of unthinking callousness, not a deliberate atrocity, but it gave an edge of horror to the news that reached Madras.

Despite the imminence of formal war with France in Europe, and the renewal of hostilities which this would undoubtedly bring to the Coromandel coast, the Council at Madras decided to send the strongest possible expedition north to re-establish the Company's position in Bengal. In October 1756 a force of 1,800 European soldiers and sepoys sailed under the command of Robert Clive, now a lieutenant-colonel and Governor of Fort Saint David as a result of his exploits against Dupleix's forces in the Carnatic. Calcutta was recaptured without undue difficulty at the beginning of 1757, and a half-hearted attack by Siraj-ud-daula's army beaten off. A peace treaty was signed with the Nawab which confirmed the Company's rights in Bengal, but did little to guarantee a permanent settlement. The Nawab was undefeated and unrepentant, and news of the declaration of war between Britain and France made an alliance between him and the French in Bengal a possibility which boded ill for the British position. Clive's negotiations with Siraj-ud-daula for permission to attack the French settlements only took a favourable turn when the threat of Afghan incursions into Bengal brought home to the Nawab the disadvantages of waging war on two fronts. With the Nawab's reluctant acquiescence Clive attacked and captured Chandernagor, and the fall of this centre of French trade and influence was followed by the surrender of the other French establishments in Bengal.

This sudden collapse of French power brought a radical change in the alignment of forces in Bengal. Unless the Nawab could persuade Bussy in the Deccan to send help, the French capitulation had deprived him of his natural ally against the British – and this at a time when Clive had decided that as long as the revengeful Siraj-ud-daula ruled in Bengal there could be no security for the British. To Clive the matter was more than ever urgent because of the necessity to concentrate

British forces in the south, where open fighting between British and French forces on the Coromandel coast could not be long delayed. He determined to join a conspiracy of discontented nobles and influential Hindu bankers against Siraj-ud-daula, and to support the claims of Mir Jafar as Nawab. His justification for this move was summed up in a letter to the Governor at Madras: 'From the tyranny, cowardice and suspicion of the Nawab no dependance can be had upon him. . . . I am persuaded there can be neither peace nor security while such a monster reigns.'

Action was not long delayed. In June 1757 Clive and his army of 3,000 sepoys and European troops marched towards the Nawab's encampment at Plassey, and in the subsequent engagement routed Siraj-ud-daula's army of 50,000 men. Opinion in Britain, where victories in the Seven Years War were as yet few and far between, was expressed by Pitt when he spoke in the House of Commons of 'Clive, that heaven-born general', who 'was not afraid to attack a numerous army with a handful of men with a magnanimity, a resolution, a determination and an execution that would charm a King of Prussia and with a presence of mind that astonished the Indies'. In reality, the British triumph was not quite the heroic feat of arms which the disparity in numbers would suggest. For so decisive an encounter Plassey was an undistinguished affair, 'an intrigue rather than a battle'. The British suffered about twenty fatal casualties, the Nawab's army five hundred or so; and there was none of the appalling slaughter which characterized so many Indian battles. Clive himself showed less audacity than in his earlier campaigns, but the vast host confronting him, with its heavy cannon, great fighting elephants and massed cavalry, was impressive only in outward appearance. Although the artillery was under French direction, the infantry was badly equipped and undisciplined; and what fighting spirit the army may have possessed was undermined by the fact that several of its commanders (who included Mir Jafar) were party to the plot against Siraj-ud-daula. A few days after the battle Mir Jafar was acclaimed as regent, and Siraj-ud-daula was hunted down and quickly killed before the British could intervene.

It seemed that Clive had attained his objective. As he solemnly informed Mir Jafar on the occasion of the latter's installation as Nawab, now that a wise and good ruler was on the throne the British would return to Calcutta, where they wished only to follow their commercial interests. But the situation was not as stable as Clive's remarks implied. Within six months of Plassey, Clive was writing home that Mir Jafar had shown himself to be an incompetent and imprudent ruler who had already provoked three rebellions. Too much had happened in the previous eighteen months for Clive to put the clock back to the reign of Alivardi Khan. Having struck at the roots of the Nawab's authority and prestige by deposing one ruler and installing another, the British could not simply withdraw and hope all would be well. As Bussy had found in the Deccan, intermittent interference in the affairs of an Indian state was not a feasible policy. Once the first step of military intervention had been taken, there was no logical stopping-place until the European power became complete master of the Indian government.

The Struggle in the Carnatic

While these momentous developments were taking place in Bengal, fighting had broken out again between British and French forces in the Carnatic. The departure of Clive and his 1,800 men in 1756 had seriously weakened the East India Company's military position on the Coromandel coast; and when in September 1757 a squadron from France with a thousand regular soldiers on board arrived at Pondicherry the British were thrown on to the defensive. At first the French restricted themselves to minor operations, but in April 1758 the discrepancy between the British and French forces was further increased when a second French squadron, commanded by the Comte d'Aché and carrying another thousand troops, reached Pondicherry. Also on board was the Comte de Lally, the new Commissioner-General, with powers over all French establishments and forces in India. Lally came with the avowed intention of destroying the British position in India, and after his arrival the war took on a more ruthless aspect, closer in character to the struggle being waged for supremacy in North America than the earlier limited hostilities between the British and French trading companies.

Despite the presence of the French regiments Lally's task was a formidable one. Although greatly outnumbered in the Carnatic, the British had a squadron at sea under Vice-Admiral Pocock. This had already shown its worth by intercepting d'Aché's fleet off Pondicherry and forcing it to fight its way into port. Moreover, in Bengal the British were now dominant in a region far richer than any the French possessed, and finance was to be an important consideration in the campaigns which lay ahead. Nor was the task of driving out the British Lally's sole concern. He was also burdened with instructions to reform the whole system of French administration in India, an intimidating undertaking at the best of times. The man expected to succeed where the talented Dupleix had failed hardly possessed the stature necessary to accomplish these tasks. The son of an Irish Jacobite, Lally was energetic and forthright; but he was impetuous and sadly deficient in those qualities of judgement and tact essential to a man in his position.

At first the numerical superiority of French forces in the Carnatic enabled Lally to win some deceptively easy victories. After a month's siege Fort Saint David surrendered in June 1758, and Arcot and Cuddalore also fell to the French. But financial stringency and the presence of Pocock's squadron on the coast prevented Lally from moving on to besiege the most important British settlement, Madras. Instead, he turned south towards Tanjore on what was in effect a plundering raid, from which he returned in August in undignified haste on receiving news that Pocock's squadron had defeated d'Aché in an action off the southern Coromandel coast. Although the engagement had not been as disastrous for the French as first reports suggested, d'Aché's squadron suffered enough damage and casualties to make its commander doubtful whether it could put to sea again as an effective fighting force. These setbacks did nothing to improve personal relations among the French leaders. Lally and d'Aché, both proud, jealous men, followed the normal pattern of French army–navy relations in this period by displaying bitter hostility towards each other. Furthermore, Lally had antagonized the Company council at Pondicherry by his contemptuous criticism of its actions, and had alienated Bussy, the outstanding Frenchman in India, by recalling him from the scene of his successful rule in the Deccan to help with the campaign in the Carnatic.

Clearly, much depended on the attack on Madras which Lally now decided to launch. The fortifications of Fort Saint George were stronger than they had been when the place fell to the French in 1746, and the garrison, commanded by Clive's old mentor Stringer Lawrence, was determined and well-supplied. For three months French forces besieged the fortress, suffering heavy casualties and losing troops through desertion, until in February 1759 the arrival of a

British squadron from Bombay forced the dispirited French army to retreat. The valour of the Madras defenders, coupled with British command of the sea at a vital moment, had inflicted a crushing blow on French hopes in the Carnatic.

Worse was to follow, for the departure of Bussy and most of his forces from the Deccan had seriously weakened the French position in that region. A revolt against the French in the Northern Circars was supported by British forces sent by Clive from Bengal, and French-led armies were twice routed. These defeats in the Northern Circars and Lally's failure before Madras had a dire effect on the French position in the Deccan. The Subahdar of the Deccan, Salabat Jang, who had been effectively supported and controlled by Bussy for eight years, opened negotiations with the British. In May 1759 he signed a treaty by which he agreed to expel the French from his domains, and granted territory in the Northern Circars to the East India Company. A little more than a year after Lally's arrival at Pondicherry with orders to expel the British from India, French influence in the subcontinent was confined to a narrow strip along the Coromandel coast. Clive had expelled the French from Bengal before Lally reached India, and now the Deccan and the Northern Circars had been lost.

Although the number of soldiers in the service of the British Company was only half that of the French, it was difficult to see what Lally could accomplish without further help from Europe. Throughout 1759 lack of money hampered and restricted his plans. He had difficulty in buying supplies, in meeting the normal expenses of government, in paying his troops. The resentment of his European soldiers at their arrears of pay was shown in several mutinies and in the constant trickle of deserters to the British ranks. Attempts to enlist the support of Indian rulers foundered when the financial plight of the French was realized. Relief finally reached Pondicherry in September 1759 when d'Aché's fleet, bringing men, supplies and money, came into port; but the circumstances of its arrival brought little cheer. Although the French fleet of eleven battleships was the strongest naval force yet seen in Indian waters, it had been intercepted and badly mauled by a smaller British fleet under Pocock. The damage done to his ships had a demoralizing effect on the French admiral. D'Aché was a firm believer in the traditional French maritime doctrine of the importance of retaining 'a fleet in being'. To preserve his ships was in his eyes more meritorious than risking them in battle; and on receiving reports that

Pocock was expecting the arrival of additional warships d'Aché left Pondicherry for Mauritius, and never returned. The French had finally and conclusively lost command of the sea, and this at a moment when the British were using the sea-lanes to bring reinforcements from Europe and Bengal.

Only a series of swift military victories could restore the French position in the Carnatic, but the chances of this diminished with the appointment as commander of the British forces of one of the finest European soldiers to serve in India, Eyre Coote. In January 1760 the British and French armies met at Wandiwash in a battle which ended in complete victory for the British. Disheartened French forces gave up one place after another, until they were driven back into their last stronghold at Pondicherry. Deprived of any hope of help from France (which had worries enough in Europe, North America and the Caribbean) and hindered by acrimonious quarrels between Lally and French company officials, the garrison found itself in a hopeless position. First blockaded, then besieged, and finally pounded by siege artillery, Pondicherry surrendered in January 1761, and British engineers began the work of demolishing the town almost immediately.

The blasting of the buildings and fortifications of Pondicherry symbolized the end of short-lived French visions of empire in India. Greater resources, superior leadership, and command of the sea, had gained victory for the British in India as in North America. At the Peace of Paris the trading settlements which the French had possessed in India in 1749 – that is, before Dupleix's advance – were returned, but with the proviso that the French were not to build fortifications or station troops in Bengal. Moreover, France recognized the British-supported rulers in the Deccan and the Carnatic. The French were to be allowed to return as traders, but political mastery lay with the British. As the Indian historian, Dr S. P. Sen, has written, 'The dream of Dupleix had come true, but for the benefit of his adversaries.'

6

Expansion in India and
the Eastern Seas 1763–1793

THE THIRTY-YEAR period between the Peace of Paris and Britain's declaration of war on revolutionary France saw the disintegration of the first British Empire as the North American colonies rebelled and gained their independence. An empire invincible a generation earlier collapsed in apparent ruin, and a trail was blazed which in time the overseas possessions of other European powers were to follow. Yet the importance of the American Revolution should not obscure the fact that the loss of the Thirteen Colonies was counterbalanced by the extension of British trade and dominion on the other side of the world – in India, the East Indies, China and the Pacific. This process began before the American Revolution, and continued long after it. The traditional division of British colonial history into two periods separated by the watershed of the American Revolution still has some historical significance; nevertheless, what was a period of defeat in the West for the greatest of the European imperial powers was one of purposeful expansion in the East.

The main stimulus to this expansion was the increasing pace of industrialization in Britain. Manufactured goods were being produced more cheaply than in any other European country, and industrialists were eager to find new markets for their products. India, China and the little-known lands of the Eastern Seas seemed to offer tempting opportunities; for in exchange for British manufactures (it was hoped) eastern goods would be brought back for home consumption and for re-export to continental Europe. The expansion of the British economy, which was helped by low interest and insurance rates, by the growth of population, by investment and the development of new machinery, is reflected in the trade statistics. By 1750 Britain was already a thriving industrial and commercial nation; yet in the next half-century both imports and exports trebled in value. Britain's competitive supremacy was further strengthened by her naval power, which enabled her to win and hold trade and bases in time of war.

The fast-growing empire in the East was not to be one of territorial occupation and white settlement. Even before the American Revolution criticisms had been heard that settlement colonies were troublesome, costly to administer, and potential industrial competitors. The model to be copied was rather the Dutch seventeenth-century empire: a network of carefully chosen trading and naval bases, secured by alliances with native rulers, and protected by sea-power. The ideal proved as difficult for the British to realize as it had been for the Dutch, and nowhere was this more clearly revealed than in India.

Warren Hastings and the Consolidation of British Power in India

The British took swift advantage of their successes in the Seven Years War to establish more firmly their position in eastern India. But military triumphs brought political problems of the utmost complexity. Clive departed for home in 1760 (to become Baron Clive of Plassey), leaving behind him in Bengal an uneasy partnership between the East India Company and successive Nawabs. The overbearing attitude of Company officials, and disputes over finance and internal trade, finally precipitated a war which decided the political future of Bengal. Company forces won at Buxar a victory the equal of any achieved by Clive; it set the seal on the Company's military predominance, and gave birth to intoxicating visions of the Company emerging as a great territorial power. When Clive returned to India in 1765 he found himself cast in the unfamiliar role of a restraining influence on the hotheads in Bengal who were planning a march on Delhi. Militarily this was feasible, but Clive hesitated before the political implications. He calmed the excitement, and substituted for the proposed advance on Delhi a negotiated agreement with the Emperor – by now an empty title rather than a power. Under the terms of this agreement the Company received the grant of the *diwani* (the right to collect revenue) in the rich territories of Bengal, Bihar and Orissa. Formal political dominion remained with the Nawab, but the 'dual system' of government introduced by Clive left the Company effective master of a great Indian state more populous than France.

This move had far-reaching effects on the East India Company. Once in control of rents and taxes in Bengal, it was no longer a mere trading company. Its most important and profitable activity in India was the collection of revenue in Bengal. Alone among the European powers in India, the British possessed a territory capable of producing a revenue sufficient to cover civil expenses and pay for armies which were colossal by normal British standards (by the end of the century the Company had 150,000 troops in India on regular establishment). The Company in India had a self-sufficiency and military strength which gave it a massive superiority over its European rivals. The foundations of British rule in India had been laid.

However, this lay in the future. For the moment, the Company's predominance in Bengal was veiled; but there was no escaping the fact that the authority in Moghul India which collected revenue was traditionally responsible for more general questions of administration. Although Clive had no wish to see the Company involved in the internal administration of Bengal, the implications of the new position are plain to see in his remarks about the Nawab:

> Nothing remains to him but the name and shadow of authority. His name, however, this shadow, it is indispensably necessary we should seem to venerate. . . . Under his sanction every encroachment that may be attempted by foreign powers can effectually be crushed without any apparent interposition of our own authority.

British authority in Bengal was real, if hidden, but the East India Company of the period was ill-equipped to tackle the problems of government which its victories had brought it. In London the directors and shareholders were mainly concerned with trading profits, and with the opportunities for patronage which the Company afforded. In India the Company's servants exploited their new power to accumulate private fortunes. Clive, whose immense wealth gained during the campaigns of the Seven Years War had made him an authority on the subject, commented on his return to Bengal in 1765: 'Such a scene of anarchy, confusion, bribery, corruption and extortion was never seen or heard in any country but Bengal, nor such and so many fortunes acquired in so unjust and rapacious a manner.'

Clive had shown the way with his acceptance of large sums of money from Indian rulers, and his example was followed by men with far less in the way of positive achievement to excuse their greed. The system of payment by the Company to its servants at this time was summarized by a later Governor-General in the words, 'small salaries and immense perquisites'. The Company's military superiority in Bengal removed all restraints from its servants. The acceptance or extortion of 'presents', and participation in private trading, made men rich in two or three years. Fortune-hunters rarely make good administrators, and pressing problems of government in a state where the basis of native authority had been destroyed were ignored in the race for private gain. Wealth was amassed at the expense of the inhabitants of Bengal, and the Company's servants represented (in Macaulay's damning words) 'the strength of civilization without its mercy'.

Ironically enough, it was Clive who was sent out to put an end to corruption. The poacher had turned gamekeeper with a vengeance. Clive pursued his policy with an apparent lack of embarrassment and a firmness which aroused intense resentment, and at one stage provoked a mutiny of the Company's military officers in Bengal. But drastic though some of Clive's actions were, he could only diminish, not eradicate, the evils he was sent to cure. In 1767 he left India for the last time, and after a few years of frustration in England which culminated in a parliamentary attack on his earlier conduct in Bengal, he committed suicide in 1774. Clive will always be remembered as a *conquistador* rather than a statesman. The importance of his career lay not in measures of imaginative government, but in his military victories and the extent of territory he brought under British control. The exploits of this masterful adventurer directed British attention to India in a wholly unprecedented fashion; the days of unobtrusive trading had gone for ever. It was left to others to follow Clive's feats of arms by building a solid administrative structure in the territories he had helped a reluctant Company to acquire.

The main burden of this task fell on one of the most controversial figures in the history of British India, Warren Hastings. When Hastings became Governor of Bengal in 1772 he found the state in deplorable condition. To the west the warlike Marathas were on the move again after a period of quiescence in the 1760s, and represented a menace which might assume frightening proportions at any time. Within Bengal famine had brought appalling misery to a people already suffering from the misrule and oppression of the Company's servants and the Nawab's officials. As a Company man admitted, 'this fine country is verging towards its ruin'. British dominion, it seemed, had only added to the confusion and despair in India. Finally, Hastings had to face the handicap that the Company through which he had to exert sovereign power over an enormous area still possessed the structure and outlook of a trading organization.

One of the Governor's first acts was to end the unpleasant farce of the dual system of government introduced in 1765, and to take over direct exercise of the administration. Power and responsibility were to go hand in hand. Efficiency, order and justice were to replace the tangled mess of corruption and self-seeking which Hastings found on his arrival. Policy was to be laid down and stringently supervised from Calcutta, and not left to the whims of Company servants in the out-lying regions. A beginning was made to the complex task of providing a fairer and more efficient system of tax collection, though this was a baffling problem with which the Bengal administration struggled until a long-term settlement was reached under Cornwallis. The privileged position of Company servants in local trade was abolished, though private trading still remained permissible for all except the Governor and Council. New courts of justice were established, based as far as possible on the recognized laws of the country.

The driving force behind these reforms came from Hastings himself. There were flaws in his character. He was often arrogant, and some-times ruthless (the execution of one of his Indian political opponents on a charge of forgery – a capital offence in England but not in India – was not far removed from judicial murder). But on the whole Hastings's virtues far outweighed his defects. He was a first-rate administrator, with that rare ability to construct a general framework of policy, and then to fit into it the details of administration. To an orderly and lucid mind was added an untiring energy and zest for business. It was one of the tragedies of Hastings's career that the task begun in so promising a fashion was interrupted, first by internal dissension, and later by grave external dangers.

For a time the most significant developments were in Britain, where tales of oppression in India, rumours that the Company was almost bankrupt, and the sight of returned Company officials – the 'nabobs' – flaunting their wealth, led to mounting public disquiet. Anxiety about the Company's position and conduct was reflected in Parliament, where Indian affairs became a hotly debated topic, and a series of Select and Secret Committees of the House of Commons investigated the complex problems of Indian government. Quite apart from the financial crisis into which the Company had run itself through the payment of extravagantly high dividends, its expansion in territory and power posed unprecedented problems to the home government. No private trading corporation had ever achieved such a position before. Edmund Burke later pointed out that the East India Company had become much more than a commercial organization; it was 'in reality a delegation of the whole power and sovereignty of this nation sent into the East'. As such it had to be brought under control, and an attempt to do this was made in the Regulating Act passed by Parliament in 1773.

The Act was the first tentative move towards an arrangement by which the state controlled the main lines of Indian policy, while the Company continued to supervise trading activities and the details of administration. Among other changes a Supreme Court of Justice was established in Bengal, whose members were nominated by the Crown. Its original purpose was to protect the native population from oppression by the Company's servants, but the difficulties of defining which Indians fell into this category soon led to its trying to exercise jurisdiction over many Bengalis who were completely unfamiliar with English law. The most important feature of the Act was that it established the post of Governor-General in India (and named Hastings as the first holder of the office), with certain powers over the other presidencies at Madras and Bombay. The centralized control over the three main areas of British power which Clive had always urged had come a step nearer realization. The Governor-General was to be assisted by a council of four, also named in the Act. Decisions were to be taken by majority vote – a serious weakness in the Governor-General's position if confronted with a hostile council. Only one of the councillors nominated was a Company man; the other three appointments were political ones.

From the beginning there were wrangles between Hastings and the three non-Company men, in particular Philip Francis, a man who, in Macaulay's phrase, 'mistook malevolence for virtue'. Francis followed what he believed was the intention of the home government in pro-pounding a system under which the exercise of British dominion would be confined to the defence of Bengal and the region's external trade. Internal administration would be left to the rehabilitated Indian rulers in the localities. Hastings denied the practicability of this policy, first laid down by Clive, and now pressed once more by Francis. He refused to accept that the British could exercise ultimate control over the region, and receive its revenue, without intervening in the morass of internal government. Reforms in the spheres of justice, administration and tax-collection – a scene described by Hastings 'as wild as chaos itself' – were all essential. Genuine differences of policy between the two men were sharpened by a bitter personal feud, and for six years Hastings dissipated his energies in an exhausting struggle for dominance in the council, while the work of reform ground to a standstill.

At the same time as the Governor-General's authority within Bengal was being attacked and undermined, he was faced with growing dangers outside, and these were the more harassing now that he held a superintending responsibility for Bombay and Madras. In external affairs commercial rather than territorial expansion was Hastings's ideal. Characteristic of his outlook was the sending of a mission to Lhasa in 1774 in an attempt (unsuccessful, as it proved), to open commercial relations with Tibet, and establish a staging-post on the overland route to China. At the same time contact was made with Ali Bey, ruler of Egypt, about the possibility of sending dispatches to Britain by way of Suez. But despite his lack of enthusiasm for territorial expansion, Hastings was fully prepared to adopt an attitude of belligerent defiance in face of threats from other Indian states. He regarded diplomacy as a more effective and cheaper weapon than military force, and favoured strengthening the Company's position by a series of alliances with neighbouring powers. The policy of static defence urged by some members of the council he regarded as dangerous, if only because the Company's territories had no easily defensible natural frontiers.

Under Hastings the Company found itself at war on both sides of India. From 1771 onwards the buffer state of Oudh, north-west of Bengal, was increasingly exposed to Maratha raids, and Hastings's efforts to strengthen Oudh led him into a dubious war of aggression on behalf of its ruler. The Carnatic was threatened by the hostile ruler of Mysore (Haidar Ali), the Marathas, and the Nizam at Hyderabad. In the west the imprudent intervention of the Bombay council in Maratha affairs resulted in a war which Hastings felt bound to support, and which dragged on in exhausting fashion until 1782. Little was gained in material terms; but the waging of a prolonged war against the formidable military power of the Marathas, at a time when the Company was involved in hostilities with the French and with other Indian powers in the Carnatic, brought a new respect for the Company's strength.

Renewed Anglo-French Rivalry

The long wars against the Marathas were the more serious because of the threat to the British position in India which came with French intervention in the American War of Independence. The French position in India was admittedly weak, even though in 1770 the Crown had taken over responsibility for the India trade after the *Compagnie des Indes* failed to achieve solvency in the post-war period and was abolished. Pondicherry on the Coromandel coast had been rebuilt after its destruction by the British in the Seven Years War, but it had no pretensions to being a strong military centre. In Bengal the French settlement at Chandernagor had been stripped of its fortifications in conformity with the terms of the Peace of Paris. Nowhere could the French match the British in military strength. However, this did not deter some French officials, and French adventurers in the service of Indian princes, from resurrecting Dupleix's old schemes. Dozens of plans were sent home, intended to reverse the verdict of 1763. Usually these involved the shipping of men and money to India, and the building of a French-supported coalition of Indian princes against the overweening power of the British Company. But the projects were ignored, and for more than a decade the French government showed little interest in its Indian possessions.

Not until 1776, when de Sartine became Minister of Marine and Colonies in France, was any serious thought given to the possibility of restoring the French position in India. Even then, so slow was the French reaction to the opportunity offered by Britain's distraction in America that when war broke out between Britain and France in 1778 nothing had been done to prepare for a French offensive in India. The priorities of the French government were the same as those of the British: the main theatre of war was in North America and the Caribbean, and it was there that forces must be concentrated. This attitude was a more serious blow to French hopes in India than to the British, for the East India Company was able to deploy forces far superior to the French in numbers and quality. Before the war French observers had written home warning the government that the British possessed close on 10,000 European troops and 60,000–70,000 sepoys, supported by good artillery and efficient naval forces.

Hastings, whose comment on the British reverses in America was that they made it the more necessary to uphold Britain's interests in the East, quickly took the offensive on the outbreak of war; and soon all the French possessions in India had fallen to Company forces. In the next three years the French, preoccupied with campaigns in North America and the Caribbean, let slip fine opportunities in India, where the Company was still involved in war with the Marathas and Haidar Ali of Mysore. At the time when the Company was hardest pressed the French government made no move, and not until 1781 did it finally decide to send strong naval and military forces to India. Though belated, this decision was part of an ambitious plan to restore the balance of European forces in India as it had been in Dupleix's time. The French commanders were to negotiate alliances with Haidar Ali and other Indian princes, with an eye to setting up a confederacy against the British. In March 1781 a fleet left France for Indian waters under the command of Suffren, a commander of genius whose offensive spirit was rare among French admirals. Unfortunately for French hopes, the land forces commanded by Bussy (Dupleix's famous lieutenant of earlier days) did not leave Europe until the end of the year.

Even Suffren arrived too late to take advantage of the precarious position the British had been in. The Maratha war was slowly dying, and the British had just captured from the Dutch Trincomalee in Ceylon – the best port in eastern Indian waters, and one which Suffren had to re-take before he could use it as his base. The Seven Years War had shown the importance of command of the sea in the Indian theatre of war, and while awaiting Bussy's arrival Suffren met the British fleet commanded by Hughes in a series of hard-fought actions. Suffren's brilliance was matched by Hughes's dogged courage, and neither side was able to claim decisive victory. When Bussy at last reached the scene he found that he had no suitable base of operations on the mainland, no firm allies among the Indian powers, and that Haidar Ali had just died. He was thrown on the defensive south of Pondicherry, and before any fighting of consequence could take place the war had ended.

Although under the terms of the Treaty of Versailles the French recovered their trading stations in India, moral victory lay with the

British. The hope of Vergennes, French foreign minister, that the clock could be put back to 1754 had been completely frustrated. The East India Company had shown that it could withstand the land and sea forces of a powerful European enemy, and the armies of several of the strongest Indian princes; and this at a time when the home government was in dire straits. Inspired by Hastings, who remained resolute in spite of distracting personal feuds, the Company emerged as the strongest single power in India. There were still fewer than 5,000 Europeans in the Company's civil employ, but in terms of wealth and power the Company had advanced far since the days when it had existed on sufferance in the shadow of the Moghul Empire.

Last Years of Peace in India

After the crisis of the Maratha, Mysore and French wars had been met and overcome, there was little to keep Warren Hastings in India. The affairs of Bengal were a continual subject of debate at Westminster, and Hastings smarted under the frequent criticisms of his government. The long years of hard work in a debilitating climate, the struggle with hostile councillors, and a succession of external dangers, had taken their toll of his health and patience. The reforming zeal had died, and in 1785 he returned to England.

After Hastings retired criticism of his actions in India increased, stimulated as much by the personal animosity of his enemies as by the genuine moral indignation of Edmund Burke and other idealists who viewed both the theory and practice of Hastings's rule in India with abhorrence. In 1788 Hastings faced impeachment on charges of gross misconduct in India. After a spectacular opening session the trial dragged on for year after year; what had been the sensation of London became the bore of London. Finally in 1795 Hastings was acquitted. The whole affair was a rank injustice to a man whose occasional acts of harshness and duplicity were far outweighed by his services both to the Company and to the people of Bengal. Hastings's critics have invariably ignored the fact that it was rapacious Indian rulers who smarted most under the weight of the Governor-General's authority. The working out of his revenue policy in Bengal was to bear hard on the peasants, but in other ways his rule brought them a measure of security in a cruel world.

The publicity the trial gave to Hastings's alleged crimes helped to obscure the fact that the real damage being done by the British in India was of a more general economic nature. The supremacy of European traders and financiers brought hardship, if not ruin, to many of their Indian counterparts. The economic subordination of vast areas of India to European interests was to be as damaging in the long term as the early years of oppression and misgovernment. (The ruthless operation of economic forces was clearly demonstrated in the early nineteenth century when British machine-made cloth flooded into India to destroy the livelihood of the hand-loom weavers.) In the same way, the impact of the most vigorous and self-confident nation in Europe had a disintegrating effect on Indian society. Later accusations that the British deliberately strove to break down the national unity of India have little weight as far as this period is concerned. Caste, religion, locality – these had far more significance in Hastings's day than 'the nation', and help to explain the comparative ease with which the British were able to dominate area after area. Innovations were resisted, life in many parts went on much as before, but slowly and often unconsciously British administrators were effecting changes which struck at the foundations of traditional Indian society.

Hastings's accusers might be little interested in these general factors, but the trial served one useful purpose. It showed that the actions of British officials in India did not lie outside the law. Although Hastings was innocent of the cruder charges of corruption and cruelty brought against him, his impeachment was a warning that the activities of British subjects in India might at any time be brought under close scrutiny. This same theme – later to be refined and developed into the concept of 'trusteeship' – ran through the India Act of 1784. The Act established a close measure of control by the state over the East India Company, which was left in charge only of trading affairs and Indian patronage. Final authority for all political, military and revenue matters was transferred to a Board of Control in London which consisted of a Secretary of State, the Chancellor of the Exchequer, and four Privy Councillors. In India the Governor-General was given powers which Hastings had often requested but never received. There was no direct declaration of sovereignty, but the ultimate responsibility of Parliament for the government of those parts of India dominated by Britain was firmly laid down in the Act. The short-lived period of rule by a trading company over millions of Indians was over.

The first Governor-General to serve under the new system which, with some modifications, was to last for seventy years, was Lord

Cornwallis, a soldier of ability despite his surrender to the Americans at Yorktown. His strength of character, powers of judgement and known honesty introduced a new spirit into the turbulent affairs of Bengal. Advised by a small group of experts, Cornwallis introduced a new land and revenue system which helped the region to regain its old prosperity though it brought hardship to many of the peasants once again. He reformed the judiciary, and ruthlessly stamped out the corruption with which Hastings had grappled for so many years. The salaries of Company servants were increased, and private trading by the administrative staff prohibited. Integrity was the keynote of the Cornwallis administration, and the beginnings appeared of that tradition of devoted public service which was one of the happier features of British rule in India during the nineteenth century.

Other distinctive characteristics were also evident. Even in India, the centre of Britain's eastern empire, the British were not settlers in the sense that they intended to make a permanent home there for themselves and their heirs. One day they hoped to go 'home' to England, and though many never did, the thought of return was always present. Their determination to remain aloof from the local environment had its unattractive side, but it was undoubtedly a source of strength to the British position in the East. There was little inter-marriage with Indian women, and no attempt to adopt an Eastern mode of life. Under Cornwallis the gulf between Englishman and Indian widened when the Governor-General ordered that higher administrative posts were to be reserved for Europeans. To the British traders, officials and soldiers in India the mother country was always the first concern, and the indifference shown (for example) by some of the Portuguese settlers and traders in the East to the fate of their homeland horrified the patriotic Briton in India.

In external affairs there was little positive attempt under Cornwallis to extend the Company's domains. Neither the British government nor the Company wanted further territorial acquisitions. Renewed hostilities against Mysore, during which Tipu Sultan, Haidar Ali's aggressive son, lost half his territory, hinted that it might be impossible to call a halt to the process of expansion; but Cornwallis was able to retire in 1793 with the knowledge that he had kept intervention in Indian affairs outside the Company's boundaries to a minimum.

K

The China Trade

Although India was the centre of the East India Company's growing territorial empire, the Company's commercial activities were being developed most rapidly in China, where it had carried on a regular though limited trade since the beginning of the century. The most valuable commodity exported was black China tea, which in Britain became the universal drink of rich and poor alike. The amount of tea sold by the Company in London rose from less than 100,000 lbs at the beginning of the century to 8 million lbs in 1770, and this quite apart from the considerable quantities smuggled into the country.

Trading conditions in China were different from those in any other part of the world visited by European traders. Unlike its counterpart in India, imperial authority in China remained strong and arrogant throughout the eighteenth century under the Manchu dynasty. To the government at Peking China was still the Middle Kingdom, the centre of the world, and the Europeans were barbarians who came from outer darkness. The normal attitude of the Chinese authorities to 'foreign devils' was one of disdainful indifference. European traders were restricted to the single port of Canton, where factors of the several European trading companies – British, French, Dutch, Imperial, Swedish and Danish – negotiated with approved Chinese merchants. The companies had factories on the river-bank outside the city walls, and their personnel were not allowed to enter the city itself. All transactions were carried out under the suspicious eye of Chinese officialdom, and at the end of the trading season, when the Indiamen had sailed for Europe, the factors were banished to Macao, the Portuguese settlement at the mouth of the Canton river.

The various European companies endured the restrictions and humiliations for the sake of the valuable trade in tea; but this too was conducted on an unsatisfactory basis. Since access to the interior was prohibited, the genuine two-way trade which was the economist's ideal was impossible to establish. There seemed little demand for western manufactures in China, which was essentially an agricultural, self-sufficient country. Its upper classes could obtain luxury goods through the Chinese trading junks which sailed the trade routes of the Eastern Seas, or by way of the overland caravans. The East India Company, with its growing territorial and administrative responsibilities, had become too large-scale and inflexible an organization to contend with the frustrations of such a market. As its revenue from Bengal increased it shed many of its less lucrative trading activities, and lost interest in the difficult business of exporting British manufactures to the East. Indiamen often went out in ballast, and as far as the important China trade was concerned the Company simply shipped silver to Canton to pay for most of the tea bought there. The trade 'gap' thus opened up was only kept within reasonable bounds by the activities of the Country Traders, private European merchants engaged in local Asiatic trade (the monopoly of the East India Company applied only to goods shipped around the Cape of Good Hope). Working with ships manned by lascar crews, they covered the whole vast area between India and the China Seas and brought into Canton an amazing variety of commodities at competitive prices. Bengal cotton was the most important of these, but it was supplemented by a long list of exotic products specially collected for the China market: sandalwood and ivory from India, camphor from Borneo, birds' nests, sago and pepper from Java and Sumatra, spices from the Moluccas, and from the smaller islands agates, pearls, sharks' fins, blackwood, coral, beeswax and tortoise shells.

The scale of the East India Company's trade in tea, supported by a huge home demand, together with the business expertise of the Country Traders, gave Britain the leading place in the China trade; but this position was far from unassailable. Britain's supply of silver was dangerously dependent on relations with Spain and its great silver-producing empire; and in any event its export to pay for a luxury commodity was frowned upon by economists at home. One answer to the problems of the China trade seemed to be the establishment of commercial bases in the seas between India and China, and after the Peace of Paris earnest consideration was given to a number of schemes put forward by individuals in the Company's service which were directed to this end.

The Dutch were still the most important power in the East Indies, but their influence, though widespread, was not dominant everywhere. Lacking the stimulus of European competition in the area west of the Philippines, they had been content to hold a few key points. As a result there were many places in the maze of islands of the Malay Archipelago, where the Country Traders were already active, which might be turned into British bases. These, it was anticipated, would become distributing centres for British manufactures, and also for opium and other Indian products. In return, the region would supply the commodities in demand in China, and these would pay for the tea bought at Canton. A chain of trade would be forged linking Britain, India, the East Indies and China in a self-supporting and highly lucrative system.

But first a base had to be found, and this proved no easy task. Manila, captured from Spain in 1762, would have served, but it had to be returned at the end of the war. In 1763 Alexander Dalrymple, one of the East India Company's most enterprising servants (whose activities as a geographical theorist are discussed in the next chapter), took possession of Balambangan, a small island lying off the north coast of Borneo. The island was ceded to the Company by the Sultan of Sulu, who in 1764 granted the Company the whole of North Borneo. The Company appeared to have taken a gigantic eastward step, across and north of the Dutch sphere of influence, and stopping just short of the Spanish-dominated area of the Philippines. However, the enterprise never succeeded as a commercial venture. The British government was uneasy about the region's proximity to the Spanish and Dutch possessions at a time of tense diplomatic relations in Europe. The Company was preoccupied with difficulties in India, dubious about the wisdom of acquiring territory so remote from its centre of power, and did not establish a post at Balambangan until 1773. Fraud by the Company servants led to heavy financial losses, and quarrels with the Suluans finally ended in an attack on the little settlement which brought about its hasty evacuation in 1775.

Dalrymple's vision of a flourishing entrepôt in the Borneo region, trading with both India and China, and linking the two areas in a way highly profitable to the Company, vanished. From the islands attention turned to the mainland, and particularly to Cochin-China, a region which held an advantage over Balambangan in that Chinese merchants regularly traded there. A reconnaissance was carried out, but before any serious attempt to establish a base could be made the War of American Independence had spread into eastern waters. Cochin-China was left unexploited by the British, and in the next century became the centre of France's new eastern empire.

No desire to found a territorial empire of settlement can be glimpsed in these undertakings. Dalrymple had stressed as early as 1769 that the lesson to be learned from the unrest in North America was that commercial attention should be directed towards regions far distant

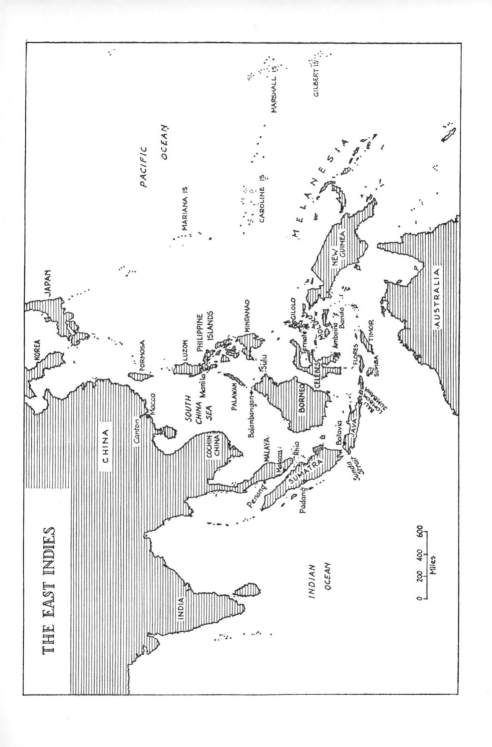

THE EAST INDIES

from white colonists, and that trade, not settlement, must be the objective. Once war was joined in the 1770s, many echoed Warren Hastings's remark that the setbacks in America made the compensating work of empire-building in the East all the more necessary; but outside India this was to be a non-territorial empire of trade. It was universally agreed that a network of commercial and strategic bases would be more profitable and less troublesome than the disappointing settlement colonies of the American type.

By 1780 Britain was at war with France, Spain and Holland, and her eastern empire looked dangerously vulnerable. It was dependent on a long line of oceanic communication which was supported by only one small base between Britain and India – Saint Helena in the south Atlantic. The more important bases at the Cape of Good Hope and Ceylon were Dutch, and Mauritius belonged to the French. Farther east the Dutch controlled the vital strategic channels of the Sunda and Malacca straits, the gateways to the East Indies and the China Seas. In the event the British were more successful than they had a right to expect. An attempt on the Cape came to nothing, but the Dutch bases at Trincomalee in Ceylon and Padang in Sumatra were captured, and efforts were even made to foment uprisings against the Dutch in Celebes. In a more peaceful sphere of competition the period of the American war marked the final triumph of the British Country Traders over their European rivals. Taking full advantage of the East India Company's influence in some of the richest regions in India, and spurred by the expanding Company trade at Canton, the British traders by the end of the war years dominated the Country Trade in eastern waters.

In the peace treaty of 1784 between Britain and Holland all captured territory was returned except the Dutch settlement of Negapatam (south of Madras). During the course of a generally disastrous war Britain's eastern empire had remained intact, and it was the weakness of the Dutch empire before a European enemy which had been most clearly revealed. Even so, the new Dutch hostility was a disturbing feature which spelt danger to the British in the East, especially since French influence in Holland was growing steadily. Although militarily weak in the East, the Dutch held important strategic bases which in French hands would be a deadly menace to Britain's eastern empire. This realization helped to sustain the British quest for a base between India and China, for the Company's position in India was also at stake.

The naval clashes in Indian waters had shown once again how grievous a disadvantage Britain suffered from the want of a good harbour on the east coast of India. During the period of the north-east monsoon ships had either to retire to Bombay on the west coast, or risk destruction on the exposed Coromandel coast. This weakness was serious enough even when the French, with their nearest base 3,000 miles away at Mauritius, were in the same position; but if the French were given permanent use of the nearby Dutch harbour at Trincomalee or could sweep into the Bay of Bengal from ports in western Sumatra, then it might become an insuperable handicap.

These considerations prompted the renewal of the search for a base east of the Bay of Bengal after the war. One of the most powerful ministers in the new post-war administration led by the Younger Pitt was Henry Dundas, and he gave government encouragement to the efforts of Company men and private individuals who were striving to build a great trading empire along the Asiatic sea-routes. Dundas saw that, although the new empire was a maritime one, its heart was Bengal. The economic and financial resources of that area gave British enterprise an invaluable springboard for expansion eastward, and its defence became an anxious consideration in Dundas's planning. Finally, it was decided to establish a defensive and commercial outpost at Penang, an island just off the west coast of the Malay Peninsula, near the Malacca Straits, and not too far distant from Bengal and the Coromandel coast. It was occupied in 1786, and although in the nineteenth century it was to be eclipsed by the rise of Singapore, it proved its worth during the long wars with Revolutionary and Napoleonic France.

Macartney's Embassy to China

At the same time as Penang was acquired, British trade with China was experiencing momentous changes. The high duty of 119 per cent on tea imported into England encouraged smuggling, and had proved a boon to the East India Company's European rivals engaged in the China trade. They had every incentive to find illegal access into the British market with its millions of regular tea drinkers. The incentive was killed when in 1784 the Pitt administration introduced the Commutation Act, which replaced the existing duties on tea by one of a modest $12\frac{1}{2}$ per cent. Apart from its financial implications at home, the Act was a deliberate move by the British government to enable the

East India Company to dominate the China trade; and the results amply fulfilled this intention.

Within a decade the amount of tea imported by the Company had more than doubled. The Swedish, Danish and Imperial companies at Canton, all of which lived mainly on the illegal tea trade into Britain, dwindled away as tea smuggling declined. The Dutch remained active competitors for a while because their East Indian possessions provided them with the spices and tin much in demand at Canton; but even their share in the tea trade was hard hit by the Commutation Act, and was finally destroyed by the French wars in the 1790s. France's China trade, which had long suffered from the lack of eastern possessions and from government apathy, also vanished at this time. Only the Americans remained unaffected by the long wars in Europe and the British mastery of the seas, and their challenge did not represent a serious threat to the British tea traders at Canton. Lucrative though it was, this trade must be kept in perspective. Britain's eastern trade in general never matched her American and West Indian trades in value, and even the fast expanding China trade accounted at the end of the century for less than 6 per cent of the country's total foreign trade.

Stimulating though the phenomenal increase in the tea trade was to British commerce in Asia generally, the difficulties which had always accompanied it were also magnified. The problem of finding goods, rather than silver, to pay for the tea remained a frustrating one. Woollens from England filled only a part of the trade 'gap'. Cotton from India proved more acceptable to the Chinese, whose spinners and weavers needed more raw cotton than was normally grown in China. The contraband trade in opium managed by the Country Traders increased enormously, and in the nineteenth century was to overtake cotton in importance (and finally in 1839–42 lead to war between Britain and China). But neither cotton, opium nor the eastern commodities imported into Canton by the Country Traders met the demands of British industrialists that the expanding China trade should be financed by the export of British manufactures. As production leapt upwards in the Britain of the Industrial Revolution, so these demands became more frequent, and pressure on the government increased.

Further dissatisfaction resulted from the multitude of restrictions and prohibitions which lay heavily on British traders in China. They were still allowed to trade only at Canton, where a great range of dues – some legal and official, many not – were exacted. Debts owed by Chinese merchants to British creditors (mainly from India) were not always honoured. The occasional British warship which anchored in the Canton river was rarely treated with the deference which the greatest sea power in the world felt was its due. Differences between European and Chinese notions of justice produced dangerous tensions (in one incident in the winter of 1784–5 a British gunner was executed after he had accidentally killed two Chinese). These tensions had always been present, but as British trade at Canton increased so resentment grew at the unco-operative attitude of the Chinese. For its part Chinese officialdom tended to fall back ever more readily behind its barriers of regulation and obstructiveness. There were straws in the wind to show that even the vastly self-confident Chinese Empire could fear encirclement. No single move by outside forces represented a direct threat, but British interest in Tibet, Dutch predominance in the Eastern Seas, Russian expansion in Siberia, and French missionary activity in Cochin-China all formed ominous ripples of activity on China's borders.

The British government was unaware of these wider considerations. It could see only that the Canton trade, as carried on in its existing form, was subject to irritating hindrances; but that if these were removed it offered unlimited commercial prospects. To this situation the government applied the normal tenets of western diplomacy, and decided to send an ambassador to the imperial court at Peking to negotiate a high-level settlement. In the first instance he was to discuss and settle the difficulties over the Canton trade – fees, imposts and questions of jurisdiction. These points were to be incorporated into a commercial treaty, which it was hoped might include wider concessions. The expansion of British trade, particularly in woollens, into the colder regions of northern China had been a British aim for most of the century; and accordingly the ambassador was to urge that the ports of northern China should be opened to British shipping. His instructions went even further. In a clause which foreshadowed the establishment in the next century of Hong Kong, the ambassador was told to ask whether a British enclave might be established on the Chinese mainland or on an offshore island to serve as a warehousing centre for British traders. In 1787 the government appointed Lieutenant-Colonel Cathcart as ambassador to Peking to carry out this mission, but the whole enterprise collapsed when Cathcart died on the outward voyage.

Far from abandoning the idea of an embassy, the Pitt administration decided to make another attempt, this time on a grander scale. George Macartney, a diplomat and colonial governor with a distinguished career, was chosen. Every precaution was taken to make the mission a success. Macartney was given an Irish viscountcy, a military escort complete with field guns to perform before the Chinese court, a collection of British manufactures from the northern and midland industrial cities, some examples of the latest technical inventions, and a selection of presents for the Emperor Ch'ien Lung which ranged from a planetarium to a novelty pistol capable of firing eight shots without reloading. Hopes were pitched at an even higher level than before the Cathcart embassy. Although Macartney's immediate objective was to put the Canton trade on a stable basis, the mission was also regarded by the government as the spearhead of a drive to open China (and perhaps even the closed world of Japan) to British trade and influence. Macartney's wit and talent would, it was hoped, enable him to strike up a friendship with the Emperor which would lead to a mutually beneficial *entente* between Britain and China. Some sceptical voices were heard even before the embassy left, especially from the ranks of the East India Company, which had been made responsible by the government for the cost of the mission (£80,000). From the beginning the Company was dubious about an embassy which, if it succeeded, might throw open the China trade in such a way as to imperil the Company's monopoly, and, if it failed, might antagonize the Chinese authorities and endanger the Company's existing trade at Canton.

Macartney left England in a 64-gun naval vessel in September 1792, and reached Chusan the following July. He arrived at Peking in September, and at the imperial court at Jehol soon after. The first British ambassador ever to reach China soon found that his mission bristled with difficulties. At one point it appeared extremely doubtful whether he would ever reach the imperial presence. After prolonged discussions about whether or not he should kotow when presented to the Emperor, Macartney was received by Ch'ien Lung in the grounds of the Summer Palace at Jehol. In a stilted ceremony the Emperor and Macartney exchanged greetings, presents and a few commonplaces (through interpreters); but all Macartney's attempts to open serious negotiations were brushed aside. George III's letter explaining the objective of the embassy was accepted, but the British requests were rejected in a letter the language of which revealed that in Chinese eyes the Emperor still ruled the world from his Dragon Throne:

> Though you live, King, far beyond the oceans, nevertheless, inspired by a humble desire to partake of the benefits of civilization, you have dispatched to us a mission respectfully bearing your memorial.
> We have perused your memorial; the earnest terms in which it is framed reveal a devout humility which we find commendable. In consideration of the long journey undertaken by your envoy we have shown him special favour, even allowing him to be introduced into our presence... Swaying the wide world, our one aim has been always a perfect governance and we are not deflected therefrom by gifts. If we have commanded that your tribute offerings are to be accepted, it was not because we have any interest in outlandish objects, but solely in consideration for the proper spirit which prompted you to dispatch them from the remote island where you live. As your envoy will have seen for himself, we are in need of nothing, we possess all things.
> We have expounded our wishes and it is now your duty, King, to respect them, displaying in the future an even greater devotion than has inspired you in the past, so that by perpetual submission to the Dragon Throne you may ensure peace and eternal prosperity for your country.

Permission was even refused to show off the latest cotton machines or to perform a military display, and it was made clear to the dejected Macartney that he was expected to leave the country as soon as possible. The mandarin who accompanied the embassy back to the coast promised to put an end to the abuses in the Canton trade, but even this minor gain failed to materialize. The mission was a costly failure, a result forecast by some of the more knowledgeable East India Company officials before Macartney left England. At home Peter Pindar penned some of his satiric lines on the venture:

> Tell me, who planned this silly expedition?
> That brain was surely in a mad condition....
> Who told our King the embassy would thrive,
> Must be the most egregious fool alive.

No point of contact had been made between two alien worlds, utterly different in custom, religion, language and outlook. The Canton trade proved a barrier rather than a bridge to any understanding between the British and Chinese governments. Both saw the Macartney mission as the thin edge of the wedge; but whereas in British eyes it conjured up possibilities of a revolution in Asiatic trade, on the Chinese side it evoked a disdainful suspicion. A Dutch embassy to Peking in 1794 received equally short shrift. The rich and intensely conservative Manchu dynasty had no intention of coming to terms with the new world of trade and power which lay outside the empire. Instead, it continued its traditional policy of keeping the clamorous European traders at arm's length, barred from contact either with the central government or the Chinese people.

Clearly, no single stroke of British diplomacy would change this attitude, and in the years after Macartney's mission the British government pursued an unambitious policy of keeping on good terms with the Chinese in the hope that one day concessions would be made. No response was forthcoming, and meanwhile friction at Canton continued. Finally it reached such a pitch that in 1816 another embassy, under Lord Amherst, was sent from London. This failed in even more humiliating fashion than Macartney's, for Amherst never even saw the Emperor, and returned home with his list of requests still in his pocket. The differences between the British and Chinese governments remained unsolved until the British extorted in the Treaty of Nanking after the Opium War of 1839–42 the concessions which they had completely failed to gain through the normal processes of negotiation. The way then lay open to European penetration, but in our period China was one of the few areas of the world engaged in trade with Europe which was able to resist the impact of western influences.

The Dutch in the East Indies

While the British, amid a hubbub of publicity and controversy, were taking the first steps towards building a new Asiatic empire, the existing Dutch empire in the East was unobtrusively changing in character. At the beginning of the eighteenth century the size of the trading network established by the *Vereenigde Oostindische Compagnie*, the Dutch East India Company, was an imposing one. Although the centre of the Company's activities still lay in the East Indies, the Dutch also traded with China and Japan, dominated the commerce of the Malay Peninsula, held posts in India, and controlled the coastal areas of Ceylon (including the valuable base of Trincomalee). Lying across the long sea-route from Europe to the Eastern

Seas was the Dutch settlement at the Cape of Good Hope, lacking a safe anchorage but important as the only port of call for refreshment between Madeira and the Indian Ocean.

The empire was one of trade rather than settlement, and until the eighteenth century the Dutch were chiefly intent on exploiting the resources of this vast area with the minimum of involvement in the region's internal affairs. Overlordship, not direct rule, was the ideal aimed at, but this was an attitude which could not endure indefinitely. The Dutch entered alliances with local rulers, and then had to support them, or – if a particular sultan proved unco-operative – a rival claimant. Here lay the seeds of change, for the result of this policy was the disintegration of native authority, increasing intervention by the Dutch to protect their commercial interests, and finally political control and territorial acquisition.

The process can be best seen in Java, the ancient centre of Indonesian civilization, and the most fertile and populous of the East Indian islands. By the mid-eighteenth century most of the island was governed from the Dutch administrative and commercial centre of Batavia (modern Jakarta) on the north-west coast. Batavia possessed a good harbour, and held a dominant strategic position near the Sunda Straits. The city which the Dutch built here was handsome and elegant, a conscious attempt to reproduce Dutch urban life, even to the familiar canals. From Batavia the Governor-General of the Indies ruled all the Dutch possessions in the East except the factory at Canton (which received instructions direct from Holland). It was the trading hub of the Eastern Seas, and through its port passed an incredibly varied assortment of cargoes. Away from Java the Company was still predominantly a maritime trading organization, although it was gradually extending its authority to the coastal regions of Sumatra, Borneo and the outlying islands.

Dutch power in the East Indies was accompanied by a ruthless exploitation of the native inhabitants, particularly in the Moluccas and in Java. The Company clung to its traditional (and by now out-moded) system of restricting production. It preferred to sell limited quantities of its eastern products at high prices in Europe rather than tackle the problems of capitalization and administration involved in large-scale production at low prices. At home this policy led to growing financial difficulties; in the East it spelt misery for the in-habitants of the islands. In the Moluccas the production of spices was cut to a quarter of the amount it had been before the Dutch controlled the area, and the result was hardship and depopulation. Even in the areas where spice production was permitted, the lot of the cultivator was far from enviable. The growers received niggardly sums of money for their products, and were forced to buy their food supplies from the Company at inflated prices. Dissatisfaction and bitterness among the growers rose to such an extent that when the demand for spices in Europe increased in the late eighteenth century the Company found it impossible to expand production. Instead, the French and British were able to take advantage of the situation by establishing clove and nutmeg plantations in their own tropical colonies.

The same restrictive policy was pursued in Java, where experiments in growing coffee had proved unexpectedly successful in the early eighteenth century. Within a few years of the first serious efforts at cultivation 12 million lb were being produced annually. The Company reacted in its usual way. It ordered plantations to be destroyed, drastically reduced the price given to the remaining growers, and limited production to 4 million lb a year. Its agents defrauded the collectors of much of the modest sum allowed them, and attempts at reform by the Governors usually foundered on the rapacity of the local chiefs. The close supervision necessary for coffee production brought an entirely new relationship between the Company and the mass of native inhabitants. The Company became a managerial as well as a mercantile organization, as concerned with agriculture as with sea-borne trade. It was at once ruler and employer, with unlimited rights over the peasant cultivators. The Company rarely interfered in details of native administration, and controlled the peasants through the chiefs, or 'regents', as they were called. As the V.O.C.'s trade declined in India, Persia and Japan, and administrative and defence costs in the East Indies mounted, so the coffee plantations of Java became increasingly important, and the Company's grip on the island tightened. This unabashed and systematic exploitation by the Dutch of the native population had few redeeming features, save for the ending of local wars in Java. Commercial profit was the only motive of government, and all else was subordinate to it.

To outsiders the V.O.C. was an impressive organization, but the colossus had feet of clay. Extension of territory was not accompanied by an equivalent growth in trade to pay for the increasing costs of government. Smuggling, piracy and fraud ate into the Company's finances, and the dividends paid by the Company had to be financed by loans. The war of 1780–3 struck a heavy, almost fatal, blow at the Company. The British seized Dutch settlements in the East, trade with Europe ceased, and most of the ships homeward bound at the outbreak of war were captured. Although the peace treaty of 1784 restored all the captured Dutch possessions except Negapatam, it stipulated freedom of navigation in the Eastern Seas – a provision which was anathema to a trading organization which had always concentrated its energies on preserving a close monopoly.

While these ominous cracks were appearing in the Company's structure in the East, at home its financial position was becoming desperate. Long discussions about reforming the Company came to nothing; and its chief hope of recovery seemed to lie in the British eagerness to negotiate a realistic division of interests in the East. The way for such an agreement was opened by the events of 1787, when after an acute crisis within the Dutch Republic the Stadholder and the Orange party emerged triumphant over the pro-French Patriot party. The same year Britain, Holland and Prussia joined in the Triple Alliance, and negotiations began to try to reach agreement on the rival overseas interests of Britain and Holland. Viewed from a national point of view the objectives of the two nations in the East were not in basic conflict. Britain's chief commercial concern was to develop her China trade; Holland's to preserve her spice monopoly. The British government envisaged a settlement which would give the Dutch commercial concessions in India, guarantee them the spice trade, and in return obtain for Britain the use or even possession of Dutch strategic bases – especially those at Trincomalee and Rhio (the latter dominated the Malacca straits in the days before the founding of Singapore). Pitt and Dundas no longer feared the Dutch as commercial rivals; the danger was rather that the Dutch might prove too weak to withstand French pressure to hand over some of their eastern bases. French activity in the Eastern Seas had grown since the end of the American War of Independence. A new East India Company was established in 1785, and in the years before 1789 no fewer than ten French naval expeditions were engaged in survey work east of the Cape of Good Hope. An Anglo-Dutch partnership in defence and trade which would buttress the British route to China, revive the flagging fortunes of the V.O.C., and keep out the French, made good sense from several points of view.

Unfortunately, the course of the negotiations was complicated by the foolish insistence of the British government that the vexed problem of Dutch trading rights as a neutral in wartime should also be discussed; and by the natural jealousies and suspicions of the Dutch. It was all too easy to portray the British proposals as an attempt to encroach on the Dutch sphere of influence, and the British request for the surrender of bases was seen as an affront to Dutch pride. Centuries of political and economic rivalry during which both countries had pursued a policy of strict commercial monopoly had to be taken into account. Even five years of patient negotiations were not enough to overcome past history and present suspicions. Negotiations broke down in 1792, and the next year war between Britain, Holland and revolutionary France started a chain-reaction of events which was to alter drastically the situation in the East.

7

The Opening of the Pacific

The Early Explorers

AS LATE as the middle of the eighteenth century the Pacific presented a series of baffling mysteries to the geographers of Europe. Centuries of sporadic exploration had traced a few routes on the maps, indicated some islands, and hinted at intriguing continental outlines; but the two chief problems of the Pacific remained unresolved. No European knew for certain whether a huge, fertile continent stretched across the south Pacific, and whether in the north an open sea-passage offered a shorter route from the Atlantic than the long haul around Cape Horn or the Cape of Good Hope.

European knowledge (as distinct from rumours) of the Pacific dated back to the early sixteenth century. It was then that the Portuguese reached the western fringes of the Pacific and built a trade empire centred on the Moluccas, with posts as far afield as China and Japan. At the same time, but 10,000 miles distant, the Spaniards began to establish themselves along the Pacific coasts of central and south America. In 1520 Magellan linked the areas of European activity on the eastern and western edges of the great ocean when he passed through the strait (later named after him) near the tip of South America, sailed across the Pacific, and after a voyage of gruelling hardship reached the Philippines. But the track of a single expedition across so vast an expanse of ocean was almost lost to sight; and although in the next two centuries Magellan was followed by other European explorers and privateers, their discoveries were limited and invariably open to dispute.

The difficulties faced by these early Pacific explorers were overwhelming. Their ships were not only small, but were often badly built, rotten with age, and manned by the dregs of the seaports. The captains themselves rarely possessed both the qualities needed to make an effective explorer: good navigational ability and decisive powers of leadership. Scurvy, the scourge of all oceanic voyages, was especially to be feared in the Pacific. The only known cure was fresh food and rest on land, but in the Pacific ships sailed for months in search of land while their crews, existing on a diet of salt meat, stale biscuits and contaminated water, sickened and died.

Even land known to exist was far from easy to find again, for navigational science was still in a primitive stage. By the sixteenth century the latitude of a ship at sea could be determined with reasonable accuracy by measuring the altitude of the sun at noon with a cross-staff, astrolabe or (later) quadrant. To discover longitude at sea was a very different proposition. No practical method was perfected until the second half of the eighteenth century when, in response to a long-standing offer by the Board of Longitude in Britain of a £20,000 award, marine timekeepers (chronometers) were at last designed which kept accurate time for years on end. Set to Greenwich time, that is time at the prime meridian – 0° longitude – the chronometer made it possible to calculate longitude in any part of the world by simply comparing local time, taken from the sun, with Greenwich time. Until the development of the chronometer sailors could only work out longitude by a complicated series of observations and calculations beyond the ability of most, or guess at it by dead-reckoning. By this time-honoured method they estimated with the help of the log the distance covered by the ship in a certain time, noted the compass courses steered, and then plotted the vessel's track on a chart. The limitations of this crude method were such that on long voyages errors of hundreds, sometimes even thousands, of miles were made. In 1588 Mendaña touched at the Solomon Islands, but so greatly underestimated their distance from South America that he was unable to find them on a second voyage; and they were not rediscovered until the eighteenth century.

Another handicap to far-ranging exploration in the Pacific was the system of trade winds, which confined the normal tracks of sailing ships to narrow belts: in the south Pacific one stretching WNW from near the tip of South America to the northern shores of New Guinea, and in the North Pacific a flattened circular route between the Philippines and southern California (the outward and homeward course of the annual Manila treasure-galleon). To venture away from these defined tracks usually involved months of beating and tacking against head-winds; and Pacific navigation was arduous enough without this drawback.

At the end of the seventeenth century maps of the Pacific were still mainly composed of blank spaces bearing the legend 'Incognita'. In the North Pacific Japan was roughly charted, but the ocean to the north and east remained completely unexplored, although rumour had it that in those areas were large populous islands whose inhabitants used gold as casually as Europeans did iron. The Pacific coast of America was known only as far north as California, and even then it was uncertain whether California was an island or a peninsula. In the South Pacific a fair knowledge had been obtained of the island groups lying on the diagonal course between South America and New Guinea, but their exact position and extent remained largely a matter of guess-work. The western half of Australia (New Holland) was known from Dutch explorations; so was the southern part of Tasmania (Van Diemen's Land), and a stretch of the coast of New Zealand. What was far from clear was the relationship between these three lands, and in particular whether any of them formed part of the great southern continent.

The concept of the unknown southern continent – *Terra Australis Incognita* – was as old as geographical science itself. In the second century A.D. Ptolemy held that there was a huge land-mass in the southern hemisphere which was joined to Africa and made the Indian Ocean an enclosed sea. The Portuguese explorers who rounded the Cape of Good Hope in the late fifteenth century disproved Ptolemy, but the map-makers of the sixteenth century (influenced by a mis-reading of Marco Polo) continued to show a southern continent. It was visualized as being far larger than the Australia of today: sometimes it was shown stretching east to west from below Cape Horn to south of the Cape of Good Hope, and north as far as New Guinea. In an age when tropical countries were expected to produce gold and silver almost as a matter of course, it was confidently anticipated that the hot northern parts of this continent would yield precious metals, while the more temperate regions farther south would be ideal for European colonization. Nor were believers in a southern continent unduly depressed by the failure of the explorers of the sixteenth and seventeenth centuries to find one. Since the discoveries were mostly confined to a narrow belt which slanted away from southerly latitudes as it left South America, map-makers merely had to push their continent slightly farther to the south. Geographers found ample compensation for this limited retreat by hinting that the islands sighted by the explorers were in fact the capes and promontories of the great land-mass which lay just over the horizon from the discovery vessels.

After Tasman's explorations in the 1640s the slow-moving course of Pacific exploration practically came to a halt. Portuguese overseas activity was mainly confined to Brazil and Africa; the Spaniards were desperately concerned with retaining and exploiting their vast American empire; the Dutch in the East Indies were preoccupied with the spice trade; and England and France had entered a period of bitter rivalry in America and the Caribbean. The only Europeans interested in the Pacific as a new sphere of enterprise, it seemed, were the buccaneers. Their ragged and disreputable ranks scarcely seemed likely to produce anyone whose observations would attract the attention of merchants and geographers, but against all probability they did. The new era of European interest in the Pacific starts with the voyages, and still more the writings, of a remarkable English mariner, William Dampier.

The Revival of Interest in the Pacific

For twelve years Dampier wandered around the world in a casual and erratic way, most of the time in the company of buccaneers, visiting the Philippines, Formosa, the East Indies and New Holland (he was the first Englishman to see Australia). Finally he returned home, and in 1697 published his journals under the title, *A New Voyage Round the World*. Readable though it was, the book was far more than a tale of high adventure; it contained a mass of careful information about the regions Dampier had visited. It was the first general survey of the Pacific by an Englishman for a hundred years, and enjoyed tremendous success, being reprinted in dozens of different editions and collections during the next half-century. Dampier caught the market at the right moment, for negotiations on the problem of the Spanish Succession were approaching a climax, and Spanish possessions in the Pacific formed part of the great inheritance which was at stake.

In London Dampier was entertained by members of the Royal

Society, consulted by the government about the possible establishment of a base on the isthmus of Darien, and then asked by the Admiralty to command a discovery expedition to the Pacific. This was a development of some importance: for the first time official interest was being taken by Britain in Pacific exploration. In return, Dampier proposed that the expedition should explore the unknown eastern coastline of New Holland. The idea was accepted, and in 1699 the first genuine expedition of exploration fitted out by the Admiralty left England. However, there were limits to the Admiralty's interest. Dampier was provided with only one ship instead of the two he had requested, and the 290-ton *Roebuck* was in the last stages of decay. Its crew was small and far from enthusiastic, probably not very different from that which accompanied Dampier on one of his other voyages, mostly 'tailors, tinkers, pedlars, fiddlers and haymakers'. Nor was Dampier himself the ideal commander. He was a careful navigator and a discerning observer, but no leader of men, and soon after the beginning of the voyage Dampier found himself sleeping on the quarter-deck at night with pistols by his side in case of mutiny. The *Roebuck* sailed round the Cape of Good Hope and on to the west coast of Australia. From there Dampier worked his way round the northern coast of New Guinea, and to the east discovered a large island (later found to be three adjoining islands) which he named New Britain. According to his instructions Dampier should now have turned southward to explore the east coast of Australia, but the condition both of the ship and its scurvy-stricken crew was so poor that Dampier decided to return. His decision was justified when a year later the bottom fell out of his vessel in mid-Atlantic, and the crew were fortunate to save their lives by scrambling ashore on Ascension Island.

In his published account of the expedition, *A Voyage to New Holland*, Dampier stressed the potential importance of New Britain as a commercial and strategic base. The island was fertile, Dampier claimed, and its position marked it as centre from which commercial enterprise might radiate to the East Indies, Australia and New Zealand. But in wartime privateering was more alluring than long-term projects of trade and settlement, and when Dampier returned to the Pacific it was as commander of a privateering expedition. He was followed by Woodes Rogers and George Shelvocke (the latter had the good fortune to capture the Manila galleon), and on their return home all three commanders published accounts of their voyages. Few discoveries were made, but the voyages caught the imagination of the literate public, and helped to inspire some of the most popular fiction and satire of the period. Swift's account of Gulliver's travels was set mainly in the Pacific, where Lilliput was situated north-west of Van Diemen's Land, and Brobdingnag (the land of giants) east of Japan. Defoe's *Robinson Crusoe*, though set in the Caribbean, owed much to the story of Alexander Selkirk, marooned on Juan Fernández Island in the South Pacific for more than four years, and then rescued by Shelvocke's expedition. In Britain the Pacific was news in a way it had not been since Drake's return in the *Golden Hind*, and the growing interest was reflected in the establishment of the South Sea Company in 1711. The company was founded to exploit the concessions expected from Spain at the peace negotiations which were bringing the War of the Spanish Succession to a close; but the Treaty of Utrecht gave Britain no commercial privileges in the Pacific. The most important concession gained by the company was the *asiento*, and this inaptly-named trading organization never sent a ship into the South Sea.

Despite the discussion and publicity in Britain about the Pacific, the French achievement in this period was more impressive from a practical trading point of view. French trade with the Pacific ports of Spanish America flourished during the War of the Spanish Succession, when France and Spain were in alliance. It was far from being an affair of single ships furtively slipping through the Strait of Magellan or round the Horn. Whole fleets sailed from Saint Malo and Nantes, sometimes ostensibly bound for China. So many ships were involved that they began to glut the market with their cargoes of cloth, silk, hardware and paper. Between 1700 and 1724 more than 150 French ships made the long and hazardous voyage. Since they normally followed as direct a route as possible to their destination in Peru or Chile, few of these vessels made any contribution to knowledge of the Pacific. At the Utrecht negotiations France promised to stop this trade (irritating both to Spain and to the other maritime powers), and it was finally suppressed in the mid-'twenties.

During the years of peace after the Utrecht settlement practical interest in the Pacific subsided. While in France government action broke the illicit trade around Cape Horn, in Britain the collapse of the South Sea Bubble had a dampening effect on distant enterprises. Daniel Defoe grumbled in 1728:

As for new colonies and conquests, how do we seem entirely to give over even the thoughts of them, as if we had done our utmost, were fully satisfied with what we have, that the enterprising genius was buried with the old discoverers, and there was neither room in the world nor inclination to look any farther.

Trade and shipping prospered, but it was the outbreak of war with Spain in 1739 which stimulated further thought in Britain about the potentialities of the Pacific.

At first, government plans for hostilities in the Pacific were on a grand scale, and had an unusually constructive look about them. A powerful expedition was to be sent around the Cape of Good Hope to the western Pacific with orders to seize and hold the Philippines. At the same time another expedition was to sail round Cape Horn to raid the Pacific coast of Spanish America, and encourage the colonists there to rise in rebellion against Spain. Once independent, the ex-colonies would negotiate favourable commercial treaties with their British liberators, or so it was assumed. The discussions afford an interesting glimpse of British hopes and ambitions in the Pacific, but as the months passed this ambitious and probably vain scheme to dismember the Spanish colonial empire and establish British predominance in the Pacific was cut down in size. The projected expedition to the Philippines was dropped, and only a small squadron of half a dozen ships under Commodore Anson left England in 1740 for the voyage round Cape Horn.

Anson's force was scarcely an imposing one. The regiment of troops promised him materialized as a pathetic rabble of raw marines and out-pensioners from Chelsea Hospital. Only three warships reached the Pacific, and on them men died from scurvy in appalling numbers: in all, 626 men out of a complement of 961 died from disease, four from enemy action. Anson's weakened forces made a series of hit-and-run raids along the Pacific coast of South America, and as a spectacular climax captured the Manila galleon off the Philippines; but there was no possibility of carrying out the original instructions to stir up discontent among the Spanish colonists. When Anson returned to England in 1744 with only one ship left, he was welcomed as a national hero. Like his privateering predecessors he had made few geographical discoveries, but the enthusiastic reaction to his voyage, the astonishing sale of the official account of his voyage, and Anson's own promotion in course of time to First Lord of the Admiralty, indicated that public and government interest in the Pacific was once more on the increase.

The Geographical Theorists

The general revival of interest in the Pacific was accompanied by demands that the mysteries of the great ocean should be solved, and by consideration of the material advantages that exploration there might bring. In the year of Anson's return John Campbell, an influential British writer on geography and trade, issued the first part of a massive collection of voyages. Campbell, writing at a time when the lack of wartime success was increasing suspicions that all was not well with British trade and enterprise, deplored the apathy of both government and merchants. Other powers, he asserted, were gaining an increasing share of world markets, and as their seaborne commerce increased so did their navies. Campbell went on to insist that two steps must be taken to arrest this decline; and both were connected with commercial expansion in the Pacific.

First, the long-sought North-west Passage must be found. In British hands a short navigable passage between the North Atlantic and the North Pacific would provide a route along which naval squadrons might pass swiftly and secretly to attack Spain's Pacific domains. In peacetime the passage would be busy with merchantmen trading with Japan, China, the East Indies and the lands of gold thought to lie somewhere in the North Pacific. Elizabethan and Stuart seamen had searched long and hard for a passage, and at the time Campbell was writing their efforts were being followed up by two discovery expeditions in Hudson Bay. One was sent in 1741 by the Admiralty, the other in 1746 by a private syndicate. Maps drawn by imaginative cartographers with an eye to a quick sale showed the passage quite clearly, but the expeditions found along the north-western shores of Hudson Bay nothing but ice and desolation. For all the confidence of Campbell and other geographers, no evidence of a passage was discovered.

In the South Pacific the obvious aim of British policy, Campbell wrote, was the exploitation of the great southern continent. He brushed aside doubts about whether such a continent existed. The Dutch, he asserted, 'are perfectly well acquainted with this southern continent, and are only reserving its use to their own good time'. Two British bases ought to be established along the route to the continent:

one at Juan Fernández where ships could refit after the arduous voyage round Cape Horn, the other at Dampier's New Britain, from which the shores of the southern continent would be easily accessible. In language characteristic of mercantilist thinking of the period Campbell concluded:

> A new trade would be opened, which must carry off a great quantity of our goods and manufactures. It would render this navigation, which is so strange and consequently so terrible to us, easy and familiar. It would greatly increase our shipping and our seamen, which are the true and natural strength of our country.

Interest was also growing in France about the southern continent. The French held some tactical advantages. Their cartographers were the best in Europe, and many of the maps which British geographers used to support their theories of northern passages and southern continents came from Paris. A curious story that a French navigator had discovered part of the southern continent years before Magellan crossed the Pacific gave France a somewhat tenuous claim to any land found. A positive step was taken in 1738 when the *Compagnie des Indes* sent Bouvet on a voyage of exploration into the South Atlantic, but his excited report that he had sighted one of the capes of the continent (actually an island) did not entice the directors to support a second expedition. French speculation on the subject was presented most persuasively by the scholarly Charles de Brosses, President of the Parlement of Dijon. In his *Histoire des Navigations aux Terres Australes* de Brosses advanced the theory of a southern continent just as dogmatically as Campbell had, although the motives behind his disquisition were slightly different. The book was intended to divert French energies away from ruinously costly European wars. In glowing terms de Brosses proclaimed the attractions of the new continent, a land where commerce would flourish, and which would provide a pure, unsullied environment where colonies might be established free from European hatreds and vices. In a famous passage de Brosses asked:

> What comparison can be made between the execution of a project such as this, and the conquest of some little ravaged province – of two or three cannon-shattered fortresses, acquired by massacre, ruin, desolation, bought at the expense a hundred times greater than that needed for the whole of the discovery proposed?

By an ironic chance de Brosses received an immediate answer to his query, for his *Histoire* was published in 1756, the opening year of the Seven Years War.

This urbane scholar was not necessarily pointing the way to peaceful co-existence between Britain and France. For all his breadth of vision, de Brosses was as nationalistic and commercially aggressive in his own way as Campbell. He was insistent upon the superior nature of French culture and civilization; and in the pages of his book the links between discovery, trade and seapower were stressed as pointedly as in any work by British mercantilist writers. A great French empire was to be built in the South Pacific, and it was noteworthy that its proposed bases were the same as those suggested by Campbell – Juan Fernández and New Britain. It seemed as if the national rivalry of France and Britain could be no more eliminated from the Pacific than from Europe, America and India. In an age of fierce competition between nations for commerce and colonies, exploration involved a great deal more than the satisfying of geographical curiosity.

Forerunners of Cook

The Seven Years War put an effective stop to schemes for Pacific exploration, but in both Britain and France discovery expeditions were set in motion soon after the conclusion of peace in 1763. The results of the war, indeed, had brought a new eagerness to examine the unknown stretches of the Pacific. Although Britain had acquired vast overseas territories at the peace settlement, and a period of quiet assimilation might have been expected, the national energies released in the successful war now sought new outlets. The vision of Pacific domination held out by Campbell and others was an alluring one, and the attack on Manila in 1762 had shown the seriousness of British interest. Discovery and possession of *Terra Australis Incognita* would set the seal on Britain's position as the mightiest imperial power Europe had ever known. Defeated France had no less strong a motive. The southern continent offered compensation for the humiliating losses suffered in America and India. The French foreign minister, Choiseul, summed up his government's attitude when he warned that France would never allow Britain alone to found new colonies in distant parts of the world; France would insist on her right to do the same. French and British geographers still corresponded with each other, explorers of the two countries were to meet and part on friendly terms; but beneath the exchanges of mutual compliments national rivalry ran deep and strong.

This was demonstrated in telling fashion within a short time of the Peace of Paris. A private expedition, commanded by Bougainville, a distinguished soldier and diplomat who had fought with Montcalm at Quebec, sailed from France in late 1763 for a secret destination. In 1764 a British naval expedition under Commodore Byron left England, also for a secret destination. Unknown to each other, the two expeditions were heading for the same area – the Falkland Islands. The islands had first come into prominence when the official account of Anson's voyage, published in 1748, pointed out their strategic value. A year or so later only strenuous Spanish protests stopped a British project to set up a base in the islands. Now the scheme was revived in Britain, where the First Lord of the Admiralty, Egmont, described the Falklands as 'the key to the whole Pacific Ocean' because of their dominant position just east of the Strait of Magellan. Egmont overstated the islands' importance, but his words revealed one of the motives behind the 1764 expedition, as did the solemn statement in Byron's instructions that 'nothing can redound more to the honour of this nation as a maritime power, to the dignity of the Crown of Great Britain, and to the advancement of the trade and navigation thereof, than to make discoveries of countries hitherto unknown'. For his part, Bougainville regarded the Falklands as a stepping-stone towards the development of French enterprise in the Pacific. Britain and France set up bases on these barren islands, both frowned upon by Spain, and soon an international crisis resulted which almost led to war (see Chapter 8).

The surveying of the Falklands was only part of Byron's task. He next sailed through the Strait of Magellan into the Pacific, but he had a stormy passage through the strait, and despite his assurance to the Admiralty that he intended to cross the Pacific 'by a new track' he followed the customary WNW route. He completed his circumnavigation in record time (a year and ten months), but made few discoveries of note and ignored his instructions to sail north of California in search of the Pacific entrance of the North-west Passage. The chief interest of Byron's voyage lies in the ambitious nature of the design revealed, with its hope of establishing British control over the southern and northern entrances into the eastern Pacific; and in the Spanish reaction to the expedition.

To Spain, desperately striving to preserve the remnants of her colonial monopoly, the Pacific was *mare clausum*. Since the days of Drake English incursions into the Pacific had been viewed with particular suspicion, and Spanish sensitivity had been heightened by the capture of Manila in 1762. True, the city was promptly returned at the end of the war, but no sooner had this been done than the British were active on the opposite side of the Pacific. In a dispatch home the Spanish ambassador in London reported his conversation with a British minister soon after Byron's return, in which he had outlined in uncompromising fashion Spanish policy towards foreign intrusions into the Pacific: 'All those countries are the King's and no one may settle in them. He asked me if the whole world was Spain's; and I replied that, as to that portion, yes.'

Spanish warnings were ignored, and in 1766 another expedition was fitted out for the Pacific under captains Wallis and Carteret, who were ordered to search for the southern continent in more southerly latitudes than any previous explorer had ever ventured. After a hard passage through the Strait of Magellan the two ships were separated, and carried out individual voyages of discovery. Wallis, pushed by the south-east trade winds, and lured by the warmth and food of the Pacific islands, again followed the diagonal track of earlier explorers. His only important discovery was the delightful island of Tahiti, an earthly paradise to his crew after the cramped and stinking quarters of their ship. Before long Tahiti was to become to Europe the symbol of the beauty and romance of the Pacific islands. Not so romantic were the diseases introduced by European seamen, but at least wholesale murder of the natives was rare. Outbreaks of violence occurred. Occasionally a seaman was cut off, more often a volley of musket-fire from frightened or exasperated sailors scattered a group of islanders and killed some of them; but the wanton massacres which had disfigured the exploits of the sixteenth-century explorers were not repeated.

Carteret, meanwhile, although in a vessel so leaky and badly equipped that he could not believe he was intended to sail around the world in it, had been more enterprising than Wallis. He crossed the Pacific farther south than any other explorer had ever done, and made considerable inroads into the alleged southern continent. He rediscovered, though he did not identify, the Solomon Islands – almost two centuries after they had been first sighted by the Spaniards. He also carried out some useful surveys around New Britain, and found that Dampier's discovery consisted of at least two islands.

Again, French activity matched that of the British. In 1766 Bougainville sailed from France with a double mission. He was to hand over the French base in the Falklands to Spain, and was then to search for the southern continent. His route across the south Pacific lay midway between the tracks followed by Wallis and Carteret. He too touched at Tahiti, and his eloquent account of the idyllic existence of the islanders lent support to the fashionable enthusiasm in Paris for the 'noble savage'. From Tahiti Bougainville courageously sailed towards the unknown eastern coast of Australia, and only bore away when confronted with the dangers of the Great Barrier Reef, which girds the continent's north-east shores. A visit to New Britain showed that the land chosen by Campbell and de Brosses as perfect for colonization was less than ideal; it appeared to be prolific, noted Bougainville, only in ants, scorpions and giant cabbage trees. Nor did the expedition come across any sign of the great southern continent, and in his published account of the voyage Bougainville registered a heartfelt protest against the uncritical enthusiasm of the theoretical geographers. 'Geography,' he wrote in a celebrated passage, 'is a science of facts; no man in his study can draw up a system without the risk of making the greatest mistakes, which are often corrected only at the expense of the navigator at sea.'

The British and French explorers of the 1760s, then, added in a rather haphazard way a considerable amount to Europe's knowledge of the island groups of the South Pacific. But little progress had been made towards solving the critical issue of the existence of a great continent. The continent had receded a little farther south, that was all. New Holland remained a western outline of an immense island or islands of unknown extent. New Zealand was a squiggle on the map, perhaps an island, perhaps part of a great land-mass. Yet within a few years there was no longer any doubt. The South Pacific appeared on the maps in much the same form as it does today; and the man responsible for this amazing leap in knowledge was the greatest of eighteenth-century explorers, James Cook.

Cook in the South Pacific

Some time before the return of Wallis and Carteret the British government had decided to send another expedition to the Pacific. In

1769 the planet Venus was due to pass across the face of the sun, and astronomers were insistent that if worthwhile observations were to be obtained a set should be taken from a station in the South Pacific. The Admiralty agreed to the Royal Society's representations, and Tahiti was finally chosen as the most suitable spot for an observatory. After some discussion, and the rejection as possible captain of Alexander Dalrymple, one of the leading geographers of the day, command of the expedition was given to James Cook. Lieutenant Cook, as he was on this first voyage, had taken part in the surveying of the Saint Lawrence during Wolfe's Quebec campaign, and later made detailed charts of the intricate coastline of Nova Scotia and Newfoundland. He had studied mathematics and astronomy, and in contrast to some of his predecessors in the Pacific possessed all the professional skills needed to make an efficient explorer. The next few years were to show that in addition he was gifted with those less tangible qualities of leadership, determination and judgement which were to make him the outstanding explorer of the eighteenth century. The driving force behind this remarkable man was revealed in one of his own letters, when he referred to his 'ambition not only to go farther than any man had ever been before, but as far as it was possible for man to go'.

Cook's instructions show that the establishment of an observatory at Tahiti was only one objective of the expedition. He was also to sail southwards in the Pacific as far as latitude 40° s., since 'there is great reason to imagine that a continent, or land of great extent, may be found to the southward of the track lately made by Captain Wallis'. If he found the continent Cook was to survey its coasts, bring back specimens of its products, negotiate alliances with the native inhabitants, and with their consent take possession of the region for Britain. These orders make it clear that the scientific purpose of the voyage, though important, was not all-embracing. The published narrative of Byron's narrative had deliberately omitted the latitudes and longitudes of the Pacific islands sighted, so 'that the enemies of our country may not avail themselves of our discoveries'; and although the accounts of Cook's voyage never suffered from this unofficial censorship, the words of Dr Douglas, editor of the accounts of Cook's second and third voyages, show full awareness of the commercial and competitive aspects of the discovery voyages: 'Every nation that sends a ship to sea will partake of the benefit [of the published accounts]; but Great Britain herself, whose commerce is boundless, must take the lead in reaping the full advantages of her own discoveries.'

While Cook was away on his first Pacific voyage the case for a southern continent, and the advantages its discovery would bring Britain, were being put in their most extravagant form by Alexander Dalrymple. Dalrymple was a talented and pertinacious geographer, with a particular flair for gleaning information from old, often long-lost accounts and maps; and his own output of charts and memoirs played an important part in arousing British interest in the potentialities of the Pacific. Unfortunately, his powers of judgement were not equal to the strength of his enthusiasms, and his regrettable tendency to subordinate facts to theories is amply illustrated in his writings about the southern continent. In a work published in 1769 Dalrymple produced a few odds-and-ends of evidence which formed the basis for a gigantic claim that the southern continent probably stretched for more than five thousand miles in an east–west direction, and contained 50 million inhabitants! In a rousing climax Dalrymple asserted that 'there is at present no trade from Europe thither, though the scraps from this table would be sufficient to maintain the power, dominion and sovereignty of Britain, by employing all its manufactures and ships'.

Up to a point Dalrymple was right. If a populous southern continent existed, the character and scale of Europe's overseas trade would be radically changed; and if Britain wished to keep its position as the leading maritime and commercial nation in Europe it must be fore-most in exploiting the region. Spanish resentment at the activities of foreign vessels in the Pacific was an indication of the probable attitude of Spain, and no doubt of France as well, if either of those powers made the discovery. But the hopes and fears concerning the southern continent which Dalrymple and other writers dwelt on at such length came from a phantom world of the imagination; convincing evidence of the existence of this great land-mass still had to be produced.

Cook left England in August 1768 in the *Endeavour*, not the usual neat naval sloop or fast frigate, but a bluff-bowed Whitby collier chosen for her strength, shallow draught and storage capacity. The collier was a slow sailor, but it could carry the necessary supplies and do the close coastal work which were more important on this voyage than appearance or speed across the ocean. So unlike a King's ship was the *Endeavour* that when it arrived at Rio de Janeiro the Portu-guese Viceroy suspected that Cook was an illicit trader; and the explorer's explanation that he was on his way to Tahiti to make astronomical observations must have sounded peculiarly unconvincing. However, Cook reached Tahiti in good time, set up an observatory, and the requisite observations were made. That they were a disappointment was no fault of Cook or of any of the astronomers on the expedition.

From Tahiti Cook sailed as far south as latitude 40° s. without sighting land, and he noted that the long rolling swell coming from the south argued against the existence of any continental land-mass just over the horizon. The *Endeavour* then turned west to New Zealand, whose coasts Cook explored and mapped with meticulous thoroughness. He showed beyond any doubt that the two islands were not part of a continent; but compensation for this disillusionment came in his report that New Zealand was a fertile land with a temperate climate, inhabited by a magnificent native race, and well suited for European colonization. Cook then sailed for that region of mystery, the unexplored eastern parts of New Holland. He reached the Australian coast just north of Van Diemen's Land, and slowly sailed northward, mapping the coastline and taking possession of it in the King's name. So near the shore did Cook sail that he found himself trapped between the mainland and the converging line of rocks and shoals of the Great Barrier Reef. After a succession of hair-raising incidents the *Endeavour* escaped, and Cook then went on to sail through Torres Strait and so settle the dispute about whether New Holland was joined to New Guinea.

Cook had carried out his instructions, and more. With only one ship he had put more than 5,000 miles of previously unknown coastline on the map. The twin islands of New Zealand, the east coast of Australia, and the strait between Australia and New Guinea, had at last emerged from the mists of uncertainty and were precisely placed on the map. The careful accuracy of Cook's surveys left little room for further argument and controversy. Moreover, this tremendous feat of detailed exploration had been accomplished without the loss of a single man from scurvy. The only serious mortality on the voyage came from malaria and dysentery picked up at Batavia on the homeward voyage. Cook's journal illustrates the thoroughness with which he carried out his anti-scorbutic measures. The sailors were given only a small ration of salt meat, and butter and cheese were banned entirely. Instead, sauerkraut, vinegar, orange- and lemon-juice, soups, and

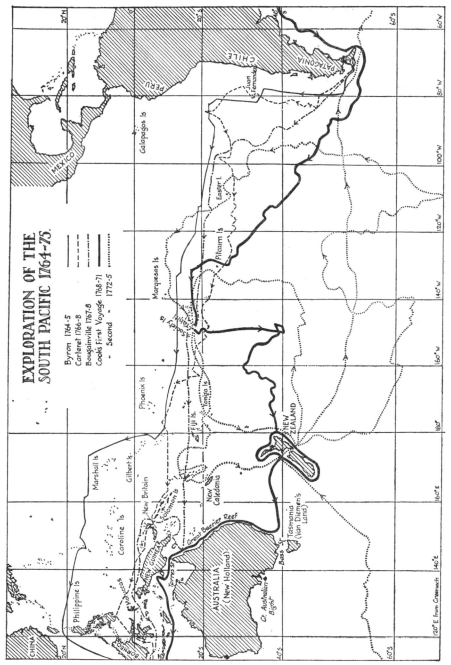

EXPLORATION OF THE SOUTH PACIFIC 1764-75.

Byron 1764-5
Carteret 1766-8
Bougainville 1767-8
Cook's First Voyage 1768-71
" Second " 1772-5

(whenever they could be obtained) fresh meat and vegetables were substituted. Cook once had men flogged for refusing to eat fresh meat. An exacting standard of cleanliness was enforced throughout the ship, and the lower decks were kept dry by stoves. Cook was no more certain of the cause of scurvy than anyone else in this period, but by combining all the known remedies for the disease, and by enforcing them with a conscientious ruthlessness, he eliminated this dreadful scourge from his ships.

On this first voyage Cook had lopped a considerable slice off the supposed southern continent, but there remained vast unexplored stretches in the southern latitudes of the Atlantic, Pacific and Indian oceans where a continent might yet be found. Pressure in Britain for another voyage mounted as reports came in that the French were again sending expeditions into the South Pacific. Four in fact visited the southern seas, hunting for continents and islands, between 1770 and 1773, but accomplished little in the way of coherent exploration. The Spaniards also had been stirred to unusual activity by fear of the effect that British and French settlements in the Pacific might have on their vulnerable South American empire. The arrival of a French vessel at Callao (the port of Lima) in 1770 which had sailed across the Pacific from Pondicherry was an unpleasant surprise, and in the same year the Viceroy of Peru sent ships to investigate Easter Island and Tahiti. Their report led to further visits to Tahiti, and the establishment of a small Franciscan mission there, soon abandoned once the Spaniards decided that the islands being discovered by Britain and France were too distant from established centres of settlement to threaten the security of South America.

So in 1772 Cook left England for the Pacific to search once more for the great southern continent, bearing with him the customary instructions to investigate, map and annex all newly discovered lands. He also carried on board chronometers, one of which was a copy of John Harrison's masterpiece, his fourth marine timekeeper of 1759, which, the Board of Longitude somewhat grudgingly decided, fulfilled the conditions laid down for the £20,000 award long on offer. The chronometer proved itself by keeping accurate Greenwich time throughout the buffetings of the long voyage, and one of the great problems of oceanic navigation had been overcome. Equipped with chronometers and improved sextants, future navigators were able to find longitude and latitude with a precision sufficient for all practical purposes. Cook's second voyage was perhaps the greatest of discovery ever made; certainly it has never been exceeded in thoroughness and comprehensiveness. From the Cape of Good Hope Cook headed south, and having at one time actually crossed the Antarctic Circle (the first navigator ever to do so), sailed east into the southern Indian Ocean, and then on to the South Pacific before bearing north to New Zealand. Cook had sailed around a third of the globe without sighting land.

After refitting in New Zealand Cook returned south, and resumed his easterly course in high latitudes, crossing and recrossing the Antarctic Circle, until he was not far west of Cape Horn. He had sailed through the heart of the southern continent of the speculative geographers. The size of the achievement can best be appreciated by measuring the bold approach which Cook carried through under appalling conditions – for weeks on end the ship, covered with ice and frozen snow, had to manœuvre through fog and among icebergs – against the hesitant tactics of his predecessors. Worthy seamen most of them were, but they lacked Cook's determination to stay in high latitudes regardless of conditions, and invariably edged north to the warmth of subtropical latitudes. At his farthest south Cook reached latitude 71° s., and was stopped by the ice-barrier which encircles the immense continent of the south. This was not the fertile land of the geographical theorists, but the frozen Antarctic – in Cook's words, 'a country doomed by Nature never once to feel the warmth of the sun's rays, but to lie for ever buried under everlasting snow and ice'.

By the beginning of 1774 Cook had fulfilled his instructions as far as they related to the Pacific, and might have reasonably returned home, exploring on the way those parts of the South Atlantic in high latitudes which he had not yet seen. His attitude after long months of gruelling work reveals the stature of the man. He pointed out in a journal entry that he could only justify an immediate return if the Pacific was 'so well explored that nothing remained to be done'. Since this was demonstrably not the case, he spent most of 1774 cruising over the South Pacific, investigating some of the regions still blank on the maps, clearing up disputed points, and making detailed surveys of the various island groups. He then sailed into the South Atlantic, once more into the ice of high latitudes, but discovered only the desolate islands of South Georgia and the Sandwich Group.

When he at last returned to England in 1775, again without any losses from scurvy, Cook brought with him in his maps conclusive evidence that the populous *Terra Australis* of the enthusiasts did not exist. Pacific trade would be on a much more modest scale than that envisaged by a long line of geographers and economists. One mystery of the Pacific had been solved; but another remained. The North-west Passage had still not been found, and it was to the North Pacific that, even before Cook's return, attention was turning in several different European countries.

The Spanish and Russian Advance in the North

The failure of the two discovery expeditions sent from England in the 1740s to find a passage through Hudson Bay to the North Pacific led to a reconsideration by geographers of the most effective way of finding the North-west Passage. Some were convinced that the passage's Pacific entrance might be easier to find than its eastern opening into the ice-choked bays of the North Atlantic. Support for this change in the direction of the search came from an account found in England of a voyage northward from California alleged to have been made in 1640 by a Spanish navigator, Bartholomew de Fonte. The account described how Fonte discovered an opening on the north-west coast of America in latitude 53° N. through which he sailed into a network of straits and rivers extending, it seemed, as far as Hudson Bay. The Fonte narrative was not the only one of its kind. Another account related how in 1592 a Spanish expedition piloted by Juan de Fuca had passed through a large straight in latitude 47° N. and discovered a land rich in pearls and precious metals. The absurd Fonte account was a complete fabrication, and the Fuca story had only a partial and dubious basis of fact; but so little was known of the north-west coast of America that it was difficult to disprove either narrative. In Britain and France several geographers eagerly seized on the accounts as material for maps which showed the North-west Passage winding its way from Hudson Bay or Baffin Bay through the North American continent, and emerging into the Pacific somewhere along the coasts of (modern) British Columbia or Washington.

Discussion about the location of the western entrance of the passage coincided with the revival of interest in the Pacific after the Seven Years War, and it was part of Byron's task in 1764 to search for a strait north of California which would take him into the Atlantic. Byron made no attempt to do this, and for the next ten years interest was focused on the South Pacific; but the Admiralty did not forget its northern plan. In 1773, while Cook was away on his second voyage, a naval expedition was sent north past Spitsbergen on a hair-brained attempt to find an open passage across the North Pole to the Pacific. The expedition naturally failed, but the government's continued interest and a hint of its future intentions were shown in a bill passed through Parliament in 1775. This modified a bill passed thirty years earlier which had offered a reward of £20,000 for the discovery of a navigable North-west Passage. The earlier bill had limited the award to private vessels; the new bill, significantly, extended it to naval expeditions. That same year Cook returned from the South Pacific, and needed little persuasion to take up a challenge that had defied Europe's finest navigators for almost three centuries. He agreed to command a new expedition to search for the Pacific entrance of the North-west Passage; and at the same time auxiliary expeditions were to be sent to Baffin Bay to survey the passage's eastern entrance.

In theory Cook's expedition was a secret one, but the Spanish government soon began to pick up rumours about it, and treated them with the utmost gravity. For some years Spain had been watching anxiously the northern limits of its American territories. At first, Russian activities in the far north caused most concern. By the end of the seventeenth century the energetic Cossacks had reached eastern Siberia, and when Peter the Great visited France in 1716 he was closely questioned about the geography of the region between Asia and America. He rejected proposals that foreigners should pass through his territories to carry out explorations along the coasts bordering the Pacific, but promised that the Russian government would undertake the task. Shortly before his death in 1725 the Tsar drew up instructions for the Danish commander of a Russian discovery expedition, Vitus Bering. These stressed that the main purpose of the expedition was to determine whether Asia and America were joined by a land-bridge in the north. Three years later Bering reached the strait which now carries his name, but haze hid the American shore, and he failed to bring back irrefutable evidence on the question of the separation of the two continents.

On Bering's return the Russian government decided to organize a second, more ambitious expedition. It was to complete the explorations made by Bering off the easternmost extremity of Asia, investigate the position and trend of the north-west coast of America, and discover whether the rich and populous islands rumoured to lie between north-east Asia and north-west America did in fact exist. In searching for these imaginary lands in 1741, Bering's two ships from Kamchatka went far out of their way, and became separated, with disastrous results. The Alaskan coast of America was sighted by both vessels, but no detailed exploration was carried out (one member of the expedition commented that ten years of preparation had resulted in ten hours of exploration). On the homeward voyage Bering's vessel was wrecked on an island where the explorer and many of his crew died.

The survivors brought back with them lustrous sea-otter skins which fetched high prices in China, and the explorers were soon followed by fur-traders. In crazy boats held together by leather thongs, often without compass or charts, they worked their way along the chain of bleak islands which stretches from Asia to North America. Although losses from storm, disease and native attacks were heavy, profits were high; and by the 1760s the Russians had reached the Gulf of Alaska, though they were not yet established on the American mainland. When Catherine II became Empress in 1762 there was a brief revival of official interest in the region, and one or two discovery expeditions were sent out, though they brought back little in the way of trustworthy information.

The Spanish government was far from certain about the extent and permanence of these Russian advances to the north, but it was sufficiently concerned to ask its ambassador at Saint Petersburg to report on the matter. Although at the beginning of the seventeenth century Spanish explorers had sailed as far north as latitude 43° N. along the Californian coast, during the next one-and-a-half centuries only Lower California was permanently settled. Inland, the Colorado and Gila rivers marked the limits of Spanish settlement. Now, the alarming dispatches it began to receive from Saint Petersburg, together with reports that Byron had been on the coast north of California, determined the Spanish government, under the vigorous rule of Charles III, on a general expansion along the Pacific coast of North America. Foreign settlements in Upper California might endanger the silver mines of New Spain, and a North-west Passage in foreign hands would turn the flank of the whole Spanish position in the Pacific. Then there was another disturbing possibility: Britain's strong position in the eastern half of the North American continent after the Seven Years War made more likely an overland thrust to the Pacific.

Moved by these considerations, Spain for the last time advanced the frontiers of its great American empire. Directed by José de Gálvez, the able *Visitador-General* of New Spain, seamen, soldiers and priests moved north along the coast and inland to occupy Upper California. By 1770, spurred by reports that the British were searching for a river which ran from Lake Superior to the Pacific, and that the Russians were fitting out fresh expeditions, the Spaniards had occupied San Diego and Monterey; and six years later they founded the first settlement in San Francisco Bay. Once established at San Diego and Monterey, the Spaniards sent probing expeditions along the coast to the north. Rumours of every kind increased their general feeling of insecurity. A squadron from Russia's Black Sea fleet was to be sent round the Cape of Good Hope to Kamchatka in order to carry out operations along the north-west coast of America; British vessels were coming across the North Pole into the Pacific (a reference to the unsuccessful expedition of 1773); British traders from Hudson Bay had advanced so far west that they had made contact with the Russians on the Pacific coast.

Spanish vessels cautiously coasted the shores of modern British Columbia, though without making any very thorough search, and in 1775 one reached Alaska, and took possession of the region for Spain. To the Spanish authorities the reports brought back by these northern expeditions were reassuring. No trace of foreign activity or of the North-west Passage had been found; but the resultant feeling of relief was short-lived. In the spring of 1776 the first news of Cook's proposed expedition to the North Pacific reached Madrid. Again, rumour ran wild: Cook intended to open up trade with New Spain; he was on his way to find the North-west Passage; he was even (according to one French Foreign Ministry report) bound for Kamchatka to help the Russians conquer Japan. A stream of instructions from Madrid to Antonio Bucareli, the Viceroy of New Spain, reflected Spanish nervousness over this new development. At first Spanish officials along the coast were merely ordered to watch Cook's movements and be cautious about giving him supplies. Next they were ordered to refuse Cook admittance to Spanish ports. Finally, they were told to detain and imprison the explorer when his expedition reached California.

There was some justification for this increasing alarm by the Spanish government. It is true that an important reason for the Pacific explorations was a desire to discover the facts about all quarters of the globe. The part played by the Royal Society in Britain in encouraging exploration was a sign of the new spirit of dispassionate investigation; and so were Cook's meticulous surveys of 1774, when he was well aware that no discoveries of great commercial or strategic value remained to be made in the South Pacific. But there were other motives as well. Trade followed exploration, and for Spain – with an empire stretching from Chile to California, and westward to the Philippines – this had unwelcome implications. The North-west Passage had always been of interest to the British because of its potential importance as a trade route, and the discovery by Cook of a navigable passage would have been of added commercial value in this period because of the East India Company's expanding trade with China.

Then there was the strategic motive. The Admiralty's decision to send expeditions into the North Pacific and the Arctic at a time when the American colonies were close to rebellion, and the international situation was worsening, was probably influenced by considerations other than those of academic interest in the existence of a North-west Passage. When hostilities with Spain threatened, the thoughts of British ministers invariably turned to the tempting prospect of raiding unprotected Spanish settlements and shipping in the Pacific; but always there was the difficulty that expeditions sailing round Cape Horn gave advance warning of their intentions. A naval expedition entering the Pacific through a northern passage would give no warning, and even if the passage was ice-free only for a few months each year this would not present the obstacle to naval raiders that it would to merchants looking for a regular trade route. The efforts of the British government to establish a base at the Falklands had shown its eagerness to secure an entrance to the Pacific. That base had been abandoned in 1774, but the discovery of a northern route into the Pacific would more than compensate for loss of control over the longer southern one.

Cook and the North-west Passage

Cook left England in 1776, sailed round the Cape of Good Hope, crossed the Pacific by way of New Zealand and Tahiti, and reached the north-west coast of America early in 1778. The most unexpected feature of his instructions was the recommendation to sail north to latitude 65° N. before searching for the passage. That is, Cook was to ignore the 2,000 miles of almost unexplored coastline which Byron had been ordered to investigate, and where the straits associated with

Fonte and Fuca were thought to lie. The main reason for this shift in the direction of the search lay in a remarkable overland journey made in the period between the voyages of Byron and Cook by Samuel Hearne of the Hudson's Bay Company. Hearne travelled on foot from Hudson Bay to the shores of the Arctic Ocean without crossing any strait, or even a large river; and this was the very region through which the straits allegedly discovered by Fonte and Fuca would have to pass if they opened into Hudson Bay. Hearne's explorations confirmed that no strait would be found through the American continent, but the possibility remained that one might be found along its northern shores, which Hearne was the first European to reach.

Because of Hearne's explorations the naval sloops searching for the Atlantic end of the passage were sent, not to Hudson Bay, but farther north to Baffin Bay. If the course of the passage lay through Baffin Bay, along the northern coast of America, and into the Pacific through Bering Strait, it would be 3,000–4,000 miles long – too long to be of much practical use. But a Russian map published in 1773 claimed to show another way from the Pacific into the Arctic Ocean apart from Bering Strait. The map, constructed by von Stählin, Secretary of the Saint Petersburg Academy of Sciences, was based on the discoveries made by Russian traders east of Kamchatka. It marked Alaska, not as a long peninsula, but as an island. North America ended in longitude 140° w., and between it and Alaska lay a wide strait through which ships could pass into the Arctic Ocean. Nor did Cook need to fear serious obstruction from ice; theorists in Britain assured him that the ice of the Arctic seas was formed when the frozen rivers of the continental land-masses broke up in the summer, and that it was a short-lived phenomenon. Accordingly, Cook's ships were not strengthened to meet ice.

The fallacy of this last piece of speculative reasoning had already been demonstrated by the time Cook reached the North Pacific: heavy ice in Baffin Bay twice prevented the expeditions sent there from even beginning their search for the passage. Cook, of course, knew nothing of this, and he spent the summer of 1778 engaged in hazardous exploration along the Alaskan coast, searching every opening for the short cut to the Arctic Ocean promised by Stählin's map. No strait was found before Bering Strait was reached in August, far to the west. Cook sailed through it and turned north-east, hoping even at this late season of the year to make some progress towards the Atlantic. Hopes of doing this were dashed when after only a week's sailing the ships sighted a massive barrier of ice. The second theory on which Cook's instructions had been based had also collapsed; the twelve-foot wall of ice confronting the ships, stretching away as far as the masthead lookouts could see, was plainly not the summer creation of the few rivers of the land to the south. It was a permanent, if shifting, barrier, and an impassable one for ships not specially strengthened for work among ice.

As Cook turned south to spend the winter at the newly discovered Sandwich Islands he expressed his feelings in his journal. Of Stählin's preposterous map he remarked that it was 'a map that the most illiterate of his illiterate seafaring men would have been ashamed to put his name to'. The frustrations of the wasted season, the rigours of the surveying work along the Alaskan coast, and the realization that there was little hope of claiming the £20,000 reward, told on Cook and his crew alike. While some of the men sent Cook a letter protesting about the food restrictions he had imposed, Cook made exasperated references in his journal to his 'mutinous, turbulent crew'. This outbreak of mutual irritation was no doubt a passing affair, but it perhaps contributed to Cook's death at Hawaii in February 1779. The explorer showed less than his usual tact and caution in dealing with the natives, and was killed in a scuffle on the beach.

The blow was the heavier in that Cook's second-in-command was dying of consumption; but with the help of William Bligh, a superb seaman if (later) an unlucky captain, the ships sailed north again. That the expedition should return to the desolate Arctic seas was a tribute to the training Cook had given his officers, but the task was an impossible one. This time the ice-barrier was encountered even farther south than the previous year, and after the ships received a severe battering from loose ice-floes their commanders decided to return. The expedition arrived back in England in 1780, and it was a final testimony to the greatness of the dead commander that on a voyage lasting more than four years not one man had died of scurvy.

There were many more voyages of exploration to the Pacific before the end of the century. Most notable were Vancouver's expedition to the north-west coast of America to complete Cook's survey, an ambitious Spanish venture under the Italian Malaspina, and a tragic French expedition commanded by La Pérouse which disappeared with all hands. These and other expeditions did useful, sometimes distinguished, work of a detailed nature; but after Cook the main features of the Pacific were known. In less than thirty years of exploration many myths had been exploded, and an immense amount of factual information accumulated. The Pacific had been revealed. The reasons for this surge of exploration are not easy to list in order of importance; indeed, attempts to separate the various strands of motive are probably more misleading than helpful. Without the investigating zeal of a Cook or a Bougainville, the scientific curiosity of the learned societies of Europe, the advances made in navigational techniques, and the tremendous popular interest in the Pacific, the voyages of exploration would not have taken the magnificent form they did. But it is equally true that to the governments or merchants who financed the expeditions the strongest motive was the hope of strategic or commercial advantage over foreign competitors.

Settlement and Trade in the South Pacific

The discovery of a fertile, populous southern continent and a navigable North-west Passage might well have revolutionized Europe's overseas trade. Explorers found neither continent nor passage; but even so their surveys and reports provided an effective stimulus to European enterprise in both the South and North Pacific, if on a less ambitious scale than once contemplated.

Cook had written of the east coast of Australia in terms which were an open invitation to colonize the region, and in 1788 the first British settlement was established at Port Jackson in New South Wales. Although the colony was the foundation-stone of a new British empire in the South Pacific, the decision to settle the area was not part of any far-sighted design. Nor were the first colonists those envisaged by Cook. They were convicts, whose accommodation had become an urgent problem for the British government once the rebellion of the American colonies put an end to transportation across the Atlantic. Various alternatives were suggested as places of banishment – the West Indies, Canada, West Africa, even Gibraltar – but all were rejected, and finally New South Wales was chosen.

The possibility of settling Australia was raised unofficially several times after Cook's first voyage. One memorialist of 1783 pointed out the advantages of New South Wales both as a settlement colony and a base for trade into the Eastern Seas, and claimed that his scheme 'may in time atone for the loss of our American colonies'. After its American experiences, however, the government was in no mood to encourage enthusiastic speculation of this sort. Its motives in establishing a settlement were sternly practical, and were summed up by the Prime Minister, William Pitt, in 1791: 'It was a necessary and essential point of police to send some of the most incorrigible criminals out of the kingdom. No cheaper mode of disposing of the convicts could be found.'

Government policy does not always dictate the course of events, and from the beginning there was pressure, both in England and Australia, for free settlers to be sent out as well as convicts. The first Governor of New South Wales, Arthur Phillip, remarked before he sailed, 'I would not wish convicts to lay the foundations of an empire,' and although he saw no free emigrants during his governorship, slowly the character of New South Wales as a penal colony changed. In 1792 permission was given for officers of the garrison to receive land-grants; and from 1795 onwards free settlers began to arrive in a small trickle which after the Napoleonic Wars swelled into a flood. Sheep-farming formed the backbone of the economy, and as other colonies were established along the coast the political map of Australia began to take the shape we know today. Thirteen hundred miles distant, New Zealand had to wait longer for colonists. Not until the 1840s was there settlement on any scale in these islands which Cook had described, almost three-quarters of a century earlier, as ideal for European colonization.

Although of the lands discovered in the South Pacific only Australia and New Zealand were suitable for intensive settlement, whalers and traders soon appeared among the island groups farther north and east. By the second half of the eighteenth century the Greenland whalers could not meet the growing demand for oil, and Cook's report of whales in far southerly latitudes soon attracted British and American whalers to Antarctic waters. They used the recently mapped Pacific islands for victualling, watering and refitting; and paid with fire-arms and liquor – a lethal combination for many of the islanders. The demoralizing activities of the whalers were repeated by the European traders who arrived among the islands before the end of the century. At first they searched for sandalwood, and for dried sea-slugs and birds' nests for the gourmets of China. Later they took copra and coconut fibre for use in the manufacturing industries of Europe.

Often these whalers and traders were the rejects of society, violent and unscrupulous. Their uncontrolled activities did incalculable harm, and since European governments refused to accept responsibility for the Pacific islands, the only resistance came from the missionaries. As early as 1797 the London Missionary Society sent missions to Tahiti, and American and French societies quickly followed suit. Although it is easy to scoff at their conscientious efforts to introduce European middle-class conventions, manners and even clothes among the Pacific islanders, the missionaries were a powerful protective influence against the ruffians who often visited the islands. In a more subtle way, their teachings had perhaps as great a disintegrating effect on the traditional societies they found as the ruinous influence of the whalers and traders. Nevertheless, until European governments began to annex and administer the islands in the late nineteenth century, the missionaries performed a valuable task. They reported the misdeeds of Europeans to the home government concerned, used their considerable influence in Europe to insist on action being taken, and on occasion saved some of the island peoples from extinction.

Great-Power Rivalry in the North Pacific

A close connection between exploration and exploitation is also to be found in the North Pacific. Cook's ships returned from the unsuccessful attempt to find the North-west Passage in 1780, and accounts of the voyage were soon on sale. All mentioned that the sea-otter skins casually collected by the sailors along the north-west coast of America had fetched high prices at Canton. A skin in good condition, perhaps obtained from a native for a few beads, might sell for a hundred dollars in Canton. Clearly, good profits might be expected from an organized trade, and expeditions were fitted out for the north-west coast, first by British merchants in China and India, and then by others in Europe and the United States (now fast becoming an important maritime power in its own right). Within a few years so many vessels were trading in the region that, as Washington Irving described it in his novel *Astoria*, 'it was as if a new gold coast had been discovered'.

Some of the first trading vessels to reach the coast from England were commanded by Cook's men, the only ones with first-hand knowledge of the area. As more ships of different nationalities appeared on the coast, and as the Russians began to establish permanent trading settlements in Alaska, competition grew fierce, though actual violence was rare. The British expeditions were independent ventures, but were often closely associated with the East India Company. Furs from the north-west coast seemed to provide an answer to the perennial problem of finding goods which the Canton merchants would accept in exchange for tea. At this time the demand for furs in China was partly met by overland trade with Russia. Many of the furs brought from Russia had been purchased in London, which had been supplied in turn from Canada or Hudson Bay. Extraordinary though it seems, furs were reaching China by the long and costly route of North America – London – Saint Petersburg – Canton; and to short-circuit it, the East India Company began to ship furs from London direct to Canton by sea. Even so, this was a lengthy business, and the Company soon saw the advantage of sending furs to China from the north-west coast of America, a voyage of only six to eight weeks. It accordingly licensed traders to go to the north-west coast (which lay within the Company's official area of monopoly), and to bring back furs which would be sold at Canton by the Company's resident factors.

The Company's hydrographer in London at this time was none other than Alexander Dalrymple, formerly the most ardent believer in the great southern continent. He now reappeared with another ambitious and imaginative scheme. The most important fur-trading company in America was the Hudson's Bay Company; the biggest trading company in the Pacific was the East India Company. Why not, asked Dalrymple, amalgamate the two, and combine the experience of the Hudson's Bay men in collecting furs with the advantages the East India factors in Canton possessed for selling them? One difficulty was that although since mid-century Hudson's Bay Company explorers and traders had steadily been pushing their way westward, between their most westerly post and the Pacific coast stretched a thousand miles of unknown but probably mountainous country. The only practical means of transporting furs over that distance was by water – in short, the North-west Passage, or a river and lake version of it. If necessary, argued Dalrymple, this route could be used in reverse, and furs from the Pacific coast sent to Hudson Bay for rapid shipment to Europe. The fact that his old antagonist, Cook, had stated that no North-west Passage existed was the more incentive for Dalrymple to find one; but in fairness to the geographer it must be said that his schemes were not mere fantasy. He himself was able to show that there were some major inaccuracies in the latitudes and longitudes given by Samuel Hearne in his account of his journey to the Arctic Ocean; and together with the doubts now cast on Hearne's reliability came news from the Pacific that some of the fur-traders on the coast had found evidence which seemed to point to the existence of a North-west Passage after all.

In 1778 Cook had hurried along the north-west coast of America until he reached latitude 60° N., where he began detailed exploration. He naturally assumed that the shores glimpsed to starboard during his voyage north were part of the American mainland, but the traders who followed him began to query this. They were the first to admit that they were employed to trade, not explore, and that any discoveries they made were incidental to the main purpose of their voyages. However, many of them had sailed with Cook, and were deeply interested in the questions which had drawn their old commander to the North Pacific. The solid, unbroken coastline marked on the maps of Cook's third voyage they found to be cut by innumerable gulfs and inlets, two of which corresponded in position to those alleged to have been discovered by Juan de Fuca and Bartholomew de Fonte.

To Dalrymple these reports furnished additional ammunition for use in his campaign to persuade the government to send a naval expedition to the north-west coast to find that strait which Cook had negligently failed to discover. The matter, Dalrymple informed various ministers, was urgent. More and more American vessels from Boston were reaching the coast after the long haul round Cape Horn. On land the Russians were pushing south from their bases in Alaska, and the Spaniards were advancing north from California. If they met, then British traders would be squeezed out, and neither the Hudson's Bay Company nor the Canadian traders would be able to secure a Pacific outlet. A government-supported union of the East India Company and the Hudson's Bay Company, on the other hand, would give British traders a strength and mobility which would enable them to dominate the North Pacific and North-west America.

Critics were not slow to point out the similarity between these arguments and the geographer's earlier outpourings on the subject of the non-existent southern continent; but the derision with which Dalrymple's proposals were received in some quarters ceased when news reached England of the Nootka Sound incident. Despite increasing activity by traders from several nations on the north-west coast, the Spaniards still clung tenaciously to their old claim that they possessed the entire Pacific coast of the Americas. This claim was based on the fact that Spanish expeditions were the first to discover those western shores, and that they fell within the sphere of influence granted to them by the Pope and the Treaty of Tordesillas in the late fifteenth century. From Cape Horn to Alaska the coast was Spanish, regardless of whether there were Spanish settlers in a particular region or not. The British, comparative latecomers on the scene, staunchly upheld the opposing doctrine of effective occupation. They refused to recognize rights inherent in prior discovery, and had no interest in the Pope's division of the world between Spain and Portugal centuries earlier. Unless a region was actually occupied the British insisted on the right to trade and settle there, and this claim was advanced in the East Indies as well as in North-west America. The right to trade and establish posts in any region not occupied by other Europeans – in brief, the ignoring of the vast spheres of influence sketched out by the Spaniards and Dutch in an earlier age – was a cardinal feature of British policy in the late eighteenth century.

The Spanish claim was a difficult one to enforce against trading ships which touched at various points along an intricate coastline, and often did not even put men ashore; but in 1788 a British trader, John Meares, made a new departure when he established a small trading settlement at Nootka Sound (on what is now Vancouver Island). The next summer the base, together with four trading vessels and their crews, was seized by a Spanish force sent north to thwart an expected Russian attempt to establish a base at Nootka (in 1788 a Spanish expedition had, for the first time, encountered Russians on the north-west coast).

Clearly, the seizure at Nootka would be a test case. So seriously did both the Spanish and the British governments take the matter that they were prepared, as a last resort, to go to war over what appeared to be an unimportant skirmish many thousands of miles from Europe. But much was at stake: not only the Pacific fur trade, but the general question of territorial rights on the north-west coast. As Dundas remarked in the House of Commons, 'We are not contending for a few miles, but a large world.' To the Spanish foreign minister Florida-blanca the episode was yet another example of British efforts to under-mine the Spanish empire, and it is true that Pitt pressed for a settlement which would include rights of access by British traders into the Spanish colonies. The British government adopted a toughly belligerent attitude, and Spain, prepared to fight yet another rearguard action in defence of her traditional pretensions in America, suddenly realized that her French ally was in no position to offer help at a time of revolution and upheaval within France. For the second time the Bourbon Family Compact had proved meaningless. As in 1770 over the Falklands Islands dispute, France was unwilling or unable to intervene, and faced with a mobilized British fleet, the Spanish government had little alternative but to renounce its claims. In October 1790 the Nootka Sound Convention was signed, by which Spain agreed to return the British post and vessels, and recognized the right of foreign subjects to trade anywhere more than thirty miles distant from a Spanish settlement (in effect, this opened the whole of the north-west coast).

The Convention was followed by action by both governments on the north-west coast itself. The Spaniards were already carrying out extensive explorations to discover the extent of foreign activity, and whether the rumours about the existence of a North-west Passage had any substance; and in 1792 a British naval expedition arrived on the coast under the command of Captain Vancouver. Vancouver, who had sailed with Cook on his third voyage, had a dual task: he was to receive from the Spanish commandant at Nootka the surrender of the British post there, and he was to explore the coast northward as far as latitude 60° N. in an attempt to find a waterway into the interior suitable for commerce.

This part of his task Vancouver performed with a thoroughness worthy of his old commander, but neither he nor the Spanish explorers found any sign of a passage. A Spanish officer commented on reports of a passage that they seemed 'to have no other foundation than the madness or ignorance of some one devoid of all knowledge of either navigation or geography'. Vancouver was equally forthright. At the end of three seasons of painstaking exploration along the north-west coast he wrote that since he had been sent on a fool's errand it was appropriate that he had sailed from England on 1 April. Vancouver had not wasted his time, however. For the first time the north-west coast had been mapped in detail, and Vancouver's precise surveys showed beyond doubt that no navigable shipping route existed between the Atlantic and Pacific oceans. While he was carrying out his explorations a Canadian fur-trader and explorer, Alexander Mackenzie, reached the coast a little to the south of Vancouver's ships

N

after making the first overland journey by a European across the continent to the Pacific. He was the forerunner of the traders of the North West Company, whose penetration from Montreal to the far west was of inestimable value in laying the foundations of a Canadian nation which one day was to stretch from ocean to ocean. He too had found no strait during his explorations. If a North-west Passage existed, it must lie far to the north, among the ice of the polar sea; and it was there in the next century that British seamen finally found it.

On the issue of the restoration of the British post at Nootka Vancouver met difficulties, and broke off negotiations, much to the irritation of the British government. Vancouver, far distant in the Pacific, was not to know that by 1793 Britain and Spain were in alliance against revolutionary France. The incident at Nootka which had led to the international crisis of 1790 was fast fading into obscurity, and in 1794 Britain and Spain signed a second convention agreeing to the mutual abandonment of Nootka Sound.

Ironically, the nation which reaped most benefit from the dispute was the United States, which had not been involved in the negotiations at all. As Britain became more deeply involved in war with France, so her trade on the north-west coast dwindled. The region was dominated by the American fur-traders, some of whom were now arriving overland as spearheads of the American drive towards the Pacific (Lewis and Clark made the first overland journey between the United States and the Pacific in 1804–5). After 1815 the race for domination of the north-west coast lay between Britain, the United States and Russia. Spain was out of the reckoning, for every Spanish colony along the seaboard, from Chile in the south to Mexico in the north, had risen in revolt. Russia, which had traders but no genuine settlers, was confined to Alaska, and Britain and the United States came to grips over the region farther south. In 1846, after threat of war had brought the long-standing 'Oregon Question' to a head, the dispute was settled peacefully by a treaty between Britain and the United States which fixed the boundary line along the 49th parallel. Britain received Vancouver Island and the whole of modern British Columbia, while the United States compensated itself for any disappointment over the treaty terms by conquering Upper California from Mexico and (in 1867) by buying Alaska from the Russians.

IV

THE COLONIAL EMPIRES
IN AN AGE
OF REVOLUTION
1763–1815

Introduction

UNTIL THE Seven Years War European overseas expansion in the eighteenth century followed a predictable enough course. A few new colonies were founded, some new trade routes were opened; but in general energies were devoted to a more intensive exploitation of existing colonies, and to a fierce struggle between Britain, France and Spain for their control. The benefits which stemmed from the possession of an overseas empire were taken for granted, as was the continued subordination of the colonies to the mother country.

The fifty years after the Peace of Paris saw a series of dramatic changes which transformed this pattern of development. While in India, the Eastern Seas and the Pacific, imperial expansion brought areas under European rule or influence on a scale not known since the Spanish and Portuguese exploits of the sixteenth century, in the western hemisphere revolution in America and Europe shattered the old empires. The imposing British empire of 1763 disintegrated as the American mainland colonies rose in rebellion; and after this shock imperial attitudes could never again be the same. Doubts about the value, morality and permanence of colonial empires grew, and, though temporarily muted by war between 1793 and 1815, they were never to disappear.

The French Revolution and its aftermath had their effects overseas as well as in Europe. The old French colonial empire, torn by rebellion within and attacked by enemies without, almost disappeared for the period of the wars; and the same fate befell the Dutch colonies. For a moment it seemed as if Napoleon might restore France to greatness as an imperial power, but after 1803 his attention turned again to Europe. In America the Spanish empire, which had held together under Charles III during the dangerous years of rebellion in the British colonies to the north, began to crumble as war ravaged the homeland; and together with Brazil the Spanish colonies moved towards independence.

187

Of the imperial powers of Europe which had fought for dominance in the eighteenth century Britain emerged supreme. The loss of the American colonies was more than counterbalanced by gains in other parts of the world. Britain's merchants dominated the trade routes in time of peace; her armed fleets controlled them in time of war. With her massive financial and industrial resources Britain was able to engage in full-scale war against France on the continent, and at the same time enlarge her colonial and commercial empire overseas. By 1815 Britain's imperial predominance was unchallenged, and the nation had entered an era of unprecedented growth in which her overseas empire and trade played an indispensable part.

8

Reorganization and Rebellion in the Americas 1763–1789

The Franco-Spanish Alliance

DEFEAT IN the Seven Years War and the strains of negotiating peace with a triumphant Britain weakened but did not dissolve the Family Compact between France and Spain. Both Charles III of Spain and the dominant French minister the Duc de Choiseul had one overriding aim in common: a war of revenge against Britain. In October 1762 Choiseul had sketched out his future plan of campaign when he wrote that peace must be made, regardless of the cost in lost territory, and that France and Spain must then work together for a renewal of hostilities against Britain in five years' time. Defeat in one war was to be accepted in order to prepare the way for success in the next, and the work of rebuilding the French navy began immediately after the peace settlement.

In London the future appeared in a different light. It was hoped that so convincing a demonstration of British strength in the war, and the leniency of the peace settlement, would remove any danger of a renewed Bourbon military alliance against Britain. The Family Compact of 1761 had brought only disaster to Spain, and ministers believed that Charles III would recognize the advantages of an amicable understanding with Britain, particularly in the commercial sphere. This optimistic dream soon vanished before the realities of the overseas situation, and in the face of Charles III's determination to retaliate against the steady encroachment of British traders in the Spanish empire. The disappearance of French dominion in Louisiana left Spain's Central American territories dangerously exposed to the British along the banks of the Mississippi. The British settlers and traders in turn saw only that the Spanish presence along the far bank of the Mississippi blocked their westward expansion. In the Caribbean British contraband traders were likely to become more active than ever now that the Florida peninsula and the strategic ports of Mobile and Pensacola were in British hands. Nor was the situation eased by the continued irritant of the British logwood cutters in the Gulf of Honduras. Finally, the sending of British discovery expedition into the Pacific was bound to arouse suspicions that Britain was aiming at the commercial and political penetration of the Spanish empire.

To both France and Spain the enemy was the expansionist power of Britain. During the century British overseas pretensions had swollen to what were now regarded as intolerable proportions. The French diplomat and explorer Bougainville expressed a common sentiment when he declared that the British were seeking that world hegemony which they had once accused Louis XIV of trying to attain. In face of the threat presented by a great commercial nation backed by a mighty navy, Charles III overlooked the rough treatment he had received from the French during the peace negotiations, and fell in with Choiseul's general strategy. Ricardo Wall, a leading minister who had persistently advocated a better understanding with Britain, was replaced by the Francophile Marqués de Grimaldi; and the next seven years saw a close working alliance between the Spanish and French governments.

The most urgent task was to put the Spanish empire on a more secure economic and military footing, and here French advisers had an important role. The French ambassador to Spain, the Marquis d'Ossun, established a harmonious relationship with Grimaldi, and constantly encouraged the task of reform. The French agent-general of marine and commerce at Madrid, the Abbé Béliardi, produced in 1763 his 'Grand Mémoire sur le Commerce des Indes', which listed the weaknesses of Spain's colonial empire, and suggested the appropriate reforms. French technical experts were sent to Spain, among them Gautier, one of Europe's leading ship-designers, whose work equipped the Spanish navy with some of the finest warships of the day. Choiseul from Paris and d'Ossun in Madrid pressed the claims of able Spanish officials, among them the forceful *Visitador-General* of New Spain, José de Gálvez.

At the same time Charles III never lost control of policy. Choiseul's grand design for a union of the economies of France and Spain, in which both countries would share the benefits of the Spanish colonies, lay dormant. Charles III was no more willing for his empire to become the milch-cow of France than of Britain. His ideal was a strong and prosperous Spain working with France against Britain, but not subordinate to her partner. Steadily the work of reform went forward, but spectacular results could not be expected within a year or two. The end of the five years' grace Choiseul had thought to give Britain after the peace settlement of 1763 came and went without any hostile move. Choiseul, indeed, was not a free agent. Renewal of war with Britain was not to the taste of all Frenchmen, and the hostility of rivals at court had a cramping effect on Choiseul's wider ambitions. It was a sign of his difficulties that so little money was available for his ambitious ship-building programme that no fewer than fifteen new ships of the line had to be financed by public subscription.

Charles III had none of these particular domestic problems, and as the reforms began to take effect so Spanish self-confidence grew. The days when Spain was the sick man of Europe now seemed far distant, and Charles III's ministers adopted an uncompromising attitude towards Britain. New regulations were introduced with the intention of eliminating British participation in Spanish trade, both in Europe and overseas. No concessions were offered on the vexed question of the ransom for Manila, captured by the British in 1762 and returned a year later. Vigorous protests were made to Britain about the discovery expeditions which were roaming the Pacific. In North America British rights of navigation on the Mississippi were questioned at every opportunity. It was against a background of contention and bickering that in 1770 a crisis was reached in Anglo-Spanish relations over the wind-swept group of islands in the South Atlantic known to the Spaniards as the Malvinas and to the British as the Falklands. Interest in the strategic possibilities of the islands had been growing since Anson's voyage during the War of Jenkins's Ear, and at the end of the Seven Years War British and French expeditions set up small bases in the group (see Chapter 7). The danger to Spain from these foreign posts was summed up by the British First Lord of the Admiralty in plain if over-sanguine terms: 'This island must command the ports and trade of Chile, Peru, Panama, Acapulco, and, in one word, all the Spanish territory in that sea. It will render all our expeditions in those parts most lucrative to ourselves, most fatal to Spain.' Negotiations between Madrid and Paris led to the handing over of the French settlement, Port Antoine, to Spain in 1767, but the British refused to budge, and hinted that Spain ought to recognize British sovereignty over the whole group. Spain's answer came in 1770 when one of her new and energetic colonial governors, Bucareli, launched from Buenos Aires an attack on the British post at Port Egmont, and forced the garrison to abandon it. Although Bucareli appears to have acted on his own initiative, his move was clearly in keeping with his government's general attitude over the Falklands, and both sides prepared for war.

In Britain Bucareli's exploit produced a public uproar which was exploited by the parliamentary opposition in a way ominously reminiscent of 1739. In Spain Charles III accepted that this was the *casus belli* which he and Choiseul had long been awaiting. But of the three governments involved, only the Spanish was unreservedly in favour of war. In Britain the new North administration, knowing the deplorable state into which the navy had been allowed to fall since 1763, had no wish for war; and was supported by those who failed to see the importance of the Falklands. Horace Walpole characteristically referred to the disputed territory as 'a morsel of rock that lies somewhere at the bottom of America', and speculated that 'by next century we shall fight for the Dog Star and Great Bear'. The decisive developments were in France, where Choiseul's advocacy of support for Spain was counterbalanced by the arguments of his political opponents that war would bankrupt France. Louis XV, with memories of the disasters of the Seven Years War still fresh, for once stood firm against his formidable first minister. No conceivable French interest seemed to be involved in the Falklands, and Choiseul's plan for revenge on Britain had been personal rather than official policy. Choiseul was dismissed, and a chagrined Charles III was forced to negotiate. The British base was restored, though in 1774 the British government (having learnt from hard experience that the Falklands were not the profitable acquisition they had seemed a few years earlier) withdrew the garrison on grounds of expense. Only a flag and an inscription were left to uphold the claims of British sovereignty.

For the time being the Family Compact had been deprived of its force. In France the chief advocate of a war of revenge against Britain had fallen from office; in Spain Charles III was outraged by the French desertion, and pursued an independent course of action. Despite this coolness, the underlying motives which had brought France and Spain into close alliance in the years before 1770 remained unchanged.

British expansion still posed a threat to both nations, and as the dispute between Britain and her American colonies flared into open warfare so the danger grew that France and Spain would intervene.

The American Revolution

The Peace of Paris in 1763 marks one of the highwater levels of British power in the modern period. France and Spain had been decisively defeated by the skilful deployment of limited military forces and by the strength of the mightiest navy the world had yet seen. The victor of the Seven Years War was prosperous as well as powerful; as in other wars of the century the ability to finance a continental ally had helped to gain success overseas. Victory had been won without resort to despotic methods. Englishmen, whether at home or in the colonies, enjoyed a greater degree of political and religious freedom than the subjects of any other empire. The American colonies were virtually self-governing in their internal affairs, and were expanding with unprecedented rapidity. In general, the British empire at the beginning of George III's reign set the rest of Europe an example in political tolerance, economic progress and cultural achievement. Yet within fifteen years came revolution in America which shattered the framework of the first British empire and led to the creation of a great independent nation across the Atlantic.

The growth of the American colonies brought with it problems which only first-hand knowledge could appreciate; but no British statesman of the period had ever crossed the Atlantic. If one had made the journey he would have found societies developing which differed in many respects from the one he was familiar with in Britain. The tremendous rise in population (from under 400,000 in 1713 to well over 2 million at the outbreak of the Revolution) made the colonies far less dependent on the mother country than they had been in the early days. Some were now a century or more old. Most of their inhabitants had never seen England. Many of them were not even of English stock; for there were Germans, French, Dutch and Irish in the colonies – men with no ties of sentiment binding them to the mother country. Improved communications had brought increasing contacts between the colonies, and although colonial parochialism was still strong a new conviction was emerging among some colonists that they were 'American' as well as British. Out on the frontiers were vigorous, self-reliant men who had little time for the careful rules and regulations of a remote imperial government. In the busy towns and ports merchants chafed at the paternalistic system of economic regulation imposed on colonial trade and industry. The growth in wealth of the colonies undoubtedly owed much to the protective mantle of the Old Colonial System (though the size of the debt is still debated by economic historians), but there could be no doubting the wish of many colonists in this period to run their own affairs. Self-confidence had been strengthened by the conquest of French Canada; the threat which had hung over the colonies for the best part of a century had been removed, and with it one pressing reason for loyalty to Britain.

The period of peace after 1763 was a time for the British government to tread warily, perhaps even to re-examine the traditional relationship between mother country and colonies which the growing assertiveness of the colonial assemblies had already questioned in no uncertain manner. But even before the end of the war years there were signs that British ministers were thinking along different lines. During the critical years of the Anglo-French struggle in North America the government had been careful to avoid colonial disputes which might paralyse the war effort, but from 1759 onwards it showed itself far less tender towards colonial susceptibilities. This trend was the more dangerous because the acquisition of what was almost a new empire in 1763 involved the British government in complex problems of administration, finance and defence. The latter was the most urgent. Even before the end of the war the colonies had lost interest in costly defence schemes. Yet there were still Frenchmen, defeated but not subdued, to the north, Spaniards to the south, and thousands of hostile Indians along the frontiers. The need for keeping a strong regular army in America was brutally emphasized by the 'Conspiracy of Pontiac', an attempt by a confederation of Indian tribes led by Pontiac to drive the British settlers into the sea. The weight of the fighting was borne by British regulars; and although the decision to increase the size of the army in America from 3,000 to 8,000 men had been taken before the uprising, the Indian campaigns of 1763 and 1764 strengthened the government's determination to carry out this move. This in turn was to lead to anticipated financial problems, and unexpected political ones.

One result of the Conspiracy of Pontiac was the hastening of the publication by the British government of its Proclamation of 1763, intended to reassure the Indians that unofficial white settlement west of the Appalachians would be strictly controlled. The main motive behind the Proclamation – the protection of the Indians from unscrupulous fur-traders, settlers and land speculators – was entirely praiseworthy, although some members of the government did not overlook the point that colonies confined to the eastern seaboard would be easier to control than communities expanding far into the interior. Whatever the motive, this attempt to regulate the westward movement of the colonists aroused intense resentment among classes ranging from tough frontiersmen to wealthy speculators. For the next twelve years successive British administrations pondered the problem of priorities in the vast hinterland. The interests of Indians, settlers and traders, questions of cost and defence: all had to be taken into account. For the moment, the great moving frontier of American history had been halted, and British policy appeared to be in direct conflict with the natural ambitions of the American colonists.

Meanwhile, the government was faced with a narrower but no less pressing problem, the cost of the enlarged regular army in America. The Seven Years War was the costliest Britain had ever fought. The land tax had risen to 4/- in the £ (at one peaceful period under Walpole it had stood as low as 1/-), the National Debt had doubled, and the government was being forced to introduce new and highly unpopular taxes. It seemed reasonable that the colonies, still lightly taxed in comparison, should help to meet the cost of British garrisons in America. After all, British ministers pointed out, the garrisons were there for the colonists' own defence. Reasonable the scheme might be, but it had long been recognized as politically explosive. Various governors had suggested the need for regular colonial contributions to defence costs for more than half a century, but the British government had always resisted the temptation. Now, in 1764, the Chancellor of the Exchequer George Grenville edged forward over the line which no British minister had previously crossed. On the face of it the Revenue Act of that year (usually known as the Sugar Act) was a conventional enough measure. Most of its clauses were concerned with routine adjustments of duties on colonial imports and bounties for colonial products. However, one clause raised an issue of principle: a threepence-per-gallon duty was to be levied on all foreign molasses imported into the colonies. There had been a precedent for this duty on an important branch of colonial trade in the Molasses Act of 1733; but no precedent for the fact that this was something more than the type of trade-regulation measure which the colonies had accepted, if at times irritably, for a century. The Act's preamble revealed that this was also a revenue-raising measure, for it read that it was now 'just and necessary that a revenue be raised in your Majesty's said dominions in America'.

Because the clause was in part aimed at trade regulation most colonies hesitated to query it; but three did, and used arguments that were to become increasingly familiar. Englishmen could be taxed only with the consent of their own elected representatives, in this case the colonial assemblies. With appeals to Magna Carta, the Bill of Rights, and John Locke, 'No representation, no taxation' was advanced as one of the inalienable rights of a free Englishman. For its part the British government made no effort to render this innovation acceptable, and an Act weighted so heavily in favour of the West Indian lobby (it was intended to stop the import of French West Indian molasses into the North American colonies) made nonsense of the ministerial argument that the American colonies were 'virtually represented' in Parliament. The colonial case was pugnaciously stated in the Massachusetts Assembly:

If our trade may be taxed, why not our lands, and everything we possess, or make use of? If taxes are laid upon us in any shape without ever having a legal representation where they are laid, are we not reduced from the character of free subjects to the miserable state of tributary slaves?

These fears were soon heightened, for in 1765 the British government (after discovering that the molasses duty was covering only a fraction of the cost of the American garrisons) introduced the notorious Stamp Act. Again, this was not the outrageous imposition which it has sometimes seemed. This type of tax on legal and commercial transactions had been in force in England since the late seventeenth century, and its extension to the colonies had been suggested more than once. The money raised was to be kept in a separate fund, and used by Parliament for the defence of the colonies. Like the Sugar Act, this new measure passed through the Commons with little debate and less than fifty members voted against it. The colonial petitions of protest were ignored, Grenville loftily remarking that the government was aware that no man liked to be taxed. A few appreciated the gravity of the move. Pitt later recalled his agony of mind as he lay sick and helpless while the bill was debated. On the government side Thomas Whateley, Secretary to the Treasury, spelt out the significance of the Act when he referred to it as 'a *great measure* on account of the important point it establishes – the right of Parliament to lay an internal tax upon the colonies'.

The colonists also were quick to grasp the point of the measure. There was no ambiguity about the Stamp Act. A tax was being laid on Americans which affected their everyday transactions, which was in no sense a trade-regulation measure, and which they could not escape. Apart from the principle involved, the tax would be a considerable financial burden, for returns to Britain had to be made in specie, always in short supply in the colonies (where local paper currency was the normal means of exchange). This tax on business dealings, on newspapers and on pamphlets, united some of the most vocal and influential elements in the colonies: merchants, printers and lawyers. It helped to ally the southern plantation colonies (little affected by the molasses duty) with the northern colonies; and the lead was taken in the Virginian House of Burgesses which passed resolutions claiming the rights and privileges of Englishmen, and refusing to pay taxes other than those which it had approved. The assemblies of other colonies passed similar resolutions, and in 1766 delegates from nine of the thirteen mainland colonies met at New York to discuss the situation. This 'Stamp Act Congress' passed a motion agreeing to parliamentary legislation but not to parliamentary taxation, and its stand was supported throughout the colonies by violent demonstrations which showed how high feeling was running. Rioting broke out in several cities, stamp distributors were forced to flee for their lives, and for the first time the Sons of Liberty appeared on the streets to lead the agitation. More telling as far as the British government was concerned was agreement among the merchants not to import British goods: if continued long, this boycott would strike at the roots of the Old Colonial System.

In England Grenville had resigned (over another matter), and his administration had been replaced by one led by Lord Rockingham. The importance of Grenville's ministry lies in the direct and vigorous methods he adopted to deal with the government's undoubted financial difficulties over colonial defence. These helped to stimulate a feeling in government circles that the time had come to put an end to the policy of drift which had characterized most governments of the

Hanoverian period as far as colonial affairs were concerned; but few ministers seem to have anticipated the storm of protest that arose as Grenville doggedly pursued his plan of tapping American sources of wealth direct, and by-passing the entanglements of Assembly obstructiveness. In America the years of his ministry saw the rise of aggressive politicians who came to prominence through their opposition to the new measures. Particularly significant was the sight of politicians who had previously found it difficult to combine even against the threat of French or Indian enemies now working together in the Stamp Act Congress and through the non-importation associations.

Several members of the new Rockingham ministry had been outspoken opponents of the Stamp Act, and powerful pressure was also being exerted by hard-hit mercantile interests to reach a settlement with the colonists. Yet the government could not appear to be giving way to intimidation. Helped by the hints dropped in London by the colonial agent for Pennsylvania, Benjamin Franklin, who considered that the colonists objected only to internal taxation (such as the Stamp Act) and not to every kind of Parliamentary tax and duty, the government hit on a compromise solution. The Stamp Act was repealed, and the molasses duty imposed in 1764 reduced from threepence to a penny per gallon. However, at the same time a Declaratory Act was passed insisting on Parliament's right to tax the colonists if it thought fit. Historians have long criticized this as an ungracious and provocative measure, without always examining the nature of Rockingham's dilemma. Even with the promise of the Declaratory Act it was difficult to get George III and some influential politicians to agree to repeal of the Stamp Act. It was hardly Rockingham's fault that his gesture was taken as the basis for an active policy by the men who followed him.

Rockingham's ministry was short-lived, and was replaced by one led by the ailing Pitt (now Lord Chatham), who in an unlucky moment settled on Charles Townshend as Chancellor of the Exchequer. Ministries came and went, but the financial problems remained. The new Chancellor, harassed by the difficulty of getting domestic tax legislation through the Commons, looked once more towards the colonies, now freed of the burdens of the Stamp Act. Declaring that he thought the colonial distinction between internal and external taxation to be 'perfect nonsense', he announced that nevertheless he was prepared to humour this strange whim. Revenue was to be raised by four new import duties: on paper, paint, glass and tea. These were external taxes, and if the colonists followed the line of argument put forward only the year before by Franklin they would find it difficult to oppose them. If they rejected them, then they were denying the right of Parliament to levy any kind of tax, and were well on the way to refusing acknowledgement of the sovereignty of Parliament. Townshend died soon after the new duties were passed, and never realized the extent of his miscalculation. The colonies had made clear their objections to taxes levied without their consent, and it was a foolish man who sought to probe how far they would take their opposition.

The colonial reaction to the new duties was soon forthcoming. John Dickinson's widely-read 'Letters from a Farmer in Pennsylvania to the British Colonists' denied Parliament's right to impose any kind of taxation. From Massachusetts Sam Adams's *Circular Letters* were sent to the colonial assemblies, forcefully upholding the principle of no taxation without representation. New non-importation agreements were made, enthusiastically in some cases, reluctantly and under pressure in others. Once more popular leaders stepped forward to lead resistance to the duties, and at the same time to challenge the powers of established and generally conservative leaders of colonial society. They accused the British government of undermining accepted colonial rights; for money from the Townshend duties was to be used to pay colonial governors, and assemblies would be deprived of the powerful weapon of withholding salaries from royal officials. They pointed to New York, where in 1767 the Assembly had been suspended for non-fulfilment of an earlier Act. Other measures taken by the British government added to the tension. The system of trade-regulation was tightened with the establishment in America of boards of customs commissioners and vice-admiralty courts which soon banished the easy convention of always acquitting local smugglers. In two or three years of what an American historian has described as 'customs racketeering' the seafaring classes of the American ports were permanently antagonized by rapacious coastguard and customs officials. In Massachusetts the situation became so serious that British regulars were sent into Boston, where in March 1770 five inhabitants were killed in a street clash which colonial propagandists quickly turned to good advantage. Feelings ran so high after the 'Boston Massacre' that rebellion might have broken out there and then if the redcoats had not been withdrawn.   o

In London the new North administration which took office in 1770 was confronted by an absurd and dangerous situation, in which the few thousand pounds trickling in from the Townshend duties were dwarfed by the losses to British trade (estimated at £700,000 in one year alone) resulting from the non-importation agreements. North decided to drop the controversial duties, except that on tea. This was to be kept, not because of its financial importance, but to save face – or as North put it 'as a mark of the supremacy of Parliament, and an efficient declaration of their right to govern the colonies'. The mistake of the Declaratory Act had been repeated. The concession had been made grudgingly, and the retention of the tea duty made it clear that the government did not admit to any error of principle. No lesson had been learned from the events of the previous years.

For a while there was a lull. The North government adopted a conciliatory attitude in that it did not introduce further legislation objectionable to the colonists. In America the non-importation agreements were abandoned, and with a boom in trade came a reaction against the extremism of some of the popular leaders who had come to the fore amid the excitement of the previous decade. To many moderates the zeal for colonial liberties of these men looked suspiciously like a device by which they hoped to gain power; and it is true that to Sam Adams and others the calm, disturbed though it was by occasional acts of violence and with an underswell of irritation against the trade regulations, was unwelcome. For a variety of motives they preferred to keep feelings running high, and two incidents soon brought a return to the passion and violence of the 'sixties. The first was an attack in the summer of 1772 on the *Gaspée* revenue cutter by Rhode Islanders, noteworthy because of the contemptuous treatment of an investigating commission sent to the spot by the British government, and also because the expected attack on the commission's legality was led by the Virginian House of Burgesses 400 miles away. Further evidence of colonial solidarity came with the establishment of committees of correspondence by colonial assemblies as a device for keeping in touch with one another. Then at the end of 1773 came the celebrated 'Boston Tea Party', a colourful but provocative incident which brought a crisis atmosphere once more. A foolish decision by the British government to allow the East India Company to become the main direct exporter of tea to the colonies alarmed American merchants (and smugglers), and outraged the patriot groups which had never ceased their agitation against the tea duty. A vicious campaign of intimidation was directed against the masters of ships bringing tea into American ports, and in December the cargo of one of these ships lying in Boston harbour was thrown overboard.

No government could ignore this act of calculated defiance. In March 1774 North introduced into Parliament a series of coercive measures (known to Americans as the 'Intolerable Acts'). They were deliberately retaliatory, and among their other effects was the closing of the port of Boston until compensation had been paid to the East India Company, and the modifying of the Massachusetts charter to lessen the powers of the Assembly. This attempt at retribution played into the hands of the popular leaders, whose task was made easier by the passing in May 1774 of the Quebec Act. In many respects this was a moderate and statesmanlike measure which provided for Canada to be governed in a way more familiar to most of its French-speaking inhabitants than the normal pattern of the British seaboard colonies. There was to be no elected Assembly, but a legislative council appointed by the Crown and including Roman Catholics. French law was to be observed in civil cases, and Catholic priests retained their right to receive tithes. Under the terms of the Act the boundaries of Canada were to extend south to the Ohio and west to the Mississippi. The Quebec Act genuinely appalled many Americans. It seemed to re-establish a despotic, popish colony to their north, and it confirmed fears already aroused by the novel political and economic measures of the British government, and by reports that an episcopalian system of church government was to be introduced into the colonies. Further-more, the great south-western extension of Canada laid down by the Act barred the way to the westward extension of the middle colonies. In its own right a generous measure for a defeated people, the Quebec Act was a disastrously timed piece of legislation as far as the American crisis was concerned.

Coercive measures had been introduced, but not the means to enforce them if resistance spread outside Boston, as it rapidly did. Aid was sent to Massachusetts from the other colonies, and the British commander-in-chief, Gage, with his regiments found himself bottled up in Boston, unable to move outside the township for fear of pre-cipitating open hostilities. The initiative passed out of the hands of the British government as colonial delegates met at Philadelphia in September 1774 to consider the situation. The Continental Congress –

a significant name – saw the final triumph of the popular leaders over their conservative opponents, and the transfer of policy-making from the separate colonies to a central body. In October a Declaration of Rights was drawn up which accepted the right of Parliament to regulate the commerce of the colonies, but denounced revenue-raising Acts, demanded the repeal of thirteen existing Acts (including the Quebec Act), and severed commercial relations with Britain. Moderate opponents of the Declaration were ruthlessly treated, and tarring and feathering became an accepted method of persuasion and intimidation. As the colonists collected arms, and began to drill in an amateurish way, so the North government set its face against the generous terms of negotiation urged by Burke and a few others. The King's comment to Gage on the colonists summed up the attitude of the government, of the majority of M.P.s, and (one suspects) of most politically conscious people in the country: 'We must either master them or totally leave them to themselves and treat them as aliens.'

One half-hearted attempt at conciliation was made by the government in February 1775. It evaded the crucial issue of Parliament's right to tax the colonies, and in any event by the time the offer reached America the situation had deteriorated almost beyond recall. In April British and colonial forces were involved in a running skirmish at Lexington, and lost 400 men between them. As the two sides drifted into war so the conviction grew among the colonial leaders (patriots to the Americans, rebels to the British) that independence must be their objective. Men could not be expected to suffer and die for limited rights within the British imperial system. The decision was not an easy one. At the Second Continental Congress in May 1775 only a minority favoured independence; but the growing bitterness of the fighting, and the continual propaganda attacks on the British government, slowly exerted their influence. In July 1776 the Declaration of Independence was issued, a dignified and moving call to arms (even if some of its assertions were of doubtful historical validity). The Declaration sent many waverers into the ranks of the loyalists, but for the rest it irrevocably committed them to separation and independence: 'for the support of this Declaration, with a firm reliance on the protection of divine Providence, we mutually pledge to each other our Lives, our Fortunes and our sacred Honour.'

The question remains: could this train of events have been averted? The errors of the various British administrations are plain enough. Burke summed them up in a devastating, if unfair, indictment:

> What woeful variety of schemes have been adopted; what enforcing and what repealing; what bullying and what submitting; what doing and undoing; what straining and what relaxing; what assemblies dissolved for not obeying and called again without obedience; what troops sent out to quell resistance and, on meeting that resistance, recalled; what shiftings and changes and jumblings of all kinds of men at home, which left no possibility of order, consistency, vigour, or even so much as a decent unity of colour in any one public measure.

It was the speech of a prosecuting counsel, not of an impartial observer. It ignored the actions of unscrupulous extremists in America, the long history of colonial refusals to co-operate on vital defence matters with the British government, and the dilemma of a government averse to using force save as a last resort. It is easy to condemn the British government for policies which built up in America a community of antagonism among colonies, classes and individuals who often had little in common but their fear or detestation of some British measure or other. But behind the government measures and the colonial reaction to them, behind the increase of tension, lay the inescapable fact – grasped by only a handful of British politicians – that the Old Colonial System was no longer applicable to the American colonies. In many ways they were as politically conscious and economically ambitious as the mother country. They had come of age at a time when the expulsion of the French from Canada radically altered their need for British protection. This maturity British statesmen failed to comprehend. To the complex problems posed by this unprecedented colonial development they could offer only the tightening of a system already becoming obsolete. Burke pointed the way forward with his insistence on the value of ties of kinship and common ideals; but in an age when mercantilist concepts were still dominant (in governing if not in academic circles) his words were bound to fall on deaf ears. Instead the British government reacted in the way any other European government of the period would have done, and trod the path of armed repression. The fate of the thirteen colonies no longer depended on the logic of their arguments, but on the strength of their will to fight.

The War of American Independence

The clash at Lexington in April 1775 was followed in June by the far more sanguinary battle of Bunker Hill outside Boston. The first was a skirmish, the second a full-scale effort by Gage to apply military sanctions to a problem apparently insoluble by political means. There could be no doubting the reality of the war after Bunker Hill. June 1775 also saw the appointment, as commander-in-chief of the American forces, of George Washington, a wealthy Virginian planter with campaigning experience in the Seven Years War. He could not be termed a professional soldier, but Congress had chosen better than it knew.

The war which now began presented from the beginning a series of worrying military and diplomatic problems to the British government. In essence the military problem could be simply stated: the British regular army was small, the potential area of rebellion vast. By western European standards communications in America were poor, and there was no capital whose capture would fatally wound the patriot cause. Difficulties of finance and equipment would probably keep the colonists' regular army small in size; but to counterbalance this the British army would need to receive its reinforcements and most of its supplies from a home base 3,000 miles distant across the ocean. With the probability emerging of fairly small armies harassed by supply problems and moving cautiously across a terrain much of which was wilderness, the key to the whole war was quickly seen to be the attitude of the colonial population. If, as George III and the North government suspected, defiance was confined to a hard core of dissidents, then one or two sharp defeats inflicted on Washington's little army would knock the heart out of the patriot cause. But if patriot sympathizers were either more numerous or more active than loyalists, then the British forces might find themselves committed to a sisyphean task. An area painfully subdued would rise again as soon as the army moved on, and the British would be endlessly engaged in that most demoralizing form of hostilities, guerrilla warfare.

Beyond these immediate uncertainties and difficulties loomed an even more worrying problem: the possibility of French and Spanish intervention. In France Choiseul had gone, but under his successor the Comte de Vergennes the motives for a war of revenge against Britain remained. If the colonial revolt did not quickly collapse, if more and more British forces were drawn across the Atlantic, then France would be given a tempting opportunity of redressing the balance tilted in

Britain's favour during the Seven Years War. For once, it would be Britain which would be fighting a war on two fronts. Spain too had ample reason for intervention, though Charles III was understandably hesitant about giving support to colonial rebels. The Falklands crisis had shown the bellicosity of the Spanish government, and Gibraltar and Minorca might be regained in a successful war against Britain. Unless swift and decisive victory could be achieved in America, Bourbon intervention might become a calamitous reality; but it was precisely that type of victory which American conditions made it most difficult to obtain.

Finally, there was the political situation in Britain. The triumphs of the Seven Years War had been achieved by the partnership between Newcastle and Pitt: the one managing Parliament, the other directing strategy. The situation during the American War of Independence was painfully different. The head of the administration, North, was an able politician, but he was no war leader. He was in the Walpole rather than the Pitt tradition, although he lacked the former's dominance. Given to periods of monkish introspection, North failed to provide the decisive leadership which was needed. Nor could the King supply this, though he did what he could to support and stiffen his ministers in the war effort. The main burden of the war rested on the shoulders of two controversial politicians, Lord George Germain and Lord Sandwich. Secretary of State Germain has always been an enigma – an impatient, forceful man whose career lay in the shadow of court martial and disgrace after his conduct at the Battle of Minden during the Seven Years War. First Lord of the Admiralty Sandwich had a dubious reputation for other reasons, but the charge once levelled against him of the mismanagement of naval administration has been shown to be largely unjustified. No First Lord in eighteenth-century Britain was ever faced with the mounting burdens and anxieties which weighed on Sandwich, and he emerged from the ordeal with more credit than he is usually given. The performance of individual ministers did not alter the dismaying fact that there was no supreme commander at home; nor, it seemed as the war wore on, were there leaders of the first rank in the army and navy. Washington was confronted with a series of generals of no more than mediocre ability; and the navy was riven with quarrels in which political partisanship played a disproportionate part. Adherents of the view that the hour will always produce the man will find scant evidence of it in the Britain of this period.

British strategy for the first full year of the war in 1776 was soundly based. The revolt seemed to be centred in New England, so that area was to be isolated by the British seizure of New York, and control of the Hudson valley. This move would link the British forces in Canada and along the Atlantic seaboard, and cut the rebel territory in two. Under its new commander-in-chief, Howe, the British army was being strengthened by the arrival of reinforcements from home and trained Brunswick and Hessian troops from Germany (this last was a conventional enough military transaction, but it had dire political results in the outraging of American opinion). With loyalist support it was hoped that Howe would gradually extinguish the rebellion in New England. This neat plan was disrupted by an unexpected American push north into Canada which, although it petered out before the walls of Quebec, took Montreal, and upset British preparations in Canada. Furthermore, Washington's pressure in the early spring caused Howe to evacuate his uncomfortable berth in Boston.

Despite these setbacks the British summer campaign slowly gathered momentum. New York, Rhode Island and New Jersey were all taken. New York became the centre of British strategy for the rest of the war: it had a good harbour, held the entrance of the overland route to Canada, and forced rebel forces to make a great detour around it whenever they moved in a north–south direction. It was soon shown that Washington's continentals were no match in formal battle for Howe's disciplined regulars, and the American commander avoided full-scale engagements whenever possible. For Washington it was essential to keep his army together; without it the revolution would probably collapse. Howe was not the most dashing of commanders, and with his army encumbered with baggage and an array of supporting services he spent the late summer months vainly lumbering after his more agile opponent. When Howe finally retired frustrated into winter quarters Washington struck back, and re-took most of the Jerseys. This was the only gleam of light in a depressing year for the Americans, but the fact remained that Washington's army was still in existence, and every month that the war continued increased the chances of French or Spanish intervention. Washington's force dwindled during the hard winter months – at one time he had only 3,000 men – but it would grow again in the spring, and with French arms arriving from Europe it would be better equipped than it had been in 1776.

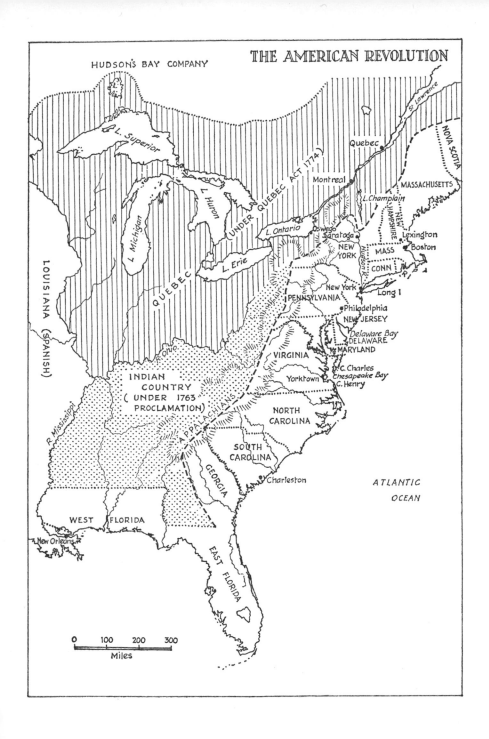

The year 1777, then, was likely to be crucial, and British strategy changed. Instead of repeating the plan of the previous year and joining with the army from Canada to crush the New Englanders, Howe decided to move south. Philadelphia was the lure, for the capture of the largest city in the colonies and the seat of Congress was expected to demoralize the rebels and leave only a hard core in New England. The flaw in the arrangement was that the British army coming south from Canada might be given a rough time by the New England forces, freed of the worry of Howe's main army striking at their backs from New York. By conducting two widely-separated campaigns the British were taking a calculated risk. After long delay Howe accomplished his objective when Philadelphia fell to him, but the victory had none of the shattering impact on the rebel cause which had been predicted. Washington's army, though hard-pressed, remained intact; and meanwhile away in the north the British army from Canada had met disaster. Its commander was Burgoyne – 'Gentleman Johnny' to his contemporaries – a rash and overbold soldier. With an army of seven thousand regulars and some Canadians and Indians he struck into the American colonies by way of Lake Champlain. Ticonderoga fell to him, but the deeper he thrust into hostile country the greater grew the dangers besetting him. There were no replacements to offset the steady drain of casualties; militia from the New England colonies were harrying him at every step; and his supply lines back to Canada were in danger of being severed. Still Burgoyne kept south, crossing the Hudson River, pushing his dwindling army ever deeper into the net of enemy forces. By mid-October Burgoyne was completely surrounded at Saratoga, with only 3,500 fighting men left, his path of retreat blocked, and many miles of enemy country between him and the British forces feeling their way north from New York. He was left no choice but to surrender, and his army was interned for the duration of the war.

The disaster at Saratoga had an effect out of all proportion to the number of men involved. A British army had been utterly and humiliatingly defeated. It was for the Americans the first real victory in a grinding war fought mainly on the retreat. The news helped to keep Washington's men going through a hard winter near Philadelphia: the British army in comfortable winter quarters not twenty miles off, the tattered Americans living on the most meagre fare in their exposed tents and log-huts. Saratoga threw into doubt the whole concept of British strategy in North America, with its confident assumption that British regulars could brush aside any continentals or militia which tried to obstruct their work of persuading areas to return to the King's allegiance. For the first time, it was seriously suggested that the British should abandon any attempt to conquer New England, and instead should hold the line of the Hudson and concentrate on clearing the middle and southern colonies. These were economically more valuable to Britain, and contained a smaller and probably less rebellious population than the northern colonies. An indication of the sudden sagging in British morale which Saratoga brought was shown in the peace proposals approved by Parliament in February 1778, which included a renunciation of Britain's claim to tax the colonies for revenue purposes. This latter was a damning comment on the policy followed by the government before 1776. The same month a more important move took place which was also linked with Saratoga. In France Vergennes had hesitated to intervene in the struggle until he was certain that the American rebellion would not collapse and leave France isolated against Britain. Saratoga was the assurance he needed, and in February treaties of alliance and commerce were signed between France and the Americans. France agreed not to make peace until American independence was assured, gave up all claims to North America east of the Mississippi, and was left a free hand in the Caribbean.

The entry of France into the war, and the probability that Spain would soon follow suit, changed the entire nature of the struggle. European waters, the West Indies and India: all now became probable theatres of war. Everywhere vital British supply lines and trade routes were threatened. America was no longer of predominant concern to the North administration, for the French might strike blows far more damaging to British interests elsewhere. The new turn given to events was reflected in the orders to evacuate Philadelphia. Clinton (Howe's successor as commander-in-chief) now held only New York and Rhode Island. Apart from these areas all the land lying between Canada in the north and Florida in the south was patriot-held. Vergennes was faced with a choice of alternatives almost embarrassing in its variety and possibilities. At this stage he was interested in lucrative overseas conquests rather than in an invasion of England. A shift in the balance of colonial power established at the Peace of Paris was the main French objective, not involvement in hard and probably profitless campaigning in the British Isles.

For a time British forces were able to stem the tide, and although Dominica was lost, Saint Lucia was captured from the French and on the mainland Georgia was recovered. As far as the American fighting was concerned, more was heard about the military potential of the loyalists, a will-o'-the-wisp that was finally to lure the British to destruction. Past experience and present circumstances ruled out the old hopeful strategy of crushing the rebellion with one or two well-aimed blows; but it was felt that an army of more than 25,000 regulars, although it might not be able to tempt Washington out of the mountains and into a decisive battle, ought to be able to fend him off while it built up loyalist support in the areas nearest the protective influence of British sea and land power.

Once more British plans were overshadowed by a move in the diplomatic sphere. In June 1779 Spain followed France into the war with the avowed intention of regaining Gibraltar and Minorca from Britain. The North government was now faced with a rebellion which pinned down most of its regular troops and many of its ships, and a union of the next two strongest naval powers in Europe. Moreover, the Bourbons had no continental distractions. Pitt's nightmare had become reality. The American war of 1776 and 1777 had turned into a struggle for overseas dominion comparable in scope to the Seven Years War. But this time the odds were heavily against Britain. There was no Pitt to direct the war effort, and the North administration was under heavy attack in Parliament. Unlike the situation in the Seven Years War, when the French navy had been destroyed before Spain became involved, the French and Spanish navies were both intact. The French navy in particular was a fine fighting force which had benefited greatly from Choiseul's rebuilding programme for ships and dockyards. Sandwich summed up a gloomy situation when he pointed out:

> England till this time was never engaged in sea war with the House of Bourbon thoroughly united, their naval force unbroken, and having no other war or object to draw off their attention and resources. We have no one friend or ally to assist us.

That home forces could not be weakened to meet the multitude of threats overseas was shown by the invasion attempt of 1779, mounted after Spanish pressure. Though the attempt was unsuccessful, for a few nerve-wracking days the French and Spanish fleets controlled the Channel with the British fleet far away to the west. The British government was in an agonizing predicament. Abandonment of the American war would involve giving up all that Britain was supposedly fighting for. Concentration on America would leave Britain's possessions elsewhere perilously exposed. The only answer was to stretch all available forces to the limit, and pray that they would be in the right place at the right time. Reinforcements were sparingly doled out, warships were carefully allocated, nowhere were resources adequate for the tasks on hand. Pressure would have grown intolerable were it not for dissensions and even treachery within the wearied patriot ranks in America, and the inefficiency of the French and Spanish war effort.

In America British efforts were concentrated on the southern colonies, where in May 1780 Cornwallis achieved a heartening success when he captured the important harbour of Charleston in South Carolina, and with it an American army 6,000 strong. It was a remarkable achievement that Britain had not fallen back entirely on the defensive, but the initiative could not be held for long. War with Holland at the end of 1780 after disputes over the Dutch supply of naval stores to France and Spain added to the government's difficulties. There was another enemy fleet to consider, and another area of operations – the North Sea and the Baltic – to provide for. In the same year the formation of the Armed Neutrality of Russia, Sweden, Prussia, Denmark and Portugal reflected the resentment of non-belligerent powers at Britain's overbearing attitude towards neutral trading rights.

On the other side the financial strain of the war was bearing heavily on France, which was in the frustrating position of being theoretically superior to her old enemy, yet unable to strike a decisive blow. In early 1781 the government decided to send the main French fleet under de Grasse to the Caribbean, from where it was to sail north to American waters. For three years Washington had been urging the French to make this obvious move, long feared by the British. It was ill luck for the British that the same summer Cornwallis decided to follow up his success at Charleston by pushing north into Virginia, where he hoped the loyalists would rally to him. Once there, he made for the coast to await orders from Clinton in New York. The spot he chose was Yorktown, at the entrance of the York River inside the great bight of Chesapeake Bay, and with exit to the sea through the narrow opening between Cape Charles and Cape Henry. There Cornwallis waited behind hastily dug entrenchments, only to learn at the beginning of September that a French fleet lay within the Capes. Unknown to Cornwallis, de Grasse had sailed northward from the West Indies in August, and now lay across the British line of retreat by sea. Superior in numbers, the French admiral was able to hold off the British fleet which arrived early in September to try to force a passage through to the beleaguered army. At Yorktown Cornwallis was trapped with 6,000 men, outnumbered two or three to one by the American and French forces surrounding him. De Grasse's fleet had not only prevented any relief by sea; it had landed French troops and artillery to support Washington. After a week of steady bombardment broken by sudden rushes by Washington's men, Cornwallis surrendered before the final assault could be mounted. As the British marched out a band aptly played 'The World Turned Upside Down'. The date was 17 October 1781, four years to the day after Burgoyne's surrender at Saratoga.

Although more than 25,000 British troops remained in America, to all intents the fighting there was over after Yorktown. The war had contained little in the way of masterly military operations. No military genius had emerged on either side. The British commanders had been burdened throughout by problems of supply, had been hampered by the restraints they had been put under in the early stages of the war when there were hopes of a settlement, and were always fearfully aware of the consequences of defeat. Most disappointing of all, the loyalists (perhaps a third of the population) had never made their mark as allies: intimidation, lack of enthusiasm or organization, and doubts about their reliability all served to make their contribution a minor one. Washington, too, was subjected to peculiarly harassing strains. Many of his men served only on short-term enlistments, and often slipped away home. Only stern discipline kept the army in being, and even so dissatisfaction over arrears of pay frequently erupted in mutiny or desertion. The militia were a cause of despair to Washington as they came and went without explanation, though at Saratoga they played a decisive part when they flocked to the scene of action to join the hard core of continentals. After the war Washington paid tribute to his continentals when he wrote that for eight years the British army had been successfully resisted by 'numbers infinitely less, composed of men sometimes half starved, always in rags, without pay, and experiencing every species of distress which human nature is capable of undergoing'. The words reveal as much of Washington as of his men. Though only a limited military tactician, he possessed those qualities of patience, tenacity and integrity which stamped him as a great leader. The part played by other American commanders and by foreign technical experts must not be forgotten; but in the end it was Washington who held the army together, nursed it in defeat, and finally led it to victory. Measured against Washington, the British generals, for all their knowledge of the formal arts of war, lacked stamina, a sense of political realities, and the devotion of their men.

In a wider context the catastrophe at Yorktown came at the end of a depressing year in which Britain had suffered setbacks in India, the Caribbean and the Mediterranean, which had seen another invasion threat, and in which discontent at the cost and course of the war had mounted at home. Yorktown, it was quickly seen, was a victory which had been made possible by the superiority of French seapower – a sobering thought for a nation which tended to take command of the sea for granted. Yorktown demonstrated to the world at large what Sandwich had long known, that Britain's naval resources were not equal to the country's commitments. To an empire based on seapower the implications of this were foreboding in the extreme. At best it meant that Britain would be unable to follow Pitt's old policy of switching forces from one theatre of operations to another, using command of the sea to obtain overwhelming superiority in one area at a time. At worst the Bourbons might adopt Pitt's strategy, and there were ominous signs that this was happening as de Grasse sailed south to the nerve centre of Britain's interests in the Caribbean.

One by one de Grasse picked off the smaller islands, Saint Kitts, Montserrat, Nevis, as a prelude to an attack on Jamaica. At home the government cut to the bone the squadrons protecting the coasts and the homeward bound trade in order to send Rodney across the Atlantic with reinforcements. In April 1782 Rodney met and defeated de Grasse just north of Dominica at the Battle of the Saints. Instead of fighting in formal line ahead Rodney broke through the enemy line in several places to give the French a foretaste of the annihilating battles of the Nelson era. Jamaica was saved, but the news of the victory came too late to aid the North government which had not long survived the news of Yorktown. The new government, headed by Rockingham, was pledged to make peace, and although the war continued, attention in Europe shifted to the negotiations.

The Peace of Versailles

For the first time in the eighteenth century a British administration entered peace negotiations from a position of military weakness. In 1762 difficult decisions had to be made as to which captured overseas territories should be handed back; twenty years later the decisions were on the much more painful subject as to which British possessions must be conceded. The American mainland empire of the Thirteen Colonies had gone, and Bourbon ambitions also threatened the other British empire of tropical dependencies in the Caribbean, Africa and Asia. The peace negotiations at this difficult period in British history were in the hands of Shelburne, never a very successful politician, but an imaginative statesman whose motives and achievements during the negotiations of 1782–3 have only recently been fully appreciated by historians.

The process of peace-making was complicated, even by eighteenth-century standards. To begin with, there were two distinct sets of negotiations: the first, the Anglo-American discussions to settle the terms of American independence; the second, the negotiations between Britain and the various partners in the continental coalition which had fought against her. France dominated this side of the negotiations, just as she had the fighting, but Spain (in particular) and Holland were far from being acquiescent subordinates. At times Vergennes found himself more in sympathy with Shelburne than with the Spanish foreign minister Floridablanca and the Spanish ambassador in Paris, Aranda. On all sides the financial strain of the war introduced an element of urgency into the negotiations: in France Vergennes at one stage warned his colleagues that continuation of the war effort for another three months would push the nation into bankruptcy. In both Britain and France the principal negotiators had to contend with bellicose groups who were convinced that perseverance in the fighting would bring triumph. A final complication was that the war was still being fought on several different fronts while the negotiations were in progress. An ambitious French drive in India, the final Spanish assault on Gibraltar, and the gathering of Franco-Spanish forces for a descent on Jamaica, were all going ahead at this time; and the fortunes of war had their inevitable impact on the attitude of the negotiators.

A view of the negotiations as a whole reveals that (contrary to popular belief at the time) Shelburne's policy generally won the day. He was insistent on a generous peace with America which would encourage the maintenance of close commercial relations, and not preclude eventual political reunion, between the two countries. As far as Britain's European enemies were concerned he advocated concessions which would remove some of the sting from the 1763 settlement, and yet preserve intact Britain's most important interests overseas. In pursuing this policy, Shelburne was helped by a series of British successes. Rodney's victory at the Saints, the repulse of the Spanish assault on Gibraltar, and the vigorous defence of British possessions in India by Warren Hastings, all strengthened Shelburne's hand at crucial phases of the negotiations.

By November 1782 the preliminaries of the settlement between Britain and her former colonies were concluded. Since Yorktown there had never been any question about the independence of the Thirteen Colonies. What was at issue was the extent of territory which was to accompany independence. Shelburne unhesitatingly met the territorial claims of the American negotiators Jay, Adams and Franklin. The fertile and largely unoccupied tracts of land between the Ohio and the Great Lakes went to the United States, not Canada (as in 1774). Shelburne would have no truck with French and Spanish moves to restrict the United States to the Atlantic seaboard, and insisted that the new nation must stretch to the Mississippi. Influenced by the arguments of the new school of economists led by Adam Smith, Shelburne argued that the Americans must be free to open up the West; the more territory they settled, the greater would be the opportunity for the import of British manufactures. To the orthodox mercantilist of the day Shelburne's policy was inexplicable, but his contention that commercial expansion need not be accompanied by a burden of administrative and defensive responsibilities was in line with British imperial trends in other parts of the globe. In a more general way, Shelburne's attitude at the peace negotiations played an important part in the formative years of the young nation across the Atlantic. His revolutionary plan for a commercial union between Britain and the United States did not long survive his fall from office in 1783, but the close economic ties between the two countries in the nineteenth century showed that the idea was not as preposterous as it appeared to many critics at the time.

Agreement with the United States did not bring peace with France and Spain any closer. Rather the reverse, for Vergennes resented his exclusion from the American negotiations, and feared that the generous concessions granted by Shelburne to the Americans would prevent the British government from agreeing to French demands. Clearly, much depended on the course of the war in the Caribbean, the Mediterranean and India. British defeats in those theatres would increase Vergennes's chances of dictating his own terms to Britain. Unfortunately for these hopes, the British fought back so stoutly that, month by month, Shelburne's hand was strengthened. Vergennes recognized the logic of the situation, and after some hard bargaining the British and French negotiators reached general agreement. Spain was the obstacle: despite the calamitous failure of her attack on Gibraltar she still presented impossibly extravagant claims, and French pressure had to be exerted before the Spanish court would agree to peace.

The Treaty of Versailles of 1783 between Britain, France and Spain (the treaty between Britain and Holland was not signed until 1784) was far from being the total overthrow of the 1763 settlement that the French and Spanish governments had happily envisaged in the first weeks after Yorktown. Britain's military recovery, the withdrawal of America from the war, Shelburne's skill, and the lack of co-ordination among the continental allies, led to a less drastic settlement than seemed at one time probable. Most of France's conquests in the West Indies were restored to Britain, only Tobago being kept (and Saint Lucia regained). New French fishing rights on the west coast of Newfoundland were less valuable than they appeared to be on paper; the main fishing stations were along the south coast and British fishermen rarely went near the west shore. In India French hopes were crushed. Vergennes's original objective of opening up extensive new French spheres of influence, with territory producing a revenue of £500,000 a year, dwindled in the peace treaty to the restoration of French trading posts, and the acquisition of a small strip of territory around Pondicherry. In West Africa the situation was restored as it had been before 1763: France regained the Senegal River area, and Britain kept the Gambia. Spain gained the Floridas and Minorca, but was unable either to press her claims to participation in the Newfoundland fishery, expel the British from the Gulf of Honduras, or get any satisfaction on the issue of British contraband trade.

The peace treaty was unpopular enough in Britain to bring down Shelburne, but examination of it shows that he had sacrificed none of Britain's essential interests. The war had proved that Britain could not at one and the same time successfully fight her own rebellious colonists and a coalition of the leading powers of Europe. But victories in the last year of the war had warned that under normal circumstances Britain was still likely to be more than a match for France and Spain overseas. In no single theatre of operations had the Bourbons taken full advantage of the predicament which confronted the British when their traditional enemies intervened in the American conflict. They had picked up a few possessions in 1783, but these amounted to little enough to compensate for the cost of the war (which in France was to be a decisive factor in the financial difficulties which led to the crisis of 1789). The United States had won independence with Bourbon help, but was in no way a client state of France or Spain. The loss of the Thirteen Colonies was a mortifying blow to British prestige, but the foundations of Britain's strength and prosperity remained untouched.

Reform and Discontent in Spanish America

As the American War of Independence drew to its close there were outbreaks of rebellion and disorder farther south in the Spanish colonial empire. These, however, never approached the importance of the independence movement within the British colonies, and in general the Spanish empire under Charles III gave an appearance of strength and coherence which it had not possessed for a century. The most cursory glance at the map will show the immense extent of the Spanish empire in America as it existed in the eighteenth century. It stretched from Chile in the south to California in the north. It embraced a wide variety of races, classes and cultures – ranging from the most backward Indian to the Spanish grandee, from the ambitious creole to the Negro slave. Its size and above all its internal tensions made it a uniquely difficult empire to govern.

The root cause of tension was the proximity of three distinct races within the empire, each with widely differing characteristics and attitudes. The Spaniard could never forget that he was the descendant of the white *conquistadores*; the Indian that he was the original inhabitant of the land; the Negro that he had been forcibly shipped from

Africa to an alien country. Stretched over this basic threefold classification was a complex pattern of further division and subdivision which brought added strains. In the early days there had been fierce conflicts between groups from different parts of Spain: between Basques and Castilians, for example. By the seventeenth century these were overshadowed by the enmity between the creoles (American-born Spaniards) and the *peninsulares* (European-born Spaniards). The creole was often wealthier and better-educated than the Spanish-born newcomer, but he could never have the same certainty about the purity of his blood and was condemned to a permanently inferior social position. There were instances of creoles who rose to high political and ecclesiastical position, but never enough to remove the sense of discrimination. Nor were the Indians in any sense one nation or people in the way that the common term given to them by the Spaniards implied. Beyond the centres of relatively sophisticated culture represented by the Aztecs of Mexico and the Incas of Peru lived a multitude of primitive tribes with no common language or religion. All they had in common was the shock of alien conquest and exploitation. Between European and Indian stood the half-breed offspring of the two races, the mestizo. He was a complex mixture of the two strains, different from both, but with some of the qualities of each, and certainly not the easiest of subjects to rule.

During the seventeenth century the growing weakness of metropolitan Spain was reflected in its overseas empire. Spanish administration in America was marked by a general laxity, by a reluctance or inability to enforce the elaborate legal system drawn up in Madrid for the governance of the overseas empire. While widespread smuggling made a mockery of the regulations designed to establish a commercial monopoly in the empire, the native population was systematically exploited in mine and plantation. The benevolent intentions of the distant Spanish government were little more than a faint ripple by the time they reached the outlying areas, and normally could be ignored with impunity. At the beginning of the eighteenth century, when the whole empire was in danger of dismemberment during the crisis of the Spanish Succession, it was riddled with corruption and inefficiency in official quarters, and undermined by dissatisfaction among the creole and mestizo elements of the population.

With the change of dynasty on the Spanish throne at the turn of the century came a change in attitude. The first two Bourbon monarchs of

Spain, Philip V and Ferdinand VI, brought a new vigour and efficiency to Spanish administration, and some evidence of this can be seen in America. The sprawling viceroyalty of Peru was reduced to more manageable size by the creation in 1717 of the new viceroyalty of New Granada, with its centre at Bogotá and including (the modern states of) Ecuador, Colombia, Venezuela and Panama. The cumbersome convoy system was modified, and an increasing number of individual sailings permitted. The Caracas Company, founded in 1728 on the model of the monopolistic Dutch, British and French trading companies, drove a flourishing trade along the coasts of Venezuela. Guided by French advisers who were influenced by the fashionable scepticism towards organized religion, the personally devout Bourbon monarchs made inroads on the powers of the Church. In America the influence of the Inquisition decreased, the number of clergy and their special privileges were reduced, and pressure was exerted on the regular orders to move away from the inhabited areas and into mission work on the frontiers.

The immensity of the task which remained was revealed in a secret report made to the home government by two young naval officers, Antonio de Ulloa and Jorge Juan, who were in Peru between 1735 and 1741. Their study of conditions in the heart of the Spanish overseas empire resulted in a scathing indictment of the colonial system. Subordinate Spanish officials were condemned for their tyranny and corruption; many of the clergy for their greed and indolence. But most ominous for the future of Spanish rule was the state of tension which the two investigators found among the white population. They could only compare the hatred which existed between creoles and *peninsulares* with that between two peoples at war with each other. The report, though undoubtedly read, remained secret. The first two Bourbons achieved a holding operation, no more. They patched up the old system, but the thorough overhaul and drastic reform which was so badly needed had to await the reign of Charles III.

Though not of outstanding intellectual calibre, Charles III was a conscientious and serious ruler who possessed the invaluable capacity of selecting able ministers to serve him. Several of the most important of these were influenced by the current ideas of the Enlightenment. They were hostile towards the Jesuits and the Inquisition, encouraged education, and favoured a policy of decentralization and free trade within the Spanish empire. Soon after the end of the Seven Years War a committee consisting of the finance minister, the Marqués de Squillace, the foreign minister, Grimaldi (both Italians) and the minister of the Indies and Marine, Julian de Arriago, met weekly in Madrid to consider plans for the improved administration and defence of the empire. Commercial affairs were studied by a junta of experts whose report of 1765 – it advocated among other reforms the opening of the trans-Atlantic trade of the Spanish West Indies (previously confined to Seville and Cádiz) to nine Spanish ports – foreshadowed a comprehensive relaxation of the old system of commercial regulation. In America the efficiency and obedience of government machinery was increased by reducing the size of the units of administration, and by making frequent use of the supervisory powers of the *visitadors* sent out from Spain.

Despite the separation of New Granada in 1717 the viceroyalty of Peru remained far too large as regional interests developed and populations grew in areas far removed from the viceregal capital at Lima. This applied particularly to the region around the Río de la Plata on the south-east coast of the continent, 2,500 miles distant from Lima. It was a frontier region facing Portuguese Brazil to the north, and had been a focal point of conflict for a century. It was also a busy centre of contraband trade, most of which came through Buenos Aires. Its hinterland, after long neglect, was developing a life and prosperity of its own. The arguments were strong in favour of making the area an independent viceroyalty, with its capital at Buenos Aires; and in 1776 this was done. The new viceroyalty included what are now Argentina, Uruguay, Paraguay and Bolivia. The silver mines of Upper Peru now came under the jurisdiction of Buenos Aires instead of Lima, and the lines of communication of an immense area of the continent east of the Andes were allowed to run towards their natural Atlantic outlet instead of being forced across the mountains to the Pacific. Accompanying this administrative move was an important commercial one. The trade of the area was released from the rigid restrictions which had previously held it in check. Freed from the restraints of Lima and of an unsympathetic commercial code, the new viceroyalty became an important part of the Spanish American empire. Population and trade increased, Buenos Aires became a boom town, and ranches began to dot the pampas.

Deprived during the course of the century of territory to the north (New Granada) and to the south-east (La Plata), Peru shrank in size and importance. Once the wealthiest region of Spanish America, it could no longer compete with the most northerly of the four vice-royalties, New Spain. This huge area, with its capital at Mexico City, came to the fore during Charles III's reign. One of the ablest of Spanish colonial administrators, José de Gálvez, spent six years in the vice-royalty as *visitador-general* before returning to Madrid to become minister of the Indies. He created a militia more efficient than any seen before in Spanish America, to ward off a series of threats – real and imaginary – to New Spain from the British, Russians, French and Indians. He carried out much-needed administrative reforms, and removed grasping and corrupt officials. He was the driving force behind the northward expansion into Upper California and along the Missouri river – the last great forward movement of the Spanish frontier in the New World. Improved techniques increased the pro-ductivity of the mines, and by the end of Charles III's reign New Spain was supplying almost half the world's precious metals. Mexico City was a flourishing centre of culture and civilization, and boasted magnificent buildings. Botanical and other expeditions into the interior were given every support by the Crown. Activity, it is true, was concentrated in a few areas. California, Texas and Florida were un-developed, sparsely populated regions with few signs in the eighteenth century of the rich states they were to become in the next century under American rule.

Relaxation of the traditional commercial system was not confined to the new viceroyalty of La Plata. Bernardo Wall, José del Campillo and other able economists urged Charles III to modernize the anti-quated system he had inherited. By 1778 the traditional monopoly of Spanish colonial trade held by a few privileged ports in Spain and America had disappeared. Direct trade was permitted between Spain and all parts of Spanish America except New Spain and Venezuela, where trade remained restricted until 1789. In 1784 further steps towards the freeing of trade were taken: duties were removed from Spanish manufactures, agricultural products and wines entering the colonies, and duties were reduced on foreign goods shipped to Spanish America from home ports. Mineral, agricultural and pastoral pro-duction expanded rapidly as a result of more efficient methods and of increased demand both within Spanish America and in Europe. Even the Caribbean islands, long neglected in favour of the great mainland provinces, experienced a quickening of economic tempo. Santo

Domingo and Puerto Rico remained countries of small white pro-
prietors, but Cuba began to move nearer the pattern of the French and
British islands. Slaves were imported in increasing numbers, sugar
plantations were established, and in the nineteenth century Cuba was
to become the most important sugar producer in the Caribbean.
Economic growth was accompanied by a more vigorous enforcement
of the laws against smuggling, and this together with the lower prices
of Spanish goods put many illicit traders out of business. As this last
development hinted, the relaxing of trade restrictions was in no way
intended to loosen the political ties between Spain and her colonies.
Rather it was an injection of reality into the make-believe world of
Spanish commercial regulation, and an attempt to boost the development of industry, trade and agriculture in Spanish America. The
passage by the British government in 1766 of the first Free Port Act
made reform the more urgent, for the establishment of 'free ports' in
the British West Indies represented yet another attempt to attract
trade from the Spanish colonies. In time, it was hoped that the British
Caribbean colonies would serve as an entrepôt for the whole of Spanish
America.

Further measures of political decentralization were taken in the
interests of better and more efficient government. The mammoth
viceroyalties were broken down into smaller administrative units in an
effort to make control from Madrid more effective – not to weaken it in
any way. An important step in this process was the introduction into
Spanish America of the intendancy system, brought into metropolitan
Spain from France during Philip V's reign. After long hesitation
Charles III's government introduced it into the overseas empire, first
for a trial period in Cuba and then, in the 1780s, into the mainland
colonies. As in France and Spain the intendant's duties covered every
aspect of government: defence, revenue, economic affairs, and justice.
Significantly, these powerful officials were invariably *peninsulares*,
and the new system had the dual objective of bringing better government to the colonists and at the same time tightening control from
Madrid.

What was not foreseen by the Spanish government was that the ideas
of the Enlightenment could not be confined to administrative reforms
emanating from Madrid. They were contagious, and their effect on
sections of Charles III's restless subjects overseas was to shake the
fabric of the empire. For long the resentment of the creoles and

LATIN
AMERICA
IN THE 18th CENTURY

San Francisco

R. Colorado

R. Missouri

Santa Fe

El Paso

R. Grande

Chihuahua
(NEW CAPTAINCY-
GENERAL 1776)

La Paz

R. Mississippi

FLORIDA
St Augustine

New
Orleans

Mexico

Vera Cruz

Acapulco

VICEROYALTY
OF NEW SPAIN
(1535)

Guatemala

Havana

CUBA
(NEW CAPTAINCY-
GENERAL 1777)

SANTO DOMINGO

PUERTO RICO

ATLANTIC
OCEAN

Cartagena

Portobelo

Panama

Caracas

Trinidad

(NEW CAPTAINCY
GENERAL 1777)

Bogotá

VICEROYALTY
OF NEW
GRANADA
(1717)

Quito

GUIANA

R. Amazon

VICEROYALTY
OF PERU
(1542)

Callao

Lima

La Paz

R. Madeira

BRAZIL

MATO
GROSSO

Recife

Bahia

PACIFIC

OCEAN

San Felix

Potosí

MINAS
GERAIS

São Paulo

VICEROYALTY
OF LA PLATA
(1776)

Rio de Janeiro

Juan
Fernandez

Valparaiso

Santiago

(NEW
CAPTAINCY-
GENERAL
1778)

R. Salado

R. Paraná

Colonia

Buenos
Aires

Montevideo

0 200 400 600 800 1000
Miles

Falkland Is

St of Magellan

C. Horn

mestizos in Spanish America had existed only as a local issue. Censorship and distance cut off these discontented subjects of imperial Spain from the liberal ideas influencing Europe in the eighteenth century. But with the advent in 1759 of an autocrat who took those ideas as a basis for many of his actions the situation changed. This was demonstrated in unmistakable fashion by the expulsion of the Jesuits from Spain and its overseas empire in 1767.

The Jesuit order had been an immense force in the Spanish colonial empire. Jesuits had dominated the universities, protected and taught hundreds of thousands of Indians in the outlying regions, and entered energetically into the commercial and cultural life of the colonies. But by the middle of the eighteenth century their enemies were strong. Their secrecy, wealth and ambition laid them open to attack by nationalists and *philosophes* alike. The former saw them as upholders of papal claims against the state monarchies; the latter viewed them as a buttress of established religion in its most reactionary form. Long-standing grievances against the Jesuits came to a head in the Iberian world in 1750, when Jesuit missionaries resisted a treaty arrangement between Spain and Portugal under whose terms territory which included Jesuit missions on the Paraguayan frontier was ceded to Brazil. Jesuit participation was also suspected in a plot against Charles III in 1766; and in 1767 he decided to follow the Portuguese precedent (of 1759) and expelled the Jesuits from his realms.

In America the measure was carried out with a minimum of publicity, but even so there were some serious disturbances. The expulsion was a sad loss to Spanish America. Some of its most devoted teachers and missionaries disappeared at a moment's notice. Thousands of Indians were left without protection. The King had shown his power, but in the long term he probably weakened rather than strengthened the power of the Crown. The expulsion caused bewilderment and resentment in America. The departure of the Jesuits from the universities left the way open for teachers favouring more radical ideas. An important spiritual link between Europe and Spanish America was severed. Finally, the Spanish Crown had raised against itself a powerful and unforgiving enemy. From their exile in Italy the Jesuits intrigued and circulated propaganda unceasingly against the ruler who had expelled them. They became natural allies for those who worked for the independence of Spanish America. The Spanish Crown had triumphed in 1767, but its victory was a Pyrrhic one.

The expulsion of the Jesuits was not the only disturbance which shook Spanish America in Charles III's reign. In 1780-1 the most serious Indian rising since the sixteenth century swept parts of Peru. Although the Spanish government had introduced new measures to regulate Indian conditions of labour, the usual difficulty of communications left the intended reforms at the mercy of local officials. In Peru in particular these flagrantly abused their powers, and in the late 1770s the burden placed on the Indians swelled to intolerable size when to the normal greed and oppression of local officials were added the financial demands of a new *visitador*, José de Areche. Intent on collecting money to support Spanish participation in the American War of Independence, Areche adopted methods which led to a terrible explosion of Indian anger and despair. The revolt was headed by Tupuc Amarú II, son of an Indian chief, and a descendant of the Incas. Although finally defeated, and mercilessly repressed, the rebels had received massive support. Armies of forty and fifty thousand men had taken the field, and although miserably equipped their size showed the strength of feeling against the government. The rebels were crushed, but the Indian population remained implacably hostile, a formidable potential ally for any future force working for independence.

Tupuc Amarú's rebellion was the more worrying because at the same time there was a revolt of the *comuneros* or townspeople in New Granada. Again the rebellion was sparked off by oppression and increased taxation, and the rebels found allies in the Indians, excited by the news of Tupuc Amarú's rebellion to the south. The *comuneros* were in turn barbarously repressed, but their revolt in so prosperous a region as New Granada was an ominous portent, the more so since representatives of the rebels had sought (unsuccessfully) British support in their struggle.

Although only Peru and New Granada experienced major disturbances, there were plots and local risings in most of the other colonies. The agitation differed from that in the British North American colonies a few years earlier in that it was produced mainly by local oppressions and abuses. As yet there was little evidence of general hostility towards measures coming from Spain. Whatever the motive behind them, these measures represented a more rational approach to economic and political problems than that experienced before Charles III's reign, whereas the greater freedom and prosperity of the British colonists before 1763 produced a very different reaction in the Thirteen

Colonies to the efforts by the British government to bring order to its imperial system. Even so, the risings were an indication that despite the reforms of Charles III the difficulties of governing the Spanish empire were growing more rapidly than the ability or wish of the metropolitan government to introduce changes. Indian bitterness had exploded in Tupac Amarú's revolt; the New Granada rebellion had shown the strength of mestizo feeling. In less dramatic fashion the creoles were undergoing a process which heightened their individuality. It would not be long before that percipient observer Alexander von Humboldt noticed that the creoles were calling themselves Americans, not Spaniards. It was on the creoles that the subtle yet powerful forces of the Enlightenment were working most strongly. French books and periodicals, and some French teachers (especially after the expulsion of the Jesuits) came to Spanish America. Syllabuses at some of the universities were liberalized. Sons of wealthy creole families studied at French universities. Literary societies were formed; a new interest emerged in scientific investigation; periodicals and newspapers were founded. In short, the creoles experienced something of an intellectual awakening, and showed themselves receptive to new and challenging ideas. The works of the *philosophes* were widely read. Voltaire, Rousseau and Raynal were all available, despite official censorship. Ideas about rationalism and equality (standards against which Spanish colonial practice measured ill as far as the creoles were concerned) were given added point by the practical example of the American Revolution. The British colonists had won their way to freedom against an imperial power stronger than Spain. Moreover, the American Revolution was essentially a conservative revolution. It was not succeeded by anarchy or mob rule; and the government of Washington and Jefferson was respectable enough to allay the fears of wealthy creoles about their fate after a revolutionary war.

The reign of Charles III, then, saw a curious mixture of developments in Spanish America. On the one hand there was an advance in prosperity which was shown both in the increased revenue coming to the Crown, and in the growing wealth of the ambitious creoles. The older cities remained impressive, and on the expanding frontiers settlements had been founded or acquired which bore names soon to become known throughout the world – San Francisco, Los Angeles, Montevideo, New Orleans. The government in Madrid had shown a more intelligent application to the problems of American government than any Spanish administration for centuries. But the reforms suffered from a fundamental weakness. They represented only a beginning of the immense task of rethinking and reconstruction needed; yet they went far enough to rock the structure of the Spanish empire in America. Some of the privileges of the Church, a conservative influence, had been whittled away. The Jesuits, stern foes of the new principles of the Enlightenment, had been expelled. The power of the viceroys – for centuries the symbol of Spanish rule in America – had been reduced. Spanish Americans were being taught drill and martial discipline in the new colonial militia, and this had its dangers as well as its advantages. Traditional ideas and institutions were being attacked, and not only by the reforming government in Madrid. It remained to be seen whether the uncertain blending of old and new which Charles III had substituted for the system he inherited, would develop a strength sufficient to withstand the ferment of discontent and incipient patriotism which was becoming evident in the colonies.

Portugal and Brazil

Until well into the seventeenth century Portuguese settlement in Brazil was confined to the coastal areas, particularly those around the important harbours of Rio de Janeiro, Pernambuco and Bahía. Mountains, jungle and desert made venturing into the interior a risky business, and for long the slave-raiding expeditions of the Paulistas (wandering colonists from the São Paulo region) remained the most characteristic form of European activity inland. Gradually the lines of penetration lengthened and thickened as missionaries, prospectors and cattlemen pushed inland, and fanned out over the vast stretches of the interior. As they crossed the official line of demarcation laid down by the Treaty of Tordesillas in 1494 they came into contact and conflict with Spaniards in Paraguay and the Plata region. Even so, settlement was never on a large scale. The nomadic bands of Paulistas, the small mission stations and the scattered ranches of the pioneer stockmen could not make any appreciable impression on the backlands.

The discovery of gold at the end of the seventeenth century dramatically changed this picture of a slowly expanding economy based on sugar and tobacco. Gold was first found in the hilly country behind Rio de Janeiro and São Paulo. It was alluvial gold, which could be easily washed out of the streams or found in shallow diggings; and its discovery led to a gold rush of a kind which was to become familiar in Australia, California and the Yukon in the nineteenth century. For almost two centuries the Portuguese had dreamed of the day when gold would be discovered in Brazil. Now men left the coastal towns in their thousands for the diggings, officials and priests among them. The 'diggers' were of every colour, age and social status, and were soon joined by immigrants from Portugal. Hundreds died from hardship, disease and starvation. For years lynch rule was the only form of law, and at one stage general conflict broke out between the Paulistas and the newcomers. Although officially the Crown was entitled to one-fifth of all gold discovered, little found its way into the royal exchequer during the first hectic years. Gradually, as the initial excitement died down, the Crown began to exert its authority over this tumultuous area, the famous Minas Gerais ('General Mines'). As more and more fortune-hunters poured into the mining camps, some of the first prospectors moved on and discovered other deposits as far inland as the Mato Grosso. Others found diamonds in the northern Minas Gerais. As some of the original mining areas were worked out, attention shifted to the more constructive occupations of farming and stock-rearing.

Behind the rowdy scenes of gold-rush fever lay a substantial population movement from the coast to the interior. The coastal towns and plantations were depopulated in the rush to the interior, and although this loss was made good in time, the discovery of gold had a permanent effect on the economic and social development of Brazil. The older Brazil centred on the slave-worked sugar and tobacco plantations near Bahía was challenged by a freer, rougher society with a mining and pastoral basis in the São Paulo region. The slow and erratic westward movement of earlier days was given an energetic boost. The frontiers were extended, by stockmen as well as by prospectors, and clashes with the Spaniards in the basin of the Upper Amazon and in the Plata region became increasingly frequent. A treaty of 1750 temporarily settled these boundary disputes, but not until 1777, after further outbreaks of hostilities, was a permanent settlement reached in the Treaty of San Ildefonso. The frontiers of Brazil recognized by the treaty were roughly those we know today. The old Tordesillas line had been pushed westward thousands of miles to the eastern slopes of the Andes, and Portugal was in formal possession of a country, as yet mainly unexplored, which covered half the South American continent.

Although the sudden population movement brought a temporary economic crisis, the Crown's income from gold and diamonds steadily increased during the first half of the eighteenth century. Portugal's economy did not benefit from this influx as much as might have been expected. More than half was re-exported to northern Europe to pay for imported products, particularly from Britain, which through a series of commercial treaties had long held a privileged position in the Portuguese market. Enough remained in Portugal to make John V (1706–50) one of the richest monarchs in Europe, but he frittered away much of his wealth on elaborate buildings and on a court intended to rival Versailles in splendour. More worthwhile forms of investment were neglected: for example, Portugal's African and Asian settlements remained chronically short of money. In India the Marathas overran the Portuguese settlements north of Bombay; and in West Africa the Portuguese territories suffered from an over-concentration on the slave trade (to meet Brazil's insistent demand for cheap labour).

Brazil was the heart of Portugal's overseas empire. It was the only region to which there was voluntary emigration on any scale, and at the beginning of the eighteenth century Bahía was second only to Lisbon in size. With its gold and diamonds, sugar and tobacco, Brazil formed an essential complement to Portugal's unimpressive domestic economy. But despite Brazil's growing importance the control exercised by Portugal was looser than that of Spain over its American colonies. There was no administrative and legal machinery in Brazil strong enough to resist the demoralizing influences of corruption and self-seeking at home during the reign of John V. The expansion on the frontiers, and the resultant collisions with the Spaniards, occurred in spite of rather than because of the efforts of the home government. Not until the next reign was there any real attempt to tackle the problems which had developed during the first half of the century. José I (1750–77) was not an exceptional ruler, but he gave his formidable first minister, José Carvalho (usually known by his later title, the Marquis of Pombal) a free hand with affairs of state. Energetic and dictatorial, Pombal pursued a ruthless policy of centralization and reform which followed closely the Colbertian model of the previous century.

Conditions in Brazil were investigated by Pombal's brother, and swift action taken. Strenuous efforts were made to encourage agriculture, mining and commerce. Monopolistic trading companies were set up in an attempt to compete with the British traders working through Lisbon. Royal control was extended to meet the expansion of the frontiers. Captaincies were established in the new towns of the interior, and in 1763 Rio de Janeiro replaced Bahía as the viceregal capital. Better appointments and closer scrutiny improved the working of the administrative machinery; and more efficient collection of taxes increased the Crown's income. Pombal's motives were the same as those as Charles III of Spain: better government, tighter royal control and an increased revenue. But he never succeeded in overcoming the basic problems of government posed by the vast distances and the local feelings of Portugal's subcontinental possession across the Atlantic. A chain of decision-making which stretched from the Mato Grosso to Lisbon, where Pombal insisted on personal control of all details of government, resulted in impossibly long delays. In Brazil the Crown had neither the officials, soldiers nor administrative machinery to exercise a firm control over its subjects. The result was a splitting of authority between local rulers, official and unofficial – captains-general, landowners, militia captains, missionaries – each more or less absolute in his own domain.

Just as administration was less systematic than in Spanish America, so racial and social divisions were less rigid. The same racial groups made up the population: Europeans (both creole and peninsular Portuguese), Indians and Negroes – with the customary half-breed mixtures. But relations between and within the racial groups produced a different situation from that to be found in the Spanish colonies. Although the *peninsulares* monopolized most of the high administrative, ecclesiastical and military posts, this situation was not as bitterly resented by the creole plantation-owners and merchants as it was in Spanish America. Intermarriage and miscegenation were far more common than in the Spanish colonies; for since few Portuguese women emigrated to Brazil (and even fewer to Africa and India) Portuguese settlers tended to take native wives or concubines almost as a matter of course. This mingling helped to produce a more tolerant attitude among the Portuguese towards races of a different colour, but in his famous decree of 1761 (and in succeeding measures) Pombal attempted the impossible when he laid down that racial discrimination was to be abolished within the Portuguese empire. Merit, not colour, was to be the only distinction which the Crown recognized between its Christian subjects. This was a praiseworthy attitude which had some practical effect, but the measures usually remained paper decrees. Indeed they belonged to a field which legislation was almost powerless to influence. In the Portuguese empire there never had been the same obsessive concern with purity of blood that the Spaniards had displayed, but a light skin was an asset, and a dark skin was not; and this persisted long after Pombal and his decrees. Brazilian planters continued to regard the Amerindians as a reservoir of cheap labour, and resented Jesuit attempts to protect them. Slavery was abolished in Portugal, but remained unscathed in Brazil, where the Negro slave played a more essential part in the economy than in any of the Spanish American colonies. It is true that manumission was more common than in the slave colonies of other nations, but the freed slave was subject to severe discrimination. This was to be expected: no race can enslave another, as the Portuguese had the African Negro for centuries, without developing feelings of prejudice and superiority. In their general racial attitudes the Portuguese compared favourably with the other imperial nations of Europe, but the claim by modern Portuguese propagandists that Portugal's overseas empire has never known a colour bar or racial discrimination is without historical foundation.

The Church in Brazil was neither as wealthy nor as omnipresent as in Spanish America. The Inquisition had no foothold in Brazil, and the Church rarely intervened in politics. Only in missionary work was religious activity in Brazil able to match that in the Spanish colonies. This was dominated by the Jesuits, who also controlled elementary and secondary education (there were no universities in Brazil during the colonial period) and the hospitals. Their position in Brazil made all the more debatable one of Pombal's most controversial actions, his expulsion of the Jesuits from Portugal and the overseas territories in 1759. This decision arose in part out of a tragic situation which had developed a few years earlier. The boundary treaty of 1750 had laid down that Portugal was to surrender the colony of Sacramento on the north bank of the River Plate in return for Spanish territory in Paraguay. Included in the Paraguayan area to be handed over were seven Jesuit missions, each with thousands of Indians. By the terms of the treaty the Jesuits were ordered to evacuate the missions with their inhabitants; and no attention seems to have been paid to the human misery which would inevitably result from this piece of diplomatic boundary-making. When Spanish and Portuguese forces advanced to enforce the treaty terms the mission Indians rose in revolt, and it took the Portuguese three years of bloody and costly warfare to subjugate them. Pombal was convinced that the rising was inspired by the Jesuits, and worked for revenge. In 1759 he was able to use the alleged implication of the Jesuits in an attempt on the King's life the previous year as a pretext for expelling all members of the order from Portuguese territory. In Brazil the effect was little short of catastrophic. The sudden removal of the most devoted teachers and missionaries left gaps which were never filled. There was neither an educated laity, nor a conscientious secular clergy, to take the place of the Jesuits.

In general terms there could be little comparison between Brazil and the great Spanish viceroyalties in the second half of the eighteenth century. Brazil lacked the highly-organized official structure which gave the Spanish empire its coherence. The viceroy at Rio could never match his counterparts at Lima or Mexico City in wealth, pomp and power. Culturally backward, with no institutions of higher learning, no printing presses and few libraries, Brazil felt the influence of the Enlightenment only faintly. A few educated people discussed the latest ideas, and founded short-lived literary societies. There was even a conspiratorial movement of 1789–92, although objections to taxation as much as revolutionary intent seem to have been behind it. Yet Brazil was potentially a great and prosperous country, which Portugal was not. The modest size of Portugal's resources spelt danger to her future as an imperial power; as early as 1732 a member of Portugal's Overseas Council had warned the King that Brazil could not be ruled indefinitely by a country smaller and poorer than itself.

The Beginnings of Anti-Colonialism

While the great colonial empires of the post-1763 period were subjected to violent stresses arising from local discontent or foreign attack, in Europe the nature of imperial rule was being criticized in a way never previously known. Since the first establishment of European settlements overseas isolated voices had been raised querying both the morality and benefits of colonial expansion, but not until the second half of the eighteenth century did any weighty expression of opinion emerge which can be classed as anti-colonial. In Britain and France in particular, two schools of thought became increasingly influential, though as yet they represented the views of only a minority. One objected to colonization on humanitarian grounds, and concentrated its attention on slavery and the general exploitation of native peoples. The other condemned colonization as economically wasteful, and attacked the commercial aspects of the existing colonial systems.

In France the last decades of the *ancien régime* witnessed a close and critical scrutiny of established institutions, customs and policies. As far as the overseas empire was concerned, the disasters of the Seven Years War raised doubts about the colonial and commercial objectives which had cost France so dearly. Rationalist thinkers led a reaction against the traditional mercantilist view of empire. With their emphasis on ideas of equality and respect for human dignity the *philosophes* could hardly support forms of colonization which presupposed the superiority of one race over another; but they were often inconsistent on specific issues. Montesquieu attacked slavery in *De l'Esprit des lois*; yet he supported a colonial system, based on slavery, which gave France valuable tropical commodities. Voltaire welcomed the loss of Canada, but he was an enthusiastic advocate of Louisiana's potentialities, and regretted the territory's cession to Spain in 1763.

None of the *philosophes* was primarily concerned with questions of empire; their main interests lay nearer home. The most influential work of the period which dealt exclusively with the problems and morality of overseas expansion was Abbé Raynal's *Histoire philosophe et politique des établissements et du commerce des Européens dans les deux Indes*. It was first published in 1770, ran through three editions and thirty impressions in Raynal's lifetime, and was widely read in Europe and America. The *Histoire des deux Indes* was a great hotchpotch of a book, full of inaccuracies, contradictions and long-winded digressions; but it met and satisfied a considerable public demand. It was a mine of information about the overseas territories of the European powers in every part of the world, and always Raynal was ready to point the moral. He attacked the tyranny and injustice of European imperialism whether they accompanied the activities of the Spaniards in Peru, the British in Bengal, or the French in the West Indies. He was outspoken about the cruelties of the African slave trade. The American Revolution he considered (in the third edition of 1780) to show the way to the future separation of colonies from the mother country: 'c'est l'arrêt du destin.' In this edition Raynal criticized the commercial restrictions of the colonial systems of his day, and for the first time advocated freedom of trade. Raynal's importance did not derive from the novelty of his ideas, most of which had already been expressed in some form by other writers. It was his single-minded concentration on European overseas expansion, and the vehemence with which he denounced its evils, that led one outraged supporter of the existing order to refer to 'le fanatisme de l'abbé Raynal et ses maximes incendiaires'.

Opposition to the mercantilist systems was not entirely confined to academic circles. Turgot, one of the most powerful political figures of the 1770s, had always been sceptical about the value of colonies. As early as 1750 he had prophesied that settlement colonies, as they grew to maturity, would separate from the mother country as surely as ripe fruit fell from a tree. He advocated the application of free-trade principles to the overseas territories as well as to France's domestic economy, and was appalled by the vast sums spent on colonial defence. His economic theories had political implications as well: during his tenure of office as Controller-General he seems to have favoured a policy which in time would have led to certain colonies being treated as allies rather than subordinates.

The revolt of the American colonies was enthusiastically welcomed by many Frenchmen, and not only because of the blow it struck at Britain. America seemed to provide a working example of the sovereignty of the people. The *philosophes*' dream of creating a new form of government, unhindered by existing constitutions, conventions and prejudices appeared to have become reality. The old had been swept away, and admiration for the American way of life was shown in the emigration across the Atlantic of individual radicals and reformers from many European countries. It was during the American War of Independence that the powerful hold of the new nation across the Atlantic on the European imagination was born. America emerged as a land which held out opportunities of freedom and advancement to the oppressed and under-privileged of Europe, and its distant example was an undoubted factor in the surges of political discontent which swept across Europe after 1789.

In the period before the French Revolution there was, then, a considerable volume of dissatisfaction and scepticism about France's overseas empire; but the effect of this on government policy was slight. There were occasional signs of official response to humanitarian and free trade agitation. A gesture to growing anti-slavery sentiment (which was to result in the formation in Paris in 1788 of the *Société des Amis des Noirs*) was made in 1784 with the introduction of an ordinance decreeing better treatment for slaves in the French Leeward Islands. More effective was a decision to open five more ports in the French West Indies to foreign (in effect, American) traders; two had already been opened in 1767. This was an admission that France could not supply her own Caribbean colonies with goods to the exclusion of contraband traders. There was a general uneasiness about a colonial system based on slave labour, and this was reflected in a number of visionary schemes for a new French empire in Egypt; but no fundamental change of government attitude could be detected. It could not be expected that any nation would voluntarily relinquish its hold on colonies which had been gained and defended at the cost of blood and money. The revolt of Britain's American colonies produced some pessimism in other European countries about the future of their own colonies; but the French did not fail to note the rapidity with which the British were building another empire in India.

In Britain the dispute with the American colonies, and controversy over the rule of the East India Company in Bengal, had given rise to a rather more searching inquiry into the nation's rule overseas. Even before the American Revolution there had been some doubts about the Old Colonial System, reflected most persistently in the writings of Josiah Tucker, an Anglican clergyman of a thoughtful and original turn of mind. Dean Tucker was an irrepressible pamphleteer, perhaps more highly regarded in France (where Turgot translated two of his works) than in Britain. At times a lone figure, he bravely denounced the Britain of the Seven Years War as a nation 'frantic with military glory', and deplored the obsessive mercantilism which drew nations into war for the sake of overseas territory and commerce. He argued that colonies were a distraction to the pursuit of Britain's true economic interests. In Tucker's view they were held to the mother country only by self-interest, and as they became self-sufficient they would drift or break away. Years before the American Revolution he pointed out that the removal of the French danger from Canada weakened the links between the American colonies and Britain. To control effectively the trade of colonists as vigorous as those in British North America was difficult, if not impossible. Nor did Tucker think the effort was worth making. He was one of the first writers to argue that the possession of colonies brought few economic advantages. The American colonies, Tucker asserted, would find Britain their best market and cheapest supplier even after separation. For dubious economic advantages

Britain had put a millstone around its neck, since the colonies were difficult to govern and costly to defend.

Tucker was the forerunner of a whole school of anti-colonial writers in Britain, but his scattered writings did not have the same impact that Adam Smith's *Wealth of Nations* had after its publication in 1776. In the course of a work ranging over the whole field of state and private economic activity Smith launched a fierce attack on the restrictions and monopolies of the Old Colonial System. From this he went on to cast doubts upon the value of colonial trade in general. To Smith, over-dependence on colonial commerce had harmed Britain's foreign trade, swallowed up an excessive amount of capital, and made the British economy dangerously vulnerable to the threat of separatist movements in the colonies. Like Tucker, he argued that whatever economic benefits Britain derived from trade with her colonies would continue after those territories became independent.

In his treatise Smith also examined the economic value of slave-labour, for long unquestioned. Earlier in the century an economist had referred to Britain's overseas empire as 'a magnificent super-structure of American commerce and naval power on an African foundation'. Now Smith from one direction, and the devoted band of evangelicals known as the Clapham Sect from another, began to chip away at that foundation. While Smith condemned slavery for its in-efficiency, a growing body of opinion attacked the slave trade for its inhumanity. In 1787 the Society for Effecting the Abolition of the Slave Trade was founded, and an organized campaign got under way. There was no scarcity of harrowing material, and the horrors of the 'middle passage' with slaves packed in the heat and stench of the hold 'like rows of books on a shelf' became familiar reading to thousands of Englishmen. The abolitionist movement illustrated the growing awareness in Britain of the moral questions which had been too easily overlooked by the imperial powers of Europe in their drive for territory and wealth overseas. This concern was shown in another way in the mounting criticism of the East India Company's servants in Bengal, though the Indian debates of the period were influenced by political motives and personal rancour to a far greater extent than the campaign for the abolition of the slave trade.

The American War of Independence naturally led to a further examination of the point made by Tucker and Smith that the possession of colonies threw heavy political and financial burdens on the mother country. Several pamphleteers argued that Britain's colonies were a source of military weakness, political corruption and financial weakness. A few radical writers queried Britain's right to rule distant colonies of white settlers who were not represented in the imperial parliament, and advocated the transformation of the familiar mercantilist empire into a community of self-governing states (similar in some ways to the modern Commonwealth). Britain's increasing prosperity in the years after the American Revolution, and a marked expansion in Anglo-American trade, strengthened the views of those who maintained that settlement colonies were not an economic necessity to Britain.

As in France, these various expressions of radical, free trade and humanitarian opinion had little immediate effect on government policy. The industrial developments which were to make the regulations of the Old Colonial System an unnecessary nuisance under Huskisson and Peel were still in an early stage. Until free trade was accepted in Britain there was no question of the colonies being granted political independence, for to the mercantilist their economic and political subordination went hand-in-hand. Even a government as comparatively enlightened in economic matters as that of the Younger Pitt after 1784 could not be expected to turn an ideological somersault and adopt the view that Britain's prosperity had grown in spite of, rather than through, the Old Colonial System. Under Pitt a few hesitant steps were taken in the direction of freer trade. A commercial treaty with France was negotiated in 1786, and in the next year an Act was passed which increased the number of free ports in the British West Indies (though here the main motive was still the wish to attract trade from the nearby Spanish colonies). But there were limits to the degree of innovation that could be achieved: attempts to negotiate a treaty of commercial reciprocity with the United States failed, and a Navigation Act of 1786 followed the conventional pattern.

As far as the political shape of the empire was concerned, the government's attitude was typified by the Canada Act of 1791. This was an effort to deal with the problem of a colony which now contained two incompatible elements: the original French-speaking inhabitants, and the British loyalists who had flooded into Upper Canada from the United States during and after the American Revolution. The Act divided Canada into two separate provinces, and gave each a form of representative government described by Pitt as 'the very image and transcript of the British constitution'. The comparison was not a very exact one, but there could be no doubting the seriousness of the government's effort to find a constitution which would avoid a repetition of the American troubles and keep the general direction of the colony's movements firmly under imperial control. The American Revolution hastened the already existing tendency to favour an empire of trading and defensive posts of the kind developing in the East, rather than one of populous and unruly settlement colonies on the American model. But there was not the slightest chance that the government might voluntarily relinquish any of the colonies it possessed: past history, national prestige and public opinion made this impossible. The anti-imperialists, free traders and radicals of the late eighteenth century remained a small, if articulate, minority, and the outbreak of war with Revolutionary France in 1793 almost stifled its voice.

War and Revolution Overseas 1789–1815

Upheaval in the Caribbean

THE OUTBREAK of revolution in France in 1789 could not be confined to the mother country, for the demand for liberty which it awakened was a universal one. 'Men are born and remain free and equal in rights' ran the first sentence of the Rights of Man, and this was a sentiment which accorded ill with the slave-based societies of the French colonial empire in the Caribbean. The foundation in Paris in 1788 of the *Société des Amis des Noirs* had been a warning sign that the planters' position would not remain unchallenged indefinitely; now there was a growing possibility that the revolutionary feelings coming to the surface in France would spread to the Negro slave and mulatto populations of the West Indies.

Particularly vulnerable was the great sugar colony of Saint Domingue, with its privileged planter class, restless free coloureds and huge slave population. In French possession since 1697, this western part of Hispaniola had been for half a century the wealthiest colony of its size in the world. No other Caribbean island could match its production of sugar, coffee, cotton and indigo. Fine roads, an extensive irrigation system, and plantations each employing a thousand or more slaves stretched across the fertile plain east of the capital at Port-au-Prince. Many of the French planters spent their time and money in Paris, where their ostentatious way of life gave rise to the catch-phrase 'as rich as a creole'. Contemporaries estimated that 700 ocean-going vessels visited the colony each year, and that almost two-thirds of France's colonial trade was centred there. The Spanish part of the island (Santo Domingo) was by contrast poor and undeveloped.

On the island itself the small white population of about 35,000 by no means formed a united class. A wide gulf existed between the wealthy planters, the *grands blancs*, living extravagantly if not elegantly, and the small property-owners and traders, the *petits blancs*. Set apart from both were the free coloureds, the *gens de couleur*, many of whom by now owned land and slaves. Despite their wealth they were subjected to humiliating restrictions, which tended to become progressively more severe as their economic importance increased. The clause in the original *Code Noir* of 1685 which stated that when a slave was set free he and his descendants were to have full rights of French citizenship had long been a dead letter, and when in 1787 Saint Domingue was granted its own representative Assembly the free coloureds were debarred from all participation. The growing resentment of this ambitious class of 30,000 mulattoes was the more dangerous because at the bottom of the social and economic scale lay a slave population of half a million. Nowhere were the provisions of the *Code Noir* regarding the treatment of slaves more flagrantly violated than in Saint Domingue, where planters apparently inflicted torture, mutilation and death on their slaves without hindrance. The evidence for some of the atrocity stories is thin, but enough exists to show that the planters of the island were more repressive and in some instances cruelly sadistic than anywhere else in the Caribbean. Events were soon to show that in the decades before 1789 a terrible, smouldering hatred of the whites had been built up among the inarticulate Negro slave population of Saint Domingue.

News of the revolutionary developments in France quickly had its effect on the island. The white planters saw in the confusion in France an opportunity to strengthen even further their dominant position; the free coloureds, on the other hand, hoped that the political rights being demanded by the middle classes in France would be extended to them. That the slaves might also have hopes of freedom and revenge seems not to have occurred to either the whites or the mulattoes, both intent on their own objectives. As soon as it was known that the States-General was to meet in Paris in the summer of 1789 the planters of Saint Domingue, Martinique and Guadeloupe pressed through their Assemblies for the right to be represented there. They were supported in this by a pressure-group of West Indian planters living in Paris, the *Comité Colonial*. After some discussion it was decided that ten representatives from the colonies should be admitted as deputies, six of them from Saint Domingue. In the National Assembly these colonial deputies (the first ever to appear in the central legislative assembly of a European power) soon drew the fire of the *Amis des Noirs* and other radical elements.

At first the Assembly took no action. It had problems enough inside France, and the commercial importance of the sugar islands counselled moderation in dealing with the planters. But slowly feeling rose against the planters, who in the midst of the ferment in France were clearly interested only in asserting their own privileged position. In 1790 the Assembly in Saint Domingue declared that its only link with France was the King, and that laws passed in France had no effect in Saint Domingue unless specifically approved by itself. The free coloureds were becoming increasingly impatient at the apparent lack of interest in Paris, and at one stage sent representatives to France to offer the government one-fifth of their wealth if they could be freed from discriminatory legislation on the island. The planters were unmoved by these claims, and met agitation by repression. The brutal execution on the wheel of a young mulatto leader, Vincent Ogé, brought matters to a head. In France Ogé was regarded as a martyr for the cause of freedom. The principles of the Revolution, it was widely felt, were being betrayed in the French West Indies, and in a vehement speech Robespierre (a founder-member of the *Amis des Noirs*) attacked the planter interests. In one striking sentence he declared: 'Perish the colonies if they must cost you your happiness, your glory and your liberty.' In the spring of 1791 the National Assembly at last nerved itself to a decision, and declared that all coloureds born of free parents were to have full political rights in the French colonies. The concession was a limited one. Since many free coloureds had been born of slave mothers, only a comparatively small number would have been enfranchised at this time. A way was opened for a compromise settlement between the whites and the free coloureds (and was actually adopted in Mauritius and Réunion), but the Saint Domingue planters continued their suicidal course. Far from accepting the decision of the National Assembly, they made inflammatory speeches pressing for secession from France.

Before words could become action the whole situation was transformed: in August 1791 a slave uprising burst on the northern province of Saint Domingue and soon spread to other parts of the colony. All the fears harboured by generations of West Indian planters – French, Spanish and British – became dreadful reality. Planters, their families and their overseers were massacred, and plantations put to the torch. The whites retaliated in kind, and on both sides the fighting went on with appalling savagery in which tens of thousands lost their lives and a whole land was laid waste. The bitter feelings between whites and mulattoes prevented any alliance of the landowning classes against the slaves, and in the western part of the colony whites and mulattoes were soon fighting each other. Even the whites were not solidly united: most were royalists, but some were revolutionaries. Nor did the arrival of an army from France in 1792 restore order, for the troops were split by the same political divisions that afflicted the homeland. The news of Louis XVI's execution in February 1793 led to the army's disintegration, and many officers deserted to join the Spaniards in the eastern part of the island. War with Britain made invasion of the colony an imminent possibility, and in France the revolutionary government decided that its only policy was to make common cause with the slaves, and accordingly it sent civil commissioners to the island with a proclamation of emancipation.

The war between France and Britain added a new dimension to the troubled Caribbean scene. As early as September 1791 the British prime minister, William Pitt, had received a request from the Saint Domingue planters to be taken under British protection. Pitt followed his policy of strict neutrality in the affairs of France and refused to take action, tempting though the prize must have been. Once war broke out with France in February 1793, however, Pitt showed himself to be an enthusiastic advocate of his father's strategy in the Seven Years War of striking at France's colonial empire. The coalition revolutionary France had raised against itself in Europe appeared – on paper – to be so strong that there seemed no good reason why the British government should not concentrate overseas. The French Caribbean islands were expected to be both more valuable and easier to take than they had been during the Seven Years War. In April 1793 British forces already stationed in the Caribbean captured Tobago (though they were repulsed from Martinique), and in September troops from Jamaica arrived in Saint Domingue, to be warmly greeted by the French planters. At the end of the year a strong expedition sailed from Britain for the Caribbean, and in 1794 seized Martinique, Guadeloupe and Saint Lucia. In the same year reinforcements reached Saint Domingue to complete the occupation of the French part of the island, while in European waters the French navy, weakened by political purges, lost a fleet in battle with Howe on 'The Glorious First of June' and was powerless to intervene.

It seemed only a matter of time before the whole of the French West Indian empire would be in British hands, but after 1794 British fortunes fell away sadly. In the first place, the crumbling of the French colonial empire had little effect on the determination of the French republicans in Europe to continue fighting. As France took the offensive and marched to the Rhine, more and more British troops were drawn into the continental fighting. In 1795 Prussia, Holland and Spain all made peace with France, and Britain entered a dark period when at times she alone seemed to be fighting France. In the Caribbean, meanwhile, the British were learning that warfare in a revolutionary era was very different from conventional hostilities on the old pattern. French Jacobin forces under Victor Hugues re-took Guadeloupe, and incited slave uprisings against the British occupation forces in the other conquered islands. In Jamaica the 'maroons' (descendants of fugitive slaves living in the mountains) also rose in revolt in 1795, and in Saint Domingue the British troops which poured into the island died almost as quickly as they arrived. The British campaigns in the Caribbean were accompanied by a ghastly casualty rate: 40,000 dead within three years from wounds or yellow fever (mainly the latter). The lessons of the Caribbean fighting of earlier wars had been forgotten. Uniforms, drill and equipment were the same as in Europe; medical treatment and hospital facilities were lamentable; and by 1797 losses were so high that Negro regiments were raised.

In Saint Domingue a terrible and bloody confusion reigned. Spaniards, British, French royalists, French Jacobins, mulattoes and Negroes were all engaged in fighting, burning and looting. The cardinal factor in these years was the rise to power of the Negro leader Toussaint l'Ouverture, who slowly and painfully brought order to the anarchic scene. Toussaint, a slave for almost fifty years, was a magnificent leader of men. Short and unimpressive in physical appearance, he possessed qualities of moderation, statesmanship and intellect which won him the respect even of his enemies. He was the first and one of the greatest of Negro nationalist leaders. After the first excesses of the slave revolt Toussaint had built up a disciplined force of ex-slaves who first fought for Spain and then for the French Jacobin army in the island. In 1795, when France and Spain signed a peace treaty, Toussaint's dominance was such that the French government recognized realities and appointed him Lieutenant-Governor of the island (under the nominal authority of a French Governor-General). Toussaint now turned on the remaining planters and their British allies. By 1798, helped by American supplies and by the ravages of yellow fever, he had beaten the British to their knees. The British commander made the best of a bad job by negotiating a secret commercial treaty with the Negro leader, and then withdrew the remnants of his forces. The most costly and demoralizing colonial campaign Britain had ever fought had ended.

Saint Domingue was now a colony of France in name only. Toussaint treated the various representatives sent to him by the French government with courtesy, but brooked no interference from them. The Directory in France was increasingly uneasy about the formidable Negro general who treated it in this cavalier fashion and even negotiated trade agreements with France's bitterest enemy; but it kept up a pretence of formal rule by appointing Toussaint Governor-General in 1799. By 1801 Toussaint was undisputed master of the whole island. The mulattoes had been finally subdued in one last awful massacre (for which Toussaint's responsibility is uncertain), and the Spanish part of the island had been overrun by his forces. Toussaint was now able to concentrate on the colossal task of restoring harmony and prosperity to his shattered land. A promising start was made. A campaign of mass re-education was undertaken to persuade the ex-slaves that, though free, they must still put in a hard day's work on the restored plantations. A decree issued by Toussaint in October 1800 illustrates the kind of semi-military discipline which he was trying to induce his people to accept: 'Managers, foremen and cultivators must conduct themselves as if they were officers, non-commissioned officers and soldiers, and attend to their duties exactly as if they were members of the armed forces.'

In the towns new buildings emerged from the ruins. Trade revived as American and British merchantmen flocked to the island. Some of the French planters returned, encouraged by Toussaint's insistence on the necessity of European help and by his efforts to promote racial harmony. Toussaint himself was prone to displays of vanity and arrogance which had not been noticeable in the early years of tribulation; but at the same time he was proving himself to be a leader who could rule with wisdom and moderation. The long period of bloodshed and suffering had clearly not warped the judgement nor embittered the outlook of this remarkable man. It is one of the tragedies of the history of this disturbed island that the work of reconstruction begun in so resolute a fashion was about to be ruined by the intervention of Napoleon Bonaparte, a dictator at once more ruthless and more powerful than Toussaint l'Ouverture.

Napoleon's Colonial Ambitions

As events in the Caribbean followed their terrible course, so opinion in France turned towards the possibility of establishing a new and less turbulent colonial empire nearer at hand. French traders had long been active in the Levant, particularly in Syria, and interest in Egypt as a sphere of French influence and perhaps occupation had been evident at least as early as Choiseul's ministry. By the 1780s a number of Frenchmen were stressing the potentialities of the country, nominally still a province of the Ottoman empire. In books, articles and reports these enthusiasts sketched a splendid prospect. The Nile valley, it was pointed out, was a wonderfully fertile region which could grow sugar, cotton and in fact most of the tropical products supplied by France's existing colonies. It lay across the most direct route to India, and the construction of a canal between the Mediterranean and Suez would make the area one of the key strategic points in the world. Its occupation would encourage French commercial penetration of the interior of Africa. Its proximity to France would make it easier to defend than the distant Caribbean colonies. Finally, the oppressive rule of the Mameluke Beys, under the shadowy authority of a Turkish pasha, made European intervention a civilizing necessity.

The arguments were persuasive, designed to appeal to imperialists and humanitarians alike; but the French government of the period, troubled by financial difficulties, and nervous about possible British reactions, was in no mood to launch ambitious schemes of conquest and colonization. War with Britain in 1793, and the disintegration of France's colonial empire in the Caribbean, brought a change of outlook in governing circles. French successes on the continent were not matched overseas, where Britain's naval power gave her almost complete dominance. In this situation, French interest in Egypt revived. The case for colonial expansion was most lucidly stated by Talleyrand in his 'Essai sur les avantages à rétirer de colonies nouvelles dans les circonstances présentes', read before the Institut de France in July 1797:

Everything presses for a consideration of the matter of new colonies; the example of the wisest peoples who have found them of great value in promoting tranquillity; the need of preparing to replace our present colonies in order not to fall behind the times; the expediency of placing the cultivation of our colonial products nearer their natural consumers; the necessity of forming with the colonies more natural relations, easier no doubt in new establishments than in the old; the advantage of not allowing ourselves to be preceded by a rival nation for which every one of our oversights, every one of our delays in this field, is a conquest; the opinion of enlightened men who have directed their attention and their researches to this matter; finally, the pleasure of attaching to these enterprises restless men who need projects and unfortunate men who need hope.

'Restless men who need projects': there was one such in the Mediterranean at the time Talleyrand was presenting his essay. The years 1796 and 1797 saw the astounding triumphs in Italy of the young general Napoleon Bonaparte. In the summer of 1797 the French government, in which Talleyrand had just become Foreign Minister, summoned Bonaparte back from Italy to command the expeditionary force preparing for the invasion of England. An inspection of the resources available convinced Bonaparte of the impracticability of this plan, and an invasion of Egypt became a tempting alternative. Bonaparte summed up his immediate concern in the words, 'If I remain doing nothing for long I am lost.' The conquest of Egypt, and then perhaps an advance on India, held out promise of being an exploit sufficiently spectacular to set Bonaparte high above France's other successful generals. Discussions between Bonaparte, Talleyrand and other French ministers naturally stressed the strategic and commercial motives rather than the philanthropic; to a nation envious of Britain's expansion in the East there was a strong appeal about occupying a territory so conveniently situated between Europe, Asia and Africa.

In the summer of 1798 the great venture got under way. Bonaparte sailed from Toulon with a mighty force which by the time it reached its destination was to number 55,000 men (including sailors) and almost four hundred vessels. Also on board was a remarkable array of civilian scientists, technicians, orientalists and artists which leaves little doubt about the French government's intention to make a permanent occupation of Egypt. Only an outsize measure of luck saved the armada from interception and destruction by Nelson, but Bonaparte landed safely near Alexandria at the beginning of July. Alexandria was quickly taken, the fearsome-looking Mameluke army was smashed at the Battle of the Pyramids (21 July 1798), and Cairo was captured. Bonaparte had begun the Egyptian campaign in his customary style, but the initial triumphs were soon to fade. Nelson found the French fleet at anchor east of Alexandria in Abukir Bay, and in a bloody engagement (the Battle of the Nile), which began when the British van in a daring manœuvre crossed the head of the French line and then sailed between it and the shore, all but two of the French ships were sunk, captured or driven aground. Britain once more commanded the Mediterranean and Bonaparte was trapped in Egypt.

There he was finding that the conquest of the country involved more than the seizure of Alexandria and Cairo. To the south the survivors of the Mameluke army were a constant menace under the command of Murad Bey, and after an exhausting nine-month chase General Desaix gave up the task of trying to catch them. In the zone of French occupation in Lower Egypt the peasants treated Bonaparte's efforts at reorganization with an almost total lack of interest. His policy of appointing Moslem notables as local rulers and his ostentatious respect for Islam met with little response; to most he remained an infidel conqueror. The French troops, if not afflicted with dysentery and trachoma (the latter disease blinded thousands of the army), suffered from boredom and homesickness. Bonaparte himself remained comparatively unaffected, and entered into the task of directing his civilian experts with the same zest as he showed for a military campaign. The Institut d'Egypte was created in which French scholars, artists and scientists worked together in close co-operation. Its tasks ranged from the technical to the purely academic, but the underlying aim of all its work was the supplying of the information necessary if Egypt was to be turned into a French colony. While artists discovered amid the sordid poverty of the villages of Upper Egypt the glories and splendour of ancient empires, engineers surveyed the Suez isthmus to determine the practicability of a canal. No previous European colonizing venture had been accompanied by so serious an effort to discover the history and natural resources of an overseas land; and the great 24-volume collection of descriptive material and plates, the *Description de l'Egypte*, which was published many years after the French evacuation, stands as a fitting memorial to the devotion of Bonaparte's civilian companions.

R

But to Bonaparte the Egyptian venture was losing its glitter. His advance into Syria in 1799 was halted at Acre, and Bonaparte retreated to Egypt with more than a third of his plague-stricken army casualties. In his absence rebellion had broken out, and Murad Bey was still at large. Off the coast the British blockade prevented any possibility of reinforcement. Hopes which Bonaparte might have entertained of following in the footsteps of Alexander the Great and marching on India had vanished. Gruelling campaigns against rebellious peasants and guerrillas had no attractions for Bonaparte, and in August 1799 he slipped through the British blockade in a fast frigate and returned to France (without informing his most senior officers). A month after his arrival he was First Consul of France; the Egyptian campaign had served one of its purposes at least.

Bonaparte's furtive departure had a depressing effect on the morale of the army left behind. The Egyptian enterprise was now only a sideshow, and the general left in command, Kléber, had never been enthusiastic about the colonizing aspects of the expedition. The military situation, as he saw it, made evacuation the only realistic policy. A treaty to this effect was negotiated with the Turks, but was disallowed by the British government, and in June 1800 Kléber's assassination changed the outlook once more. His successor, General Menon, was a fervent advocate of permanent French occupation, and he still clung to the ambitious hopes of 1797 and 1798. Egypt was to replace the Caribbean colonies as the main producer of tropical and subtropical commodities, perhaps with the help of settlers from stricken Saint Domingue. Gold and ivory from the interior of Africa, and the opening of trade with India, would further help to make Egypt 'the first colony in the world'.

In France Bonaparte showed a flicker of interest in his forsaken army. Tsar Paul of Russia had changed sides to become France's ally, and agreed to march south on India. Bonaparte arranged for reinforcements to be sent to Egypt to make the threat a double-pronged one, though it is difficult to see how his troops could have reached India. In the event, British command of the sea prevented them from even crossing the Mediterranean, and the whole airy scheme collapsed when the Tsar was assassinated in March 1801. The only fresh troops to arrive in Egypt were British ones, for in the same month an expeditionary force under Sir Ralph Abercromby landed at Abukir Bay. Within six months Menon had been forced to surrender to superior Anglo-Turkish forces. As a massive attempt at permanent conquest Bonaparte's Egyptian enterprise was a complete failure. Although a new European interest in Egypt had been aroused, the most lasting effect of the invasion was on Egypt itself. After a brief British occupation civil war broke out during which the power of the Mamelukes, seriously weakened during the French campaigns, was finally smashed by Mehemet Ali. With him the history of modern Egypt begins.

Bonaparte's colonial ambitions did not die with his failure in Egypt. They merely turned in another direction, and soon after his appointment as First Consul he began planning to re-establish a modified version of the old Bourbon empire in North America. Some of the aims of the new policy were revealed in October 1800 when by the second Treaty of San Ildefonso Spain ceded Louisiana to France. A year later the preliminaries of the Treaty of Amiens were signed to bring peace between France and Britain, and Bonaparte was free to put his new colonial policy into operation.

The Treaty of Amiens restored to France all her colonial possessions (the British government, though not its political opponents or the nation's merchants, had been content with acquiring Trinidad from Spain and Ceylon from the Dutch); and the importance of Louisiana now became clearer. This huge mainland colony, stretching from the Mississippi towards the eastern slopes of the Rockies, would provide the French sugar islands with the timber, meat, flour and other necessities which the United States normally supplied. A self-supporting and productive colonial empire would be consolidated, particularly if Spain agreed to cede Florida, with its harbours at Pensacola and Mobile, in addition to Louisiana. But as yet the projected empire was without its most valuable single territory: Saint Domingue was virtually independent under Toussaint l'Ouverture. This, the richest of all the sugar islands, was essential to Bonaparte's plan. Without it, the acquisition and development of Louisiana would lose most of its point. It was no coincidence that three weeks after the preliminaries of the Amiens settlement freed Bonaparte's hands in Europe, the First Consul appointed his brother-in-law, General Leclerc, commander of an expeditionary force of 20,000 men which was to sail to Saint Domingue. Toussaint l'Ouverture, who had appointed himself ruler for life in July 1801, was to be eliminated: in Bonaparte's colonial empire there was not room for two dictators. Fighting broke out soon after Leclerc reached Saint Domingue, and in a brilliant, if costly, campaign the French gradually established their ascendancy. Some of Toussaint's most important generals deserted him, and he was taken by trickery and sent to France. There he died in a prison in the Jura Mountains in 1803 from ill-health, cold and neglect.

In Saint Domingue, meanwhile, the French had not reaped much benefit from their treachery. Negro resistance suddenly stiffened when news reached the island that Bonaparte's forces had reintroduced slavery in Guadeloupe. That this was to be Saint Domingue's fate there could now be no doubt. At the same time that the fighting flared up again Leclerc's army was stricken by yellow fever. French soldiers died in their hundreds and thousands from this most terrible of tropical diseases, including Leclerc himself. His successor, Rochambeau, soon lost control of the situation, and in November 1803 was glad to surrender with the tattered remnants of his forces to a British squadron standing off the island. After the French evacuation the island was ruled by one of Toussaint's former generals, Dessalines, who exterminated the remaining whites. After his death in 1806 Haiti (as the island was now called) was partitioned between Pétion, a mulatto, and Christophe, a Negro. The island had won its independence from European control, but its inhabitants were to experience little prosperity, freedom or happiness.

The catastrophe in Saint Domingue had a profound effect on Bonaparte's colonial schemes. In the winter of 1802–3 a French expedition destined for Louisiana lay ice-bound in a Dutch port, and by the time spring came the news from Saint Domingue caused the French government to examine afresh the question of Louisiana. By now it was clear to Bonaparte that a French occupation of Louisiana would strain relations with the United States to breaking point. From the first news of the cession the Americans had viewed with concern the prospect of the Mississippi valley being occupied by the forces of Napoleonic France. Under a treaty arrangement with Spain American traders were allowed to sail down the Mississippi to New Orleans, and deposit their produce there for reshipment. New Orleans became the exit for the trade of the vast inland area drained by the Mississippi and Ohio rivers, and more American than Spanish vessels used the Mississippi. In 1802 the Spanish Intendant of Louisiana cancelled the American right of deposit at New Orleans, and French influence was inevitably (though erroneously) suspected. The American government moved closer to the British, and in Paris its representatives made tentative approaches to discover whether France might be willing to cede New Orleans to the United States.

Other difficulties were also emerging. Spain refused to cede Florida, and so deprived the French of the only good harbours on the Gulf coast. Most ominous of all, relations with Britain were deteriorating, and the whole of French experience in the eighteenth century warned of the danger of trying to fight a war with Britain on two fronts. There was little hope that a French colonial empire in America and the Caribbean could be held in the face of superior British naval power. The reports of French disasters in Saint Domingue decided the issue. Louisiana would be an embarrassment rather than an asset, and accordingly must be given up. In an effort to win American goodwill Bonaparte decided to cede the territory to the United States rather than return it to Spain. The transaction was pushed through with remarkable rapidity. In a matter of weeks Louisiana was sold to the United States for three million dollars (about four cents an acre, it has been calculated). The Louisiana Purchase was one of the great bargains of history. The way across the continent was opened to the Americans, and the cession of 1803 was to help make the United States into a great power.

From one point of view the cession was well-timed. The main negotiations were completed by the end of April 1803; the next month Britain and France were at war once more. Bonaparte's colonial ambitions had played their part in the worsening relations between the two powers, although Malta and Holland were the most contentious issues. Brought to a temporary halt in Europe, Bonaparte was directing his aggressive instincts overseas – or so it had seemed to the British – and not only to Saint Domingue and Louisiana. In 1800 a French expedition commanded by Nicolas Baudin sailed for the south Pacific, and although its main objectives were scientific the British government was bound to be uneasy about French activity along the Australian coastline. The political implications of this kind of scientific exploration were illustrated in 1807, when the narrative of Baudin's voyage gave French names to many features along the Australian coast, and named the whole region from the Great Australian Bight to Bass Strait *Terre Napoléon*. A more direct threat to British interests was Bonaparte's dispatch of General Decaen in March 1803 to take repossession of the French posts in India. This had been agreed in the Treaty of Amiens, but Decaen's notorious Anglophobia, and the extraordinary number of general officers he carried with him, seemed to indicate an attempt at a French military revival in India.

Bonaparte was no more successful in his overseas ventures than the general run of his Bourbon predecessors, and for much the same reasons. As long as his main ambitions lay within Europe he could not hope to match the British overseas. Britain's local defence forces (especially in India), and the amount of help that could be expected from the mother country, were infinitely greater than anything France could muster. Without control of the seas, Bonaparte could not possibly win mastery in the colonial sphere. The desire to beat Britain at its own game seems always to have been present in Bonaparte's thinking. In 1804–5 a characteristically ambitious plan was laid down by which the fleets of France and Spain would attack, or pretend to attack, in the Caribbean and eastern waters, while at Boulogne the invasion flotilla lay poised to strike at England. This triple threat was intended to confront Britain with a terrible dilemma about where to deploy its forces; but it was the Franco-Spanish fleet which proved unequal to its task. On 21 October 1805 Bonaparte publicly stated: 'I want peace on the continent. What I long for is ships, colonies and commerce.' That same day the Battle of Trafalgar was settling the command of the sea for the rest of the war. Nelson's victory did more than save England from invasion and give her control of the Mediterranean; it brought security for Britain's overseas possessions and trade, and allowed British seaborne forces to pick off the French colonies at leisure.

Further British Expansion in India

In India the period of the Revolutionary and Napoleonic Wars saw a decisive advance by the British after a decade of quiet consolidation and reform under Cornwallis. Although alarm at possible French intervention played its part in this renewed forward movement by the British, the major underlying cause was the condition of India itself. The French threat brought a new urgency to the situation, but sooner or later the dangerous disorder of much of India would have drawn the British into a policy of expansion and annexation if they wished to exercise any control over events.

On Hastings's retirement the directors of the East India Company had called a halt to the process of territorial expansion, but Cornwallis's war with Tipu Sultan, ruler of Mysore, in 1790–2 provided an indication of things to come. Other pointers could be found amid the political turmoil of the great subcontinent. There was still an Emperor at Delhi, but he had lost all power. In Mysore Tipu, deprived of half his lands, remained bitterly anti-British. North of Mysore lay the territories of the powerful Nizam of the Deccan, who employed French officers in his army. Almost surrounding his territory were the lands of the Maratha confederacy. These were divided between several rulers who were sometimes united, often not. They were military men who had won power through the sword, and had for long regarded the rising British power with distrust. The Company directors in London hoped that the turbulent and ambitious rulers of India would follow the lead being given and learn to live in peace. The hope was an empty one. The East India Company might be a satiated power for the moment; the same could not be said of the Indian princes in general. Britain was now one of the great powers of India, and when challenged had either to strike back or abdicate its position.

Following the outbreak of war in Europe in 1793, the French settlements in India quickly suffered their routine fate, and were overrun by the British. It was not there that danger to the British position lay, but in the numerous French adventurers serving Indian princes as military commanders and advisers. The British probably exaggerated the threat these men presented. Almost all put their private fortunes before the national interests of France, and their political objectives were ill-defined. There was little likelihood that the armies they commanded would move against the disciplined and powerful forces of the East India Company unless regular French forces took the field in India; and this was at best a distant possibility. The French government was preoccupied with the European situation, and even if it had troops to spare it would hardly risk them on the long sea-passage once the British had seized the Cape of Good Hope and Trincomalee (in 1795).

The danger came from a different, unexpected quarter. As we have seen, in 1798 Bonaparte led an expedition to Egypt, and was – theoretically at least – in a position to send troops to India either by overland route or through the Red Sea. It is doubtful how far this alarming possibility represented a real threat. Bonaparte sometimes day-dreamed of following the path of Alexander the Great, and in exile at Saint Helena he claimed that he had considered a march on India from Egypt, and would have arrived at his destination in 1800. Either Bonaparte's memory or his veracity was at fault. It seems unlikely that even after Nelson's victory at the Nile had left the French expeditionary force stranded in Egypt Bonaparte would have moved so far away from the centre of politics and war in Europe. An attack on India was a long-term project, fraught with difficulty, and would need careful preparation. Even use of the easier Red Sea route would involve serious negotiations with Tipu and other potential allies in India, as well as instructions to the French at Mauritius and Réunion to send all available vessels to Suez; but there is no evidence that any of these steps were taken.

However, the British were not to know this, and when a new Governor-General, Marquis Wellesley (Lord Mornington until December 1799), reached India in 1798 the situation appeared grave. To the south the French held possible invasion bases in the islands of Mauritius and Réunion. Within India the French advisers at various princely courts posed a worrying problem. Tipu – 'the Tiger of Mysore' – was an acknowledged enemy. And now the greatest soldier in Europe had reached Egypt, perhaps on his way to the East. It was at this juncture that reports reached Wellesley of negotiations between Tipu and the French at Mauritius. There was little substance in the negotiations; for the French on Mauritius were in no position to send effective assistance to India, and less than a hundred volunteers left to help Tipu. They were enough to seal Tipu's fate, for Wellesley decided to take action. Tipu, hoping to the last for effective French help, refused peremptory British demands to expel all French subjects from Mysore. Wellesley wrote joyfully, 'I have had the satisfaction of drawing the beast of the jungle into the toils.' In 1799 Tipu's territories were invaded by two British armies, and he was killed in battle. Part of Mysore was annexed by the British, and the rest was put under the rule of the Hindu princely family which Tipu's father Haidar Ali had dispossessed years before.

Farther north the Nizam of the Deccan accepted the British ultimatum, and agreed to a treaty under which he disbanded his forces, expelled the French, and relied on Company forces for the safety of his domains. The same firm policy was pursued by Wellesley in other parts of India. An excuse to take over the government of the Carnatic, long notorious for its oppressive rule, was found when the

Nawab engaged in allegedly treacherous negotiations with Tipu Sultan. In nearby Tanjore the ruler was left with the trappings of authority but real power passed into British hands. The important buffer-state of Oudh, north-west of Bengal, presented a more delicate problem. Its ruler was guilty of deplorable misrule, but remained unquestioningly loyal to the British cause. Here Wellesley showed himself at his most merciless. The Nawab was confronted with intolerable demands, and when he raised objections his state was stripped of its frontier areas, and he was brought under close British tutelage. The Governor-General's actions were of dubious legal and moral validity, but he showed himself utterly ruthless in driving forward to his objective. His reasons can be summed up in his own words, to be echoed by future generations of empire-builders: 'No greater blessing can be conferred on the native inhabitants of India than the extension of the British authority, influence and power.'

The methods used by Wellesley varied. Some territory was conquered in war, as in Mysore. Elsewhere – in the Carnatic, for example – the effective government of a state was taken over by the British, but the nominal ruler was allowed to retain his title, and granted a fixed revenue. Then, Wellesley made extensive use of the 'subsidiary alliance' system. In its most common form this provided for the stationing in an Indian state of British forces, which were paid for by the native ruler. It strengthened the Company's military position at no additional expense, and without formally increasing the area of British territory. In the long term it usually led to complete British domination of the area concerned. But whatever the method of control used by Wellesley, the same two considerations remained uppermost: the urgent need to exercise more direct influence over territories threatened by the French or the Marathas, and despair at misgovernment by native administrations whose power had been increased by British alliance and protection. Spurred on by these motives, Wellesley took in three years the most important steps forward by British power in India since Clive's day.

Meanwhile the French threat had practically disappeared with Bonaparte's failure in Syria, his return to France, and the defeat of his forces left in Egypt by Abercromby. The main significance of Bonaparte's Egyptian campaign as far as the British position in the East was concerned was negative. British attention was distracted away from the vulnerable islands of Mauritius, Java and Manila, which otherwise might easily have been taken in the late 'nineties when British sea-power in eastern waters was practically unchallenged. But opportunities missed in one direction were compensated for by Wellesley's advances on the Asian mainland, and by a more energetic policy along the approaches to India. Soon after Bonaparte's arrival in Egypt Indian troops established themselves at Aden to give the British control of the Red Sea. A Resident of the East India Company was sent to Bagdad, and another to Muscat. Unwittingly the French, from the time of Dupleix to Bonaparte, had played a large part in stimulating British expansion in the East. They presented the appearance, if not the reality, of danger; and the British reacted by strengthening and extending their position.

The real test of British power in India was yet to come. Across central India lay the great Maratha confederacy – a loose coalition of the strongest native military powers in India, predatory and dangerous. Maratha power stretched south to the Deccan, east to Orissa, and in the north held Delhi and the person of the Moghul Emperor in its grip. At the best of times the coalition (nominally led by the Peishwa of Poona) was an uneasy one, and between 1800 and 1802 a murderous struggle for supremacy was being fought. Wellesley, again anxious about possible French influence, intervened and threw British support behind the Peishwa. The steady expansion of British influence had already excited Maratha suspicions. The appearance of British forces in Hyderabad, after the treaty of 1800 with the Nizam, had been a severe jolt to Maratha raiders, who looked on the Deccan as a profitable hunting-ground. The new British dominance at Poona only two years later brought matters to a head. A British official pointed out that British forces at Hyderabad and Poona would be 'great bolts of a chain of defence' stretching across the Indian peninsula from coast to coast, protecting the Company's interests and the states in alliance with the Company. Maratha forces lost no time in putting the strength of those defences to the test, but they were outgeneralled by Arthur Wellesley (the Governor-General's younger brother, soon to become famous as the Duke of Wellington) and Lord Lake. As their armies won victories over the most feared fighting men in India, so the British advanced on all fronts. Imperial Delhi was reached, and there the British found the wretched person of the Moghul Emperor, old, blind and powerless. He was given an allowance, and a measure of his dignity was restored; but the Empire had gone for ever. Its ghostly title represented by the pathetic figure of the Emperor was taken under British control so that it could not be used by any other power – Indian or European – as a cloak for its ambitions. British power was strong enough to do without such a cloak. In the negotiations of 1803 territory stretching to the Jumna river and beyond was brought under British control, the influence of French adventurers active in North India was crushed, and alliances were forged with rulers whose lands bordered the new British acquisitions.

The Marathas, though defeated, were far from subdued, and war broke out again in 1804. This time there were no brilliant British victories. At home opposition mounted to Wellesley's aggressive forward policy. Appalled directors fretted about the cost, and resented the Governor-General's imperious attitude. Castlereagh, President of the Board of Control, worried about the straining of British resources in India at a time when French power was menacing Britain's national survival. In face of these criticisms Wellesley resigned, and the British advance came to a halt. There would be no abandonment of positions already won, but consolidation rather than further expansion was the policy to be followed in the immediate future.

No honours or dignities greeted Wellesley on his return home. In the awful stress of war with Napoleonic France distant exploits in India seemed almost irrelevant. For thirty years the massive achievements of perhaps the greatest of all British statesmen in India were underrated or ignored. It was left to the future Duke of Wellington to put his brother's efforts in perspective when he wrote to him:

> By your firmness and decision you have not only saved but enlarged and secured the valuable empire entrusted to your government at a time when everything else was a wreck and the existence even of Great Britain was problematical.

As Napoleon tightened his grip over Europe, so British anxieties mounted once more in the East. Under the terms of the Amiens settlement in 1802 the captured French settlements in India were to be restored, but this had not been done when war broke out again in 1803. The French still held Mauritius and Réunion, and a French squadron arrived at the islands in 1803 with a thousand regulars on board. This was an insignificant number, but the soldiers were accompanied by an unusually large number of general officers, clearly intended to raise and train sepoy troops in India. This plan came to nothing, and although Mauritius and Réunion remained troublesome centres of privateer activity there was little possibility that they would be used as bases for an invasion of India. Although Napoleon never entirely lost his eastern ambitions, and occasionally toyed with plans for a seaborne invasion of India, the situation in Europe never allowed the dispatch of an expeditionary force to so distant a centre of operations. At least 20,000 troops with a strong naval escort would be needed – as Napoleon pointed out, to send fewer would be courting disaster – and these could not be spared. Moreover, the situation in India was radically different, and from the French point of view infinitely more discouraging, from that of ten or fifteen years earlier. Many of the native powers with which the French agents had negotiated then had either disintegrated or were firmly under British control. Even the redoubtable Marathas had suffered severe defeats at the hands of the British, and were in a state of political and financial confusion which made their effectiveness as allies questionable. Schemes for an invasion of the Indian mainland were replaced by a stepping-up of commerce-raiding. The activities of daring and elusive privateers such as Surcouf were damaging to British trade, and difficult to combat while the French retained Mauritius; but they scarcely amounted to a war-winning policy.

For a time the French government considered the possibility of an overland assault on India by way of Persia, and as a preliminary to this a treaty of alliance was signed between France and Persia in 1807. A plan was sketched out for the Persian army to join a French expeditionary force of 20,000 men in a march on India, where it was hoped to rally support among the Marathas and other disaffected Indian powers. A diversionary attack might be made from Mauritius. The whole project was based on the flimsiest foundations, and the more realistic French ministers pointed out the futility of trying to re-establish French power in India. Their pessimism was soon justified. The alliance with Persia collapsed, and renewed commitments in Europe made a diversion of French resources to the East impossible. The weakness of the French position in eastern waters was finally and conclusively proved by the capture of Mauritius and Réunion in 1810.

At the peace treaties of 1814–15 France once more regained her Indian settlements, but under conditions more stringent than ever. No fortifications or troops were allowed, and France had formally to recognize the East India Company's sovereignty over the immense areas it controlled. In 1813 the Company had lost its commercial monopoly in India (though not in China), an overdue recognition of the fact that it had long ceased to be primarily a trading organization. Wellesley had set out the order of priorities years before:

> Its duties of sovereignty must be deemed paramount to its mercantile interests, prejudices and profits . . . the happiness of its subjects, the permanent improvement of its dominions, the dignity, purity and vigour of its government must take precedence of commercial considerations.

Certainly in the years ahead the Company need fear no European rivals. The tiny French posts were completely overshadowed by the mighty power of the Company, and ceased to have any political or military significance. The way lay open for British control of all India, and this was to be the theme of the next thirty years.

War and Innovation in the Dutch East Indies

The course of developments in the Dutch East Indies was permanently affected by the turn of political events in Europe which brought Holland under French domination for most of the war years. In 1793 the United Provinces went to war with revolutionary France in alliance with Britain, but within two years French armies swept across the frontier, the Stadholder William V of Orange fled to England, and a democratic government brought the newly-named Batavian Republic into alliance with France. The Stadholder had lost his authority over the homeland, but since he remained Director-General of the *V.O.C.* he claimed a measure of control over Dutch territories in the East. Soon after his arrival in England he issued the 'Kew Letters' in which he ordered all Dutch colonies to surrender peaceably to the British. The main concern of the Pitt administration was to deny the use of those territories to the French, and it pledged to restore them to Holland once the war was over.

In accordance with this arrangement the important Dutch bases at the Cape of Good Hope and Trincomalee fell under British control, as did the Dutch factories in India, and later the settlements farther east at Malacca, Amboina and Banda. Java, 'the Bengal of the Dutch' (as the British commander-in-chief of the East Indies station described it in 1796), remained in Dutch hands. So also did Ternate, most northerly of the Moluccas. These territories remained Dutch, not by virtue of their own strength, but because of British commitments elsewhere. The demand for British naval forces to protect the valuable China trade, and for land forces to defend India against a possible French invasion, left few forces available for an attack on Java.

There a piquant situation had arisen. The Governor-General and his advisers had no inclination to hand the island over to the British; but neither did they wish to see the doctrines of liberty and equality now fashionable at home eroding their position in Java. They hoped to get the best of both worlds. They would recognize the new Dutch government, but plead the special circumstances of Java as an excuse for resisting any untimely liberalizing tendencies. The manœuvre was successful. The government at the Hague swallowed its principles, and agreed that its revolutionary doctrines 'cannot be applied to the East Indian possessions of the state as long as the security of those possessions depends on the existing and necessary state of subordination of the Indonesians'.

The East India Company died a natural death when its charter expired in 1799, but the commercial principles on which it had operated continued in Java. There were proposals by a few Dutch administrators in the island, notably Dirk Van Hogendorp, to introduce a new administrative and tax system fairer to the peasant cultivator. The practice of forced cultivation and delivery, and the privileged position of the native chiefs who ruled the localities for the Dutch as Regents, were regarded by Van Hogendorp as inimical both to the happiness of the people and to the prospects of higher agricultural productivity. The issue was referred to a commission set up by the Dutch government in 1802 to examine the whole question of colonial reform, which concluded that the existing system ought to remain in operation, 'at least for the present'.

To the dominant conservative elements in the Dutch administration at Batavia there seemed little reason for change in a system which was serving them well. With the British navy controlling the sea routes, Java enjoyed a state of semi-independence; and it took full advantage of the effects of war and revolution in the West Indies to sell its coffee to neutral merchants (American and Danish in particular). The defences of the island were weak, but it was hoped that as long as Java remained obviously incapable of offensive action the British would leave the island at peace. French officers who arrived from Mauritius to take command of the island's military forces were promptly sent back. This period of profitable, if unofficial, neutrality came to an end when the new government of Louis Bonaparte (Napoleon's brother) came to power in Holland, and in 1808 sent Herman Willem Daendels to Java as Governor-General with orders to reorganize the island's government and defences.

Daendels was an ardent Bonapartist, whose military services to Napoleon had gained him the rank of marshal. A man of immense energy and stubborn will, he shook the Dutch in Java out of their comfortable complacency. The *Tuwan Besar Gunter* ('great thundering Lord') as the Javanese called him, saw the problems of the island with a soldier's eye. Fresh regiments of native troops were raised and trained in order to strengthen the army. Munition factories and fortresses were built. A new road was constructed along the length of the island which cut the journey from one end to the other from six weeks to one week, but which cost the lives of thousands of natives used as forced labour. In the administration of the island a new departure was made in that efforts were made to turn the Regents into salaried civil servants, a policy which aroused intense resentment among the Javanese aristocracy. This move towards increased control and centralization was a logical one, but it did little to better the peasants' lot. Financial necessity forced Daendels to leave the Regents in control of the native economy as before, and their activities as oppressive and extortionate middlemen went unchecked.

Finance was the Achilles' heel of Daendels's administration. To help meet the costs of reorganization and defence, Daendels ruthlessly extended the system of compulsory coffee cultivation. In justification he insisted that 'protection of the native labourer only encouraged him in his natural laziness' – a favourite maxim of Van Hogendorp's conservative opponents. Unfortunately for Daendels, it proved impossible to sell the coffee. Denmark was no longer neutral, and the British blockade held Java in a tight stranglehold. Desperate financial expedients were adopted. Paper currency was introduced, compulsory loans were extorted, great areas of land were sold to speculators. Finally, in 1810, while a British expedition was being prepared to invade Java, Daendels was recalled.

His short career in the East has been a subject of debate and controversy almost from the moment of his return to Europe (Daendels himself published a massive defence of his actions as early as 1814).

Undoubtedly his character and policies were shown in the worst possible light by the Englishman who ruled Java soon after him, Thomas Stamford Raffles. For long, Raffles's *History of Java* remained a standard work, in which Daendels's administration was continually contrasted with the beneficent nature of the author's own rule. But even if we discount the bias of Daendels's English contemporaries, he emerges as an unsympathetic and dictatorial figure who paid too little attention to the lot of the Javanese. It is to his credit that he introduced the rudiments of an improved system of justice, and tried to stamp out corruption (he exempted himself from this particular crusade); but the fact remains that he failed in his own chosen task, the mission to which all else was subordinated – the strengthening of Java against British attack.

The few Dutch and French troops on the island could not defend Java alone. Javanese help was essential, but Daendels's brusque treatment of the native chiefs had totally alienated many of them. The defence of Java was as much a political as a military problem, an elementary fact which Daendels failed to recognize. The task of his successors was seen to be a hopeless one when in August 1811 a great invasion fleet arrived off the island. It consisted of eighty ships, and close on 11,000 troops (most of them seasoned veterans of the Indian campaigns), and was led in person by Lord Minto, the Governor-General of India. The first Englishman ashore, a scholarly doctor armed to the teeth, found the coastal defences manned only by 'a flock of barn-door fowls headed by an aggressive rooster'. Batavia fell with scarcely a shot being fired, and after a spell of spirited Dutch resistance inland, plans to defend central Java collapsed when the local chiefs refused to send reinforcements. The campaign lasted only six weeks, and the conquest of Java marked the end of formal hostilities in the East. Everywhere the British were predominant. With the capture of Mauritius in one year, and Java the next, Napoleon lost his last bases in eastern waters.

After the capitulation Minto returned to Bengal, leaving 31-year-old Stamford Raffles Lieutenant-Governor of Java. Although aware that there would be considerable pressure for Java to be returned to the Dutch after the war, both Minto and Raffles hoped that Java might become a permanent British possession. This was not the intention of the East India Company directors in London, who had imagined that after the French in Java had been defeated and expelled, the island would simply be abandoned. Minto's reassurances that Java would be a profitable acquisition cut little ice with businessmen who had heard reports of Dutch financial difficulties on the island, and whose own experiences in India provided first-hand knowledge of the cost of territorial expansion. Java was invaded in no mood of empire-building; but in so remote a theatre of war the personality of the man on the spot was as important as official intentions, and Raffles had very firm ideas of his own about Java's future.

Raffles's ambition was to turn Java into the hub of a new British imperial complex in the eastern seas. From Java Britain would control a vast area stretching from India to the China Seas, and south to Australia. Aware of the danger that Java might yet be restored to Holland, Raffles used Britain's temporary position of dominance in the East Indies to negotiate treaties with local rulers. These, he hoped, would help British traders even if Java had to be given up. The Dutch, he was convinced, must never again be allowed to monopolize the trade of the region to the exclusion of the British. The island of Bangka off the eastern tip of Sumatra was occupied, and British ships sent to Japan flying Dutch colours to take advantage of the modest but unique commercial concession the Dutch held there. This last enterprise had no permanent results, and perhaps the biggest stir was occasioned by the presence on board one of the ships of an elephant – a present for the Emperor of Japan which unfortunately it proved impossible to land at Deshima.

Within Java Raffles's policies were vigorous, and in some ways revolutionary. Whatever their defects, they permanently altered the nature of European rule in Java. After Minto's departure Raffles was confronted with a country the size of England which was in chaotic condition, its external trade dead, and its treasury empty. To tackle this situation he had a professional staff of only three East India Company civil servants. Other posts were distributed either among those Dutch officials willing to collaborate, or among soldiers, doctors and other amateur administrators from the expeditionary force. Raffles's main advantage over his immediate predecessors was that with the British blockade lifted Java's seaborne trade could resume; but offsetting this was the lack of support from his superiors in India and England for anything but a policy of rigid economy.

The first task was to restore order on the island after the upheavals of invasion and battle; and this Raffles did in ruthlessly efficient

S

fashion. Incipient rebellions by local rulers were quelled by armed force, and Raffles continued Daendels's policy of reducing the privileges of the princes, though without offering them gratuitous insults as he did so. On the contrary, Raffles's interest in the language, history and customs of Java brought close relations between him and many of the local rulers. Daendels's policy of turning the Regents into salaried officials was also continued, though financial difficulties hindered the full implementation of this. At the village level, on the other hand, Raffles introduced an element of self-government when he laid down that the headman should be elected by the villagers. This was a radical innovation, though its practical efficacy was somewhat doubtful. Despite Raffles's effort to point the contrast between his administration and that of Daendels, the period from 1808 to 1816 should be seen as a whole. Under Daendels, inspired by Napoleon's reforms in Europe, the traditional Dutch pattern of ruling through the local chiefs was replaced (in theory at least) by bureaucratic government. Raffles continued this process of change, convinced that direct contact between the cultivator and his reforming administration would be more beneficial and productive than the arrangement under which Regents held a semi-independent position between the peasants and the government.

Raffles's greatest problem was the same as that which had afflicted Daendels – finance. Before leaving Java Minto had ordered that the Dutch system of forced cultivation and compulsory deliveries should be abolished. 'While we are in Java,' he declared, 'let us do all the good we can.' Raffles agreed that the Dutch system was morally evil and economically harmful, but saw that if the existing arrangements were simply ended, an immediate drop in government income would result. Apart from deploring the local implications of this, Raffles was also extremely anxious to show the British government that its new eastern acquisition was financially sound, and therefore worth consideration at the forthcoming peace negotiations. Raffles cut his way out of this dilemma with the boldest of his changes: a complete reform of the land and tax system along the lines suggested by Van Hogendorp ten years earlier. Investigations into the system of land tenure in Java persuaded Raffles that there were similarities between it and that prevailing in Bengal when it fell under British rule. He accordingly decided to sweep away the whole apparatus of compulsory cultivation and fixed sales, and to introduce in its place a general tax based upon land. First he declared the government to be the owner of all land in Java, and then arranged for land to be assigned to the village headmen, who in turn would let it to the actual cultivators. These were to be protected tenants, paying a cash rent based on the yield of the land (on average about two-fifths of the yield). By substituting a money payment for the system of barter (invariably weighted against the peasant), Raffles hoped to stimulate production and open Java to the influences of a cash economy. These, he confidently anticipated, would include a demand for cloth and other manufactured goods, which Britain would supply.

Unfortunately, the new scheme had to be introduced in haste at a time when the Java government was desperate for money. From the beginning some of the richest coffee and teak districts were exempted. The detailed surveys necessary if the individual rent assessments were to be fairly determined could not be properly carried out because of the lack of trained staff. Illiterate headmen and villagers could not cope with the arithmetical problems which the new arrangements imposed upon them. Daendels's old practice of selling land to private speculators crept in again. Short of time, money and staff, Raffles failed to make Java financially self-supporting; but the underlying advantages of the system were recognized by the Dutch, who retained many of its features when the island was restored to them.

All this activity was far from welcome to the directors of the East India Company, who viewed Raffles's financial balance-sheet with alarm. Nor was the British government, intent on establishing a strong and friendly power in the Low Country after the chaos of the Napoleonic Wars, enthusiastic about the forward policy being advocated by the forceful young Lieutenant-Governor in the East Indies. In 1814 it promised to return Java, together with the rest of the Dutch East Indies, to the Netherlands. By the time this was done Raffles had left Java, recalled after the Company and government in England had shown a growing mistrust of his actions. A bitterly disappointed man at this moment, with his career apparently in ruins, Raffles was not to know that his greatest achievement, the founding of Singapore, lay ahead of him.

The true worth of Raffles's policies in Java has always been difficult to evaluate through the mists of partisanship and patriotism that have surrounded his eventful career. The merit of individual reforms is often debatable, but these were perhaps less important than the new spirit of inquiry and reform which Raffles brought to Java. Personally as well as politically Raffles was a remarkable man. He possessed a variety of interests far beyond the range of most of his Dutch predecessors (or his British contemporaries for that matter). His published works on the East Indies suffer from attempts at self-glorification, but long remained standard works, and attracted the attention of Englishmen to a region which had long been a closed book to them. He encouraged naturalists, historians and antiquarians to carry out research in Java, and became an active President of the Batavian Society of Arts and Sciences (founded in 1778, but practically defunct during the period of the French wars). It was during the British occupation that the magnificent Buddhist shrine of Borobudur was discovered in the jungle only fifteen miles from one of the largest Dutch settlements, and surveyed on Raffles's orders.

Nor is it possible to understand Raffles and his policies in Java without appreciating the sincerity of his humanitarian sentiments. These were as much a part of him as the autocracy, ambition and ruthlessness he often showed. Raffles was deeply influenced by both of the two great driving forces which shaped the British Empire of the nineteenth century. In one respect he represented the aggressive imperialism which was to reach its peak in Cecil Rhodes; but his insistence that the first duty of a colonial government was the well-being of its subjects was the genuine voice of liberal humanitarianism. Again, circumstances frustrated many of his intentions. Although he reduced the number of slaves in Java, he could not in so short a time abolish the institution of slavery. But his whole-hearted concern for the welfare of the Javanese stood in marked contrast to the general tone of Dutch administration in the second half of the eighteenth century; and was not forgotten. Raffles's governorship of Java was both a challenge and an encouragement to many Dutchmen who followed him. Not only were some of his administrative, financial and judicial reforms maintained; a measure of the philanthropic idealism which inspired Raffles was carried over into the Dutch administration of Java after the island's restoration.

Revolution in Spanish America

When Charles III of Spain died in 1788 there were few signs that Spanish America was soon to rise in a series of revolts which were to bring it independence. Discontent and resentment undoubtedly existed, but not apparently on such a scale as to threaten widespread insurrection. Spain could take comfort in the thought that her American empire had outlived its British and French counterparts to the north. With the acquisition of Louisiana in 1763, the regaining of Florida in 1783, and a continuing extension of the land frontiers, it was now larger than at any time in its history. Under Charles III the Spanish colonies had prospered economically, flourished culturally, and been ruled more efficiently than ever before. Disorders and rebellions had shown that all was not well within this vast empire, but they had been effectively if brutally quelled.

The worst-exploited sections of the colonial population, the Indians and the Negro slaves, generally remained in a state of passive docility. Few revolutionary leaders rose from their ranks to goad their followers into action. Except in the terrible Mexican rising of 1810 neither Indians nor Negroes became a force to be reckoned with until the final stages of the Wars of Independence. The mulattoes and mestizos were more active in the revolutionary movements, but again rarely produced outstanding leaders. These came for the most part from the creoles, American-born Spaniards, whose grievances (described in Chapter 8) had not been diminished by the reorganization of colonial government under Charles III. Among the creoles the stirrings of discontent ran deeper than the Spanish government realized. The revolt of the North American colonies against a far from tyrannical British government had hinted that European colonial rule had not the permanence most people assumed. The American Revolution, with its due regard for the rights of property, had demonstrated that a struggle for political freedom need not involve violent social upheaval. At the time it had few direct effects on the Spanish colonies, but the existence and rapid growth of the United States of America formed a standing reminder of a successful revolution against one of the strongest powers in Europe.

The influence of the French Revolution on Spanish America was at once more immediate and more complex. To literate creoles, familiar with the works of Rousseau and other radical writers, the events of 1789 came as a challenge and a renewal of hope. A reaction gradually set in as the revolution turned to terror, and France appeared to be collapsing into a bloody chaos. Feelings of alarm were heightened when the forces of revolution erupted much nearer at hand, in Saint Domingue. Rousseau remained a powerful influence on men who could argue that the French Revolution had perverted rather than fulfilled his ideals, but the example of moderate English constitutionalism also made itself felt. Although some Englishmen were disturbed by the increasing authoritarianism of Pitt's government in the face of war abroad and agitation at home, Spanish Americans were generally impressed by the degree of liberty with order which the British system of constitutional government seemed to guarantee.

By the end of the eighteenth century parts of Spanish America were in a potentially dangerous state of unrest. Yet although resentment at various aspects of Spanish rule was widespread among the creoles, the determination and organization which had been evident among Britain's American colonists in the years before the American Revolution were lacking. The stimulus which turned discontent into revolution in Spanish America is to be found not in America but in the course of events in war-torn Europe. In 1788 Charles III had been succeeded by the lethargic Charles IV, ruled by a virago of a Queen and influenced by a contemptible minister, Godoy. Disaster in the war with France which began in 1793 added to the government's unpopularity, particularly when Godoy made peace in 1795 by handing over to the French Spain's oldest colony (admittedly not a very prosperous one) of Santo Domingo. The next year Spain entered a formal alliance with France, a short-sighted move which weakened the position of those striving to keep revolutionary doctrines out of Spain. It also involved Spain in war with Britain, most dangerous of all potential enemies. For long periods British seapower cut off Spain from its American colonies, where a severe economic recession was checked only by the activities of British and American traders.

At this time a name which became increasingly familiar to the British government was that of Francisco de Miranda, a Venezuelan-born Spaniard who had fought for Spain against Britain in the American War of Independence. Since then he had travelled extensively in Europe and America, living on his wits and foreign money (for a short time he served with distinction in the French revolutionary army), and dreaming of the day when the Spanish colonists would rise in revolt. Miranda was convinced that foreign help was necessary, and pinned his hopes on Britain. The Pitt administration was sufficiently interested to negotiate with Miranda and grant him a pension, but it invariably rejected or pigeon-holed the ambitious schemes he put before it. On this matter the British government was a prey to indecision. On the one hand, the strategy of a descent on Spanish America as a means of rousing the colonists in revolt had a long and honourable lineage – in the realm of paper projects, if not of action. Success would strike a damaging blow at Spain and her French ally, and would help to meet the growing clamour of British manufacturers for complete freedom of trade in the Spanish American market. But revolution in this period, even when directed against an enemy, no longer carried the satisfying implications it had in earlier days, before the horrors of the Negro uprising in Saint Domingue and the excesses of the Terror in France. Chaos on that scale in Spanish America would reflect ill on the European power responsible for encouraging it, and it would damage rather than serve British commercial interests.

The indefatigable Miranda laboured on, unmoved by these doubts and misgivings. He was the centre of a network of propaganda and correspondence, all directed towards the cause of Spanish American independence. His set of rooms in London became a meeting-place for ardent young creole visitors to Europe. For fifteen years talk rather than action dominated Miranda's life, but the events of his later years were to show that South American patriots who called him the 'Morning Star of Independence' or *El Precursor* had some justification.

In the war Spain was faring badly. The Spanish fleet was mauled by Nelson off Cape Saint Vincent in 1797, and in the Caribbean British forces captured Trinidad. More serious in the long term was that British naval domination continued to make communication between Spain and her colonies difficult, if not impossible. In Europe the relationship between France and Spain became even more one-sided as Bonaparte consolidated his position. Spain ceded Louisiana to France in 1800, only to find within three years that Bonaparte had sold the territory to the United States. A long series of Spanish defeats and humiliations reached a climax when the Spanish fleet, fighting along-side the French fleet, was smashed at the Battle of Trafalgar. The Spanish navy never recovered, and Spain's colonies in America lay open to attack by any enemy.

Miranda, who might now have been given his chance by the British government, had lost heart after successive disappointments and had gone to the United States. Although he failed to enlist the official aid of the American government he managed to collect together enough money to fit out a tiny expedition of two hundred men. With this he intended to light the fuse of a revolution in Venezuela which he confidently anticipated would spread through South America like wildfire. Instead it spluttered out in a mingled atmosphere of farce and tragedy. Miranda's men landed in Venezuela in 1805, but received little local support and beat an ignominious retreat.

Far more menacing and better-organized was a British descent on Buenos Aires in 1806. Since the reorganizations of Charles III's reign the La Plata region had known a period of unprecedented prosperity, and Buenos Aires became an obvious point of attack for any British expedition sent against Spanish America. At the beginning of 1806 a British force captured the Dutch settlement at the Cape of Good Hope, and a detachment was sent (without direct orders from London) across the South Atlantic to Buenos Aires. The main reason put forward by Sir Hume Popham, commander of the fleet, for the project was the chance 'to supply several millions of inhabitants with the manufactures of the United Kingdom'. The assault was completely successful. Resistance was slight, the viceroy reserving most of his energies for flight into the interior. British forces occupied the city, and proclamations were issued protecting private property, safe-guarding the Roman Catholic religion, and opening up free trade between the region and all British territories. In London the surprised British government gave the venture *post facto* blessing, and sent out reinforcements. They arrived to find a changed situation. Patriot forces led by Liniers, a Frenchman in Spain's service, had driven the British forces out of Buenos Aires within two months of its capture. This had been achieved without any help from the viceroy, and when he reappeared on the scene he was deposed and his powers shared by Liniers and the *cabildo abierto* (the municipal corporation). On the left bank around Montevideo the build-up of British forces continued. In all, 12,000 men were assembled, and in June 1807 a second attack was launched on Buenos Aires. The defence this time was conducted in a very different spirit from that only a year earlier. Liniers had raised and trained an enthusiastic local militia, and so fiercely was the city defended that the British forces gave up the attempt. They withdrew from Buenos Aires, then from Montevideo, and returned to England.

The episode has more than military significance. The weakness of the viceroy in 1806 had done much to discredit Spanish authority. The successful recapture and defence of Buenos Aires had come entirely from local initiative. The new self-confidence which accompanied military success showed itself in the refusal to accept the former viceroy's authority. Nor had the concessions which the British offered gone unnoticed. British troops had been resisted as alien conquerors, but the practical advantages of free trade had been seen by all in the short period when British ships commanded the Plata estuary. The Spanish flag still flew over Buenos Aires, but the days of unchallenged viceregal rule had gone for ever. The creoles had tasted freedom and the right to live and fight under their own leaders. It was not altogether unexpected that of the rebellions of 1810 the one in La Plata showed most vitality.

Coincidental with these stirring events in the Argentine, Napoleon made a move in Europe which was to prove decisive in the history of the Spanish and Portuguese empires. Fresh from his triumphs over Austria and Prussia, the French emperor decided to solve the persistent problem of Spain, where the government was trying to slip away from its unhappy alliance with France. In 1807 Franco-Spanish forces entered Portugal, forcing the Prince Regent, John of Braganza, and his court to flee to Brazil; but French troops in the peninsula were reinforced instead of being withdrawn as the Spaniards expected. A series of demands by Napoleon made it clear that he wanted complete control over Spain. In the confusion Charles IV and Godoy lost power, and the heir to the throne was declared King (Ferdinand VII). Napoleon refused to recognize either Bourbon as rightful monarch, forced both to abdicate, and proclaimed his elder brother, Joseph Bonaparte, King of Spain. It was a disastrous miscalculation. The Spanish people rose in revolt against *El Intruso* (the intruder), and a ferocious war broke out in which Spanish guerrilla forces and British regulars under Wellington took a heavy toll of the French occupation armies.

Joseph Bonaparte's authority was as little accepted in the overseas empire as in Spain. His representatives were refused entry to the colonies, and the interned Ferdinand VII was acclaimed as rightful king. Lacking consistent guidance from a distracted Spain, where the regency junta at Seville could send only occasional directives across the Atlantic, the colonies were forced back on their own devices. The machinery of government continued to operate – a tribute to the Spanish administrative system – but economically the colonies became dependent on Britain (more than ever eager to trade with Spanish America now that Napoleon's Continental System had stopped British trade with most of Europe). In this state of chaos and uncertainty the balance could not long be held undisturbed in America, where creole dissatisfaction had been growing steadily during the twenty years of ineffective government, defeat and humiliation which had followed the death of Charles III. Now, with the Spanish crown itself in dispute, creole leaders saw their chance to break free from Spain. The year 1809 saw plots and uprisings, which though unsuccessful were portents of things to come. In 1810 news reached America that Seville had fallen to French troops, and that the tenuous link between the junta and the colonies had been snapped. The same year there were four major rebellions in Spanish America: the Wars of Independence had begun.

Revolution first broke out in Venezuela, for long a vulnerable part of the Spanish empire. Its proximity to the British and French West Indian islands had brought the colony into closer contact with the outside world than was normal in Spanish America. It was there that Miranda had landed in 1805 in his unsuccessful attempt to provoke rebellion. Since that fiasco news of the events in Spain, and the arrival in the colony of Bonapartist officials, had stimulated revolutionary sentiments among the wealthy, well-educated creoles of Caracas. In April 1810 a group of conspirators overthrew the government of the Spanish Captain-General. When royalist forces in the colony rallied, and were reinforced by Spanish troops from Cuba, the revolutionary government sent an aristocratic young creole, Simón Bolívar, to London to ask for British support. Bolívar was to be the outstanding figure in the Wars of Independence – *El Libertador*, to give him the proud title by which he was soon to be known. Imaginative and impulsive, he had travelled widely in Europe, where he had seen for himself the disreputable court of Charles IV, and had suffered from the contemptuous haughtiness of the peninsular Spaniard towards the American-born creole.

The mission to London failed to win material help from the British government, now in alliance with Spain and therefore unable to support independence movements in the Spanish colonies. Although there was much unofficial sympathy for the patriot cause, Britain's main concern was to bring Spanish America securely within its sphere of commercial influence. Unlike Britain's North American colonists, the Spanish Americans were to fight their wars of liberation without foreign allies. Without outside assistance the Venezuelan revolt slowly crumbled, despite Miranda's arrival to take charge of affairs. His irresolution, the economic and political chaos of the country, and finally a disastrous earthquake (widely regarded as a divine visitation upon the rebels) sapped the strength of the revolutionary cause. By 1812 the short-lived republic had collapsed; Miranda was in Spanish hands; and Bolívar had sailed westward along the coast to New Granada.

Here the events of 1810 had also sparked off revolution. Uprisings in Cartagena and Bogotá led by ambitious creole politicians and merchants had overthrown the government of the viceroy; but as in Venezuela, the revolutionaries found the work of destruction more congenial than that of construction. When Bolívar arrived in 1812 only half of New Granada was held by the patriots, and they were hopelessly divided among themselves. Accompanied by a few hundred volunteers, Bolívar moved back into Venezuela across jungle, swamps and mountains on the first of his remarkable military exploits. But although he temporarily regained possession of Caracas the royalist forces steadily gained the upper hand, heartened by the news in 1814 that Ferdinand VII had been recognized as King of Spain. After ferocious and brutal fighting which set the pattern for the wars of independence – civil wars in which there was little discrimination between combatants and non-combatants – Bolívar abandoned Venezuela to its fate. Soon afterwards he fled from New Granada also, as the revolutionary government fell before onslaughts of veteran troops sent from Spain.

Farther north, rebellion in New Spain had met with no better success. Here Father Miguel Hidalgo, an unorthodox priest with a turbulent history of opposition to authority, led the revolt. For a moment he captured the support both of the creoles, frustrated under Spanish rule, and the Indians, with their deeper and darker grievances. The union was only a fleeting one, for the insurrection quickly turned into a racial war as the Indians wreaked an indiscriminate vengeance on the whites. The revolution had taken a different turn from those to the south, where the Indians and Negroes had generally remained outside the fierce conflict between the Spaniards. Only a few whites remained with Hidalgo and his undisciplined Indian followers. In 1811 this phase of the rebellion ended when a united force of *peninsulares* and creoles defeated the rebels, and Hidalgo himself was captured and executed. Guerrilla warfare went on for another four years, but by 1815 that too appeared to have been extinguished.

Only in the Argentine was a major rebellion successful in 1810. There the events of 1806 and 1807 had given the creoles a measure of prestige and confidence not experienced elsewhere, and they found little difficulty in overthrowing the government and setting up a junta. Nominally they owed allegiance to Ferdinand VII, but in reality they were aiming at independence. To win Buenos Aires was comparatively simple; to convert the inland districts to the revolutionary cause was a much sterner task. Already some characteristic features of modern South American history were emerging as political factors: the differences between the coastal and interior regions, and between town and country; the jockeying for political power among the revolutionary leaders; and the inability to create a stable form of government. Early hopes of gaining Upper Peru soon proved illusory, and in Buenos Aires political rivalry ran high. Although in 1816 a patriot congress declared its independence from Spain – the first Spanish colony formally to do so – the future of the new republic looked far from certain.

As war ended in Europe, and Ferdinand VII came to the throne of his ravaged country, the main dangers to imperial rule in Spanish America appeared to have been averted. Yet in less than ten years the Spanish empire in America had completely disintegrated, and had been replaced by thirteen independent states. The details of this story, and the exploits of Bolívar, San Martín and other heroes of the patriot cause lie outside the scope of this book; but the fundamental factor was the failure of the restored Spanish monarchy to win back the allegiance of its creole subjects. It soon became painfully clear that the government of Ferdinand VII envisaged, at best a return to the *status quo*, at worst a policy of repression. In 1817 revolt broke out again, and this time swept all before it. The Spanish empire in America collapsed as the British had half a century earlier. Too much should not be made of parallels between the two revolutions. The colonists, the governments and the immediate motives were all very different. But one underlying factor was present in both: a European government could not expect to hold down indefinitely prosperous and energetic colonies across the seas. Castlereagh pointed the moral when he declared in 1812 of the Spanish American situation that 'provinces of such magnitude will not longer submit to be treated as mere colonies'.

In Brazil independence came in less turbulent fashion. After his flight there in 1807–8 the Prince Regent, John of Braganza, instituted a more efficient form of government than the country had ever known in its days of distant control from Lisbon. Economically Brazil prospered after John's decision to open its ports to the merchants of all friendly nations. With the British navy blockading the coasts of Europe, this concession was in effect limited to Britain, and a treaty of commercial reciprocity signed in 1810 confirmed her traders' dominant position in Brazil's commercial life. John VI (as he became in 1816) did not return to Portugal until 1820, and although two years later Brazil became independent it did so under the guidance of the King's son Pedro, who became Emperor of Brazil. The continued rule of the Braganza dynasty, and the achievement of independence without the searing experience of civil war, help to explain why Brazil overtook the former Spanish colonies during the course of the century, and became the most important nation in South America.

As far as Spanish America was concerned, successful revolution was not the panacea for all ills. Many of the old evils remained, and new ones were added. Political instability, social tensions and economic difficulties have pursued the Latin American republics from the time of their struggle for independence to the present day. But at least the protective barrier cast round the continent by British naval power and the Monroe Doctrine gave the new nations freedom to grapple with these problems in their own way. The rivalries and antagonisms of Europe which had such traumatic effects on Asian and African societies during the nineteenth century were represented in Latin America in the mild and generally beneficial form of commercial competition.

West Africa and the Abolition of the Slave Trade

Throughout the eighteenth century, as Europeans penetrated and exploited the Americas, India and the Pacific, the African continent south of the Sahara remained largely inviolate. The two most extensive European colonies were those of Portuguese Angola and Mozambique; but the first was notable only for its slave-trading and vicious misgovernment, and the second consisted of a few decaying forts and churches. The settlement of Mauritius by the French in 1715 revived European interest in East Africa, but attempts to establish settlements on Madagascar after its annexation by Choiseul in 1768 came to nothing, and the Arabs continued to dominate the trade of the east coast of Africa. The only colony with a substantial white settler population was at the Cape of Good Hope, where by the time of the

British occupation in 1795 there were about 20,000 colonists. There, indeed, the settlers had got out of official control. In the view of the Dutch East India Company, Europeans had settled at the Cape to provide provisions for the Indiamen: the Cape was a strategic and supply base, nothing more. But it proved impossible to restrict the Boers to the area around Cape Town, and by the end of the century Boer trekkers had pushed 500 miles inland, and were already involved in conflict with the Bantu.

West Africa alone was of substantial economic importance to Europe in the eighteenth century. Only along the coast from Cape Verde to Angola were European traders active in any numbers, and despite some commerce in gold, ivory, palm-oil and gum these merchants were mostly engaged in the slave trade. Even this did not involve penetration inland. Disease, difficulties of communication, and the opposition of the African coastal tribes to any attempt by Europeans to make direct contact with the slave-producing regions of the interior, confined the traders to their ships or coastal factories. Nor did the slavers have any pressing reason for venturing into the interior. No known trade could rival that in slaves for profit, and it was easier, safer and healthier for Europeans to carry out their transactions on the coast. Along the slave coasts there were some permanent or semi-permanent European factors, and among the Africans with whom they traded some evidence of European influence in language, religion and trading customs; but after three centuries of contact European influence still did not strike deep or spread far. Only as the movement for abolition of the slave trade gathered momentum in Britain were there signs of a change in this state of affairs.

It was a striking feature of the abolitionist movement that it tenaciously pursued its objective in the midst of the bloodiest wars and revolutions the western world had known. At a time when other reform movements fell by the wayside or were repressed by the government, the abolitionists achieved success in 1807 (although slavery itself was not abolished within the British empire for another generation). The course of events in the twenty years before the slave trade was abolished makes a fine and moving story which has been told many times. The leading abolitionists were household names: Thomas Clarkson, an indefatigable researcher into the iniquities of the slave trade; William Wilberforce, Pitt's friend and leader of the abolitionists in Parliament; Henry Thornton, a widely respected banker and M.P.;

and Zachary Macaulay (father of the historian) who had worked as an under-manager on a Jamaican slave plantation. Under their direction the Society for Effecting the Abolition of the Slave Trade mounted a massive publicity campaign. Hundreds of local branches were formed, and petitions poured into Parliament demanding abolition. Every possible device was used to win public sympathy for the cause; pamphlets, poems, ballads and Wedgwood's famous cameo of the enchained Negro. In Parliament abolition was supported by Pitt, Fox and Burke.

Against the growing volume of protest the slave-trade interests fought a stout defensive action. Backed in the Commons by what one contemporary called 'the minor orators, the dwarfs and the pygmies', they held off the threat until the outbreak of war with France in 1793 brought a change of mood. Public enthusiasm for abolition faded in the face of the struggle with French Jacobinism. Reform of any kind tended to become equated with revolution, and the awful train of events in Saint Domingue was often quoted as a dire example. A French war, it was widely felt, was not the right time to knock away so long-standing a strut of Britain's commercial system. For years Wilberforce doggedly continued the struggle, though with little support in the country, until events once more turned in his favour. War against Napoleonic France had not the same ideological under-tones as war against revolutionary France, and the abolitionists were no longer branded as Jacobins. Even the opposition of the West Indian interests weakened as they saw that the trade, if continued, would help to build up the economies of Britain's newly-acquired Caribbean possessions, at the expense of their own older colonies. In Parliament Fox came into office, pledged to abolition, and in 1807 a bill prohibiting British participation in the slave trade passed through Parliament, and came into force at the beginning of 1808. (The unimportant Danish slave trade had already been abolished, and the declining Dutch slave trade was to be abolished in 1814.)

Abolition has long been regarded as a triumph for the new evangelical movement in British public life, a striking example of a nation voluntarily depriving itself of a valuable asset on grounds of moral disapprobation. Clearly, Wilberforce and his associates were moved by religious and humanitarian motives, and they provided the driving force behind the abolition movement; but other factors also need examination if we are to understand how a trade apparently so impregnable could be overthrown. The first blow at the slave-owners came with the American Revolution, which removed from the empire the southern states with their great slave plantations. The West Indian interest was deprived of a valuable ally, and this at a time when the British Caribbean colonies were beginning to lose the predominant position they had long held in the empire's commerce. The British islands had fallen far behind the French West Indian colonies as sugar-producers, and could not hope to match the low price of Saint Domingue sugar which, until the slave revolt of 1791, dominated the European market.

As the economic difficulties of the old British West Indian colonies increased, so capitalist and mercantile interests in Britain began to abandon the cause of the African slave-traders and Caribbean sugar-planters. In his book *Capitalism and Slavery* Dr Eric Williams has described how the monopolistic attitude of the West Indian planters had become directly opposed to the interests of the manufacturers and traders of Britain's expanding industrial society. Even the great slave-trading port of Liverpool was diversifying its activities, and increasing numbers of its ships were employed in bringing raw cotton from the United States to the mills of industrial Lancashire. On another aspect of the slave trade Clarkson's researches had produced statistics on the mortality rate among seamen on the slave ships which gravely weakened a favourite strategic argument that had always been used by defenders of the trade. Sometimes one-fifth of a crew was lost on a single voyage and, in the words of one naval officer with experience of the Guinea coast, the slave trade was 'not a nursery but a grave of seamen'.

The economic arguments cannot be pressed too far. From the long-term point of view the British West Indies were entering a period of economic decline, but during the war years when, it must be remembered, abolition was finally accepted by Parliament, they experienced a boom. The destruction of the sugar plantations of Saint Domingue, the high prices paid in Europe for sugar, cotton and coffee, and the increase of trade with the Spanish colonies, brought prosperity to the British islands. The slave trade itself was still lucrative, as the number of illegal traders after 1808 proved. Before abolition Britain engrossed approximately half the slave trade, which relied to a very large extent on manufactured goods. The advantages which the industrial revolution with its mass production of cheap cottons was giving British slave-traders would undoubtedly have enlarged Britain's share of the trade. Moreover, although the older British islands might no longer be good markets for slaves, this did not apply to the cotton plantations of the United States or to Brazil and Cuba. By 1840 there were probably almost twice as many slaves landing in the Americas each year as in the late eighteenth century, when an annual total of 70,000 was quite normal. Changing conditions had weakened the obstructive powers of the West Indian planter interests, but the trade which Britain renounced was a profitable and expanding one.

The withdrawal from the slave trade of the nation hitherto dominant in it had a profound effect on the nature of European interest and activity in Africa. The abolitionist campaign had already stimulated the foundation of missionary societies, the most important of which were the London Missionary Society of 1795 and the Church Missionary Society of 1799. These were soon active in Africa, where the humanitarians already had a remarkable achievement to their credit. This was the establishment in 1787 of a colony in Sierra Leone for freed slaves: first, those living in England; and later, Negro loyalists uncomfortably quartered in Nova Scotia after their flight from the former American colonies. It was hoped that the new colony would thrive 'on the true principles of commerce', trading British manufactures for African products, and spreading 'the blessings of industry and civilization' far into the interior. These high hopes were soon dashed. Many of the early arrivals in Freetown died from disease, and legitimate traders found it difficult to compete with the slave trade. The little colony survived only with the help of financial aid from the British government, which in 1808 accepted full responsibility for it. It was a useful base for naval vessels engaged in suppressing the slave trade, and became a haven for thousands of Negroes freed from the slave-ships.

After 1808 the abolitionists in Britain, together with commercial interests, were influential enough to persuade the government to press for a general abolition of European participation in the slave trade. Castlereagh raised the subject at the peace negotiations of 1814–15, and although most of the other powers expressed support for Britain's stand their unwillingness or inability to control their nationals engaged in the trade led to the extension of British diplomatic, naval and commercial activity in West Africa. Abolition brought renewed interest in other forms of trade, and this in turn helped forward the work of exploration which was essential if a realistic assessment was to be made of the commercial potentialities of the interior. In 1788 the founding, under Sir Joseph Banks's presidency, of the Association for Promoting the Discovery of the Interior Parts of Africa reflected the revival of curiosity about the geography of the African continent. Founder-members ranged from industrialists such as Wedgwood to members of the Clapham Sect. From the beginning it had government approval, for the exploration of this great continent lying alongside the vital sea-routes to the East had strategic as well as commercial significance. Banks himself had sailed with Cook on his first voyage, and had used his considerable influence as President of the Royal Society to support the Pacific discovery expeditions. The oceanic explorers had found no fertile southern continent, no navigable North-west Passage; and before the end of the century the attention of geographers and economists was turning from the Pacific to Africa. There was ample room for speculation. The African Association's 'plan' of 1790 accurately summed up the state of European knowledge of Africa:

> Notwithstanding the progress of discovery on the coasts and borders of that vast continent, the map of its interior is still but a wide extended blank, on which the geographer . . . has traced with a hesitating hand a few names of unexplored rivers and of uncertain nations.

The Association's main interest was in the Niger, whose direction, course and mouth were all unknown. Along the banks of this mysterious stream rumour placed great cities and rich goldfields: it was a lure to traders and geographers alike. Several unsuccessful attempts were made by the Association to reach the Niger across the Sahara or by way of the Gambia before it found in Mungo Park one of the first great explorers of Africa. On his first journey in 1795–7 Park proved that the Niger flowed eastward; and on his second, government-sponsored expedition in 1805–6 from which only one of his party returned alive he sailed down the river as far as Busa (800 miles from Timbuktu). Park had not answered all the questions about the Niger, but he had inaugurated an era of European exploration in Africa during which the courses of all the main rivers were to be traced in turn, and the continent opened to European settlement and trade.

British Dominance in 1815

On the strategic level the conflict between Britain and France which lay at the heart of the European war of 1803–1815 followed, almost in exaggerated form, the customary pattern of Anglo-French hostilities since the beginning of the eighteenth century. France's strength had always lain in her army, but Napoleon bestrode the continent in a way no French ruler had ever done before; Britain had usually fared well overseas, but her control of the oceans after Trafalgar gave her a dominance she had never attained even in the Seven Years War. A power supreme on land was the implacable enemy of one invincible at sea, and it was ironical how difficult the two rivals found it to get to grips with each other. Except in Spain, direct confrontations between the French and British armies were rare, and on the sea the French fleet virtually ceased to exist after defeats at Trafalgar and in the Caribbean.

As Napoleon advanced his tremendous power on land, so Britain seized the overseas possessions of France and Holland. Even before Trafalgar, the West Indian territories of Saint Lucia, Tobago and Dutch Guiana had been taken by British forces; and after 1805 the tempo of conquest quickened. Year after year the expeditions sailed, and the list of captures grew in length: the Cape of Good Hope in 1806; Curaçao and the Danish West Indies in 1807; some of the Moluccas in 1808; Martinique and Senegal in 1809; Guadeloupe, Mauritius, Amboina, and Banda in 1810; Java in 1811. Sometimes there was fighting, often there was not. Local resistance was obviously futile, and help from Europe impossible. There were no spectacular victories or dramatic feats of arms, but quietly the overseas empires of France and Holland disappeared into Britain's grasp. Helpless to stop this process, Napoleon struck back in the way most damaging to an industrial and trading power of Britain's size: by means of the Continental System he sought to close the markets of Europe to British products. In 1808 and again between 1810 and 1812 Napoleon's measures had severe effects on Britain's economy, and the war with the United States in 1812 over Britain's right to search neutral shipping added to the difficulties of British traders. But the Continental System was never complete, it could not touch Britain's empire overseas directly, and although it hindered the re-export of tropical products to Europe the demand on the continent for sugar, coffee, tobacco and cotton could not be satisfied by *ersatz* products or stifled by Napoleon's customs officials. Britain found some compensation in the markets of Spanish and Portuguese America, and was able to weather the storms which this method of economic warfare produced. During the war years in general the number of British merchant vessels increased by half, an addition of more than a million tons of shipping.

When peace negotiations opened in 1814 Britain was in a position where, as Napoleon admitted, she could have retained most of her overseas captures. Instead, Castlereagh followed the line suggested by Pitt in 1805, and used Britain's colonial conquests as a means of securing a stable settlement in Europe. To achieve a satisfactory balance of power on the continent and to establish a strong Dutch kingdom, the British government was prepared to return most of its colonial gains. A cabinet memorandum of early 1814 stated in self-congratulatory tones:

> Great Britain has declared her disposition with certain exceptions to sacrifice these conquests for the welfare of the continent, being desirous of providing for her own security by a common arrangement rather than by an exclusive accumulation of strength and power. Her object is to see a maritime as well as a military balance of power.

Apart from Tobago (which in any event had been French only since the American War of Independence) and part of Dutch Guiana, no captured colonies were kept for commercial reasons; and this despite the outraged protests of British merchants and planters with capital invested in the occupied territories. Guadeloupe, Martinique, Senegal, Réunion and the Indian trading settlements were handed back to the French; Java, Banda, Amboina, Ternate, Curaçao, Saint Eustatius and Surinam to the Dutch. Castlereagh declared the government's order of priorities when he replied to demands for the retention of territory in the Dutch East Indies: 'I am sure our reputation on the Continent as a feature of strength, power and confidence is of more real moment.' Nevertheless, there were 'certain exceptions', as the Cabinet memorandum of 1814 stated; and although these appear modest in comparison with what was handed back, they were acquisitions which Britain had aimed at for many years. Malta became British to give added control over the Mediterranean and the Levant. In the Caribbean Saint Lucia, with its fine harbour, was retained for strategic reasons. Most important of all, the Cape and Mauritius were kept to give Britain complete command of the long sea-route to India and the East. Ceylon had already been gained by the Amiens treaty of 1802, and farther east Singapore was to be acquired by Stamford Raffles in 1819. The pattern of the 1713 and 1763 treaties had been repeated: with comparatively modest ambitions on the continent Britain had used war and treaty-making as a means of damaging rival empires and enlarging her own. If the Ionian Islands, Ascension and other small territories are included, the total number of British colonies had increased from 26 to 43 since 1793. The empire of 1815 differed from that of 1763 in that it was truly world-wide. The latter had been based on the African–Caribbean–North American triangle. Now the growth of British power in India, the beginnings of settlement in the South Pacific, the increase of trade in China and the Eastern Seas, and finally the wartime acquisitions, had produced an empire which was better balanced and more strongly guarded.

The other colonial powers presented a sad contrast. The nucleus of the old Bourbon empire was restored to France, but the enthusiasm for overseas colonies and conquests had vanished. In her conflicts with Britain, France had experienced too many defeats, and known too much disillusionment to want to take up the challenge again. Her mercantile marine and navy had been destroyed, and the manpower which in Britain was flocking to the new industrial centres had in France been drained away by Napoleon's campaigns. North Africa increased its hold over the minds of some Frenchmen, but not until mid-century were there stirrings of French maritime and colonial ambitions outside the Mediterranean. The Spanish empire in 1815 was still visible on the map in its old form, but it was little more than a husk, and within a few years Spain's continental possessions in America had won their independence. There, as in Brazil, Britain was the European power which gained most from the wars of liberation. That commercial penetration of Spanish America which had been a British objective throughout the eighteenth century was accomplished at last, and the South American market became almost a British preserve. Holland had been treated generously at the peace negotiations, but never again could she rival Britain as a commercial and colonial power. In contrast to those wars of the eighteenth century in which a profitable if precarious neutrality had been maintained, the Dutch had suffered severely in the wars of 1793–1815. Subject to French domination in Europe and to British conquest overseas, Holland had experienced nothing but disaster. With the exception of the Cape and Ceylon her most important colonies had been restored, but she did not possess the industrial resources at home to be able to match Britain's competitive advantages in world markets.

If we are to understand Britain's emergence as a world power then the industrial advances at home must be taken into account as well as the formal gain of territory abroad. These were related, not separate, developments. Economic historians still debate the precise relationship between Britain's overseas predominance in the eighteenth century and the great industrial leap forward which occurred before the end of the century. One of the causes of the Industrial Revolution in Britain was undoubtedly the amount of capital available for new industrial developments from the profits of overseas enterprise, and this overseas trade relied increasingly on colonial markets and sources of supply. In 1700 four-fifths of English exports went to Europe, and one-fifth to the rest of the world; by 1800 the proportions had been reversed. While trade with the heavily protected markets of Europe remained static, that to America, the West Indies, India and the East expanded enormously. These territories took the bulk of the products of the new cotton industry, which by the end of the Napoleonic Wars accounted for 40 per cent of British exports; and in turn supplied Britain with sugar, tea, coffee, raw cotton, tobacco and other products for domestic consumption and re-export. Other industries were following the cotton industry along the path of large-scale mechanization and capitalization, and Britain's emergence as the first modern industrial nation in the world consolidated her position as the leading imperial power. Protected by the unchallenged might of a navy served by a chain of strategic bases, Britain's merchant vessels traded to all parts of the world – some formal parts of the empire, many not. Vitality, enterprise and aggressive self-confidence were shown in domestic industry and in foreign trade alike. While in London successive administrations disclaimed any desire for further territorial acquisitions, British settlers, traders and missionaries continued to extend the frontiers of European influence and power. The future domination of the world by a handful of European states is already visible in Britain's immense and expanding empire of 1815.

SELECT BIBLIOGRAPHY

Chapter 1

J. H. Parry, *The Age of Reconnaissance* (London 1963) is a stimulating general survey of European overseas expansion between 1450 and 1650. An earlier work by the same author, *Europe and a Wider World 1415–1715* (London 1949) provides a succinct introduction to a longer period. A more analytical treatment is to be found in Frédéric Mauro, *L'Expansion Européenne 1600–1870* ('Nouvelle Clio' series, No. 27: Paris 1964). This contains an excellent bibliography listing Spanish Portuguese, Dutch, English and French sources (primary as well as secondary). A briefer bibliography is J. S. Bromley and A. Goodwin, *A Select List of Works on Europe and Europe Overseas 1715–1815* (Oxford 1956).

On the Spanish empire in the Hapsburg period C. H. Haring, *Trade and Navigation between Spain and the Indies in the time of the Hapsburgs* (Cambridge, Mass. 1918) remains a standard work. A more general study by the same author is *The Spanish Empire in America* (New York 1947). Two slim volumes by C. R. Boxer discuss the salient features of Portugal's overseas empire: *Four Centuries of Portuguese Expansion 1415–1825* (Johannesburg 1961), and *Race Relations in the Portuguese Colonial Empire 1415–1825* (Oxford 1963). Bernard H. M. Vlekke, *Evolution of the Dutch Nation* (London 1951) has sections on the Dutch overseas empire. *Nunsantara: A History of the East Indian Archipelago* (Cambridge, Mass. 1944), also by Vlekke, sets the Dutch eastern empire in its historical and geographical perspective. One of several competent histories of English overseas enterprise is J. A. Williamson, *A Short History of British Expansion*, Vol. I, *The Old Colonial Empire*, 4th edn (London 1961). The standard work on England's American colonies is still C. M. Andrews, *The Colonial Period of American History*, 4 vols. (reprinted London 1964). An outline history of the early French colonies is J. F. Saintoyant, *La Colonisation française sous l'Ancien Régime*, 2 vols. (Paris 1929). H. I. Priestley, *France Overseas through the Old Régime* (New York 1939) is a rather stolid account; a better view of the working of the French colonial system

285

will be obtained in W. J. Eccles, *Canada under Louis XIV, 1663–1701* (Toronto 1964). European settlement and trade in the Caribbean are dealt with in a first-class little book, J. H. Parry and P. M. Sherlock, *A Short History of the West Indies* (London 1956).

Chapter 2

There are chapters on European overseas activity during the eighteenth century in the relevant volumes of the *New Cambridge Modern History*: VII, *The Old Régime 1713–63* (1957); VIII, *The American and French Revolutions 1763–93* (1965); IX, *War and Peace in an Age of Upheaval 1793–1830* (1965).

The subject of mercantilism is briefly introduced by Charles Henry Wilson in a Historical Association pamphlet *Mercantilism* (London 1958), and examined in detail in Eli Heckscher's invaluable two-volume work, *Mercantilism*, trans. M. Shapiro (London 1935). Studies of English and French mercantilist policies are contained in L. A. Harper, *The English Navigation Laws: A Seventeenth-Century Experiment in Social Engineering* (New York 1939), and in two books by C. W. Cole, *Colbert and a Century of French Mercantilism*, 2 vols. (New York 1939) and *French Mercantilism 1683–1700* (New York 1943). A chapter by J. F. Rees, 'Mercantilism and the Colonies', in *The Cambridge History of the British Empire*, I (Cambridge 1929) is a useful concise discussion. Theories and techniques of colonization are examined – with a wealth of quotation – in Klaus E. Knorr, *British Colonial Theories 1570–1850* (reprinted, Toronto 1963), and more briefly in Hubert Jules Deschamps, *Les méthodes et les doctrines coloniales de la France du* XVI*ᵉ siècle à nos jours* (Paris 1953).

A. T. Mahan's classic work, *The Influence of Sea Power upon History 1660–1783*, first published in 1889, is now available in paperback form (London 1965). Though outdated in places, it remains a stimulating survey of Anglo-French naval hostilities. A more recent work is G. S. Graham, *Empire of the North Atlantic: The Maritime Struggle for North America*, 2nd edn (London 1958). The development of the French navy is briefly described in L. Nicolas, *Histoire de la marine française*, 'Que sais-je?' series, No. 342, rev. edn (Paris 1961) and more fully in J. Tramond, *Manuel d'histoire maritime de la France des origines à 1815* (rev. edn, Paris 1947). Geoffrey J. Marcus, *A Naval*

History of England, Vol. I, *The Formative Centuries* (London 1961) traces the history of the British navy from its beginnings to 1783.

Overseas missionary activity from the sixteenth to the eighteenth century is comprehensively dealt with in K. S. Latourette, *A History of the Expansion of Christianity*, Vol. III, *Three Centuries of Advance* A.D. *1500*–A.D.*1800* (London 1947). A shorter and more general account is Stephen Neill, *Christian Missions* (Harmondsworth 1964). The slave trade and its effects are graphically described in Daniel P. Mannix and Malcolm Cowley. *Black Cargoes: A History of the Atlantic Slave Trade 1518–1865* (London 1963). K. G. Davies, *The Royal African Company* (London 1957) is a scholarly history of one of the most important European slave-trading companies. Gaston-Martin has written the authoritative work on slavery in the French overseas empire, *Histoire de l'esclavage dans les colonies françaises* (Paris 1948). The organization and impact of the trade in Africa can be followed in J. D. Fage, *An Introduction to the History of West Africa*, rev. edn (London 1962), or in Roland Oliver and J. D. Fage, *A Short History of Africa* (Harmondsworth 1962).

Chapter 3

The expansion of England and France in North America are dealt with, in very different ways, in J. B. Brebner, *The Explorers of North America 1492–1806* (London 1933), and H. A. Innis, *The Fur Trade in Canada*, 2nd edn (New Haven 1962). The little-known rifts between France and Spain are examined in Henry Folmer, *Franco-Spanish Rivalry in North America 1524–1763* (Glendale 1953). A reliable guide to the North American campaigns up to the end of the Seven Years War is Howard H. Peckham, *The Colonial Wars 1689–1762* (Chicago 1964). Some scattered fragments of information about Louisiana will be found in H. M. Hyde's biography, *John Law: the History of an Honest Adventurer* (Amsterdam 1948); but Law's Mississippi schemes are put into better perspective in Emile Lauvrière, *Histoire de la Louisiane française 1673–1939* (Paris 1940). John Patrick Carswell, *The South Sea Bubble* (London 1960) is a readable account of the financial and political crisis in England.

Anglo-Spanish overseas rivalry and the events leading to the War of Jenkins's Ear are analysed in an important monograph by Jean

O. McLachlan, *Trade and Peace with Old Spain 1667–1750* (Cambridge 1940), and also in the early chapters of Richard Pares, *War and Trade in the West Indies 1739–1763* (Oxford 1936), an indispensable book for any serious student of the period. French diplomacy, naval policy and overseas trade are all examined in A. M. Wilson, *French Foreign Policy during the Administration of Cardinal Fleury 1726–1743* (Cambridge, Mass. 1936). The overseas aspects of the wars of 1739–48 are best followed in H. W. Richmond, *The Navy in the War of 1739–48*, 3 vols. (Cambridge 1920). An excellent general account of the period is W. L. Dorn, *Competition for Empire 1740–1763*, edn with rev. bibliography (London 1963).

Chapter 4

The standard work on Anglo-French rivalry from 1748 to 1763 is L. H. Gipson, *The British Empire before the American Revolution*, Vols. VI–VIII, *The Great War for the Empire* (New York 1946–54). J. S. Corbett, *England in the Seven Years' War*, 2 vols. (London 1907) remains of some value. G. M. Wrong, *The Rise and Fall of New France* (New York 1928) is another older book still of service. The best account of the siege of Quebec is C. P. Stacey, *Quebec, 1759: the siege and the battle* (Toronto 1959). The multi-volume work on the North American campaigns by the American historian Francis Parkman is now generally superseded, but is still well worth reading for its detail and dramatic narrative quality. A selection from it, *France and England in North America*, has been edited by S. E. Morison (London 1956). The second volume of the most recent full-scale biography of the Elder Pitt, O. A. Sherrard, *Pitt and the Seven Years' War* (London 1955) is frankly adulatory; a more critical view of Pitt as a war leader is taken in Stanley Pargellis's short introduction to *Military Affairs in North America 1748–1765: Selected Documents from the Cumberland Papers in Windsor Castle* (American Historical Association: New York 1936). A careful monograph on the Caribbean fighting is Marshall Smelser, *The Campaign for the Sugar Islands, 1759* (Chapel Hill 1955). Two articles by Allan Christelow analyse the Anglo-Spanish conflict: 'The Economic Background of the Anglo-Spanish War of 1762', *Journal of Modern History*, XVIII (1946), and 'French Interest in the Spanish Empire during the Ministry of the Duc de Choiseul, 1759–

1771', *Hispanic American Historical Review*, XXI (1941). There is no completely satisfactory account of the Peace of Paris: the best study of the negotiations from the British and French viewpoints is Z. E. Rashed, *The Peace of Paris 1763* (Liverpool 1951).

Chapter 5

For those with little previous knowledge of Indian history, Michael Edwardes, *A History of India from the Earliest Times to the Present Day* (London 1961) is a readable introduction. Vincent A. Smith, *The Oxford History of India*, 3rd edn by Percival Spear (Oxford 1958) deals concisely in Book VII with the activities of the British in India during the eighteenth century. Vol. IV of *The Cambridge History of the British Empire*, *British India 1497–1858* (Cambridge 1929) covers the same ground more fully. The chapter on Dupleix and Bussy is of particular value, being written by Alfred Martineau, author of the standard works on the French in India during this period, *Dupleix et l'Inde française*, 4 vols. (Paris 1920–8) and *Les Dernières années de Dupleix* (Paris 1928). Henry Herbert Dodwell, *Dupleix and Clive: the Beginning of Empire* (London 1920) is a detailed narrative. A. M. Davies, *Clive of Plassey* (London 1939) is by contrast a popular biography. A more astringent work than any of these pro-European studies is K. M. Pannikar, *Asia and Western Dominance* (London 1953), which examines in highly critical fashion European activities in Asia generally. The East India Company's rise to economic predominance in Bengal is analysed in Sukumāra Bhaṭṭāchārya, *The East India Company and the Economy of Bengal from 1704 to 1740* (London 1954). A substantially different version of the Black Hole incident from that normally given in English text-books will be found in B. K. Gupta, *Sirajuddaullah and the East India Company, 1756–1757* (Leiden 1962). S. P. Sen, *The French in India 1763–1816* (Calcutta 1958) has excellent introductory chapters on the Indian political scene and Anglo-French rivalry in India before 1763.

Chapter 6

Apart from the works mentioned above, D. G. E. Hall, *A History of South-East Asia*, 2nd edn (London 1964) is a valuable reference work covering a vast area. Two biographies of Warren Hastings which can be recommended are Edward Penderel Moon, *Warren Hastings and British India* (London 1947) and Keith Feiling's weightier study, *Warren Hastings* (London 1954). Macaulay's essay on Hastings is of literary and historiographical interest. Anglo-French naval hostilities are dealt with in magisterial fashion by H. W. Richmond, *The Navy in India 1763–1783* (London 1931). G. D. Bearce, *British Attitudes towards India 1784–1858* (London 1961) is a trenchant study. On British activities, official and unofficial, in India and regions farther east, V. T. Harlow, *The Founding of the Second British Empire 1763–1793*, 2 vols. (London 1952–64) is a mine of information. Some of the conclusions of the first volume of this work are challenged in Peter Marshall, 'The First and Second British Empires: A Question of Demarcation', *History*, XLIX (1964). The Macartney mission to China can be followed in the ambassador's own journal, recently edited by J. L. Cranmer-Byng, *An Embassy to China* (London 1962). The East India Company's China trade is dissected by E. H. Pritchard, *The Crucial Years of Early Anglo-Chinese Relations 1750–1800* (Washington 1936). Two books dealing with the growth of European interest in China are W. W. Appleton, *A Cycle of Cathay* (New York 1951) and Hugh Honour, *Chinoiserie: the Vision of Cathay* (London 1961). The first volume of E. S. de Klerck, *History of the Netherlands East Indies*, 2 vols. (Rotterdam 1938) covers the period up to 1802. The tangled course of Anglo-Dutch diplomatic negotiations over eastern territories and trade is traced in Nicholas Tarling, *Anglo-Dutch Rivalry in the Malay World 1780–1824* (Cambridge 1962).

Chapter 7

Good introductions to the Pacific discoveries of the eighteenth century are J. C. Beaglehole, *The Exploration of the Pacific*, 2nd edn (London 1947), J. A. Williamson, *Cook and the Opening of the Pacific* (London 1946), and John Dunmore, *French Explorers in the Pacific*, I (London 1965). A more specialist work on French trading activities in the Pacific in the early part of the century is E. W. Dahlgren, *Les Relations commerciales et maritimes entre la France et les côtes de l'Ocean Pacifique*, I (Paris 1909). Dampier's accounts of his wanderings are to be found in John Masefield (ed.), *The Voyages of*

Captain William Dampier, 2 vols. (London 1906). British attempts to find a North-west Passage are examined in Glyndwr Williams, *The British Search for the Northwest Passage in the Eighteenth Century* (London 1962). Advances in navigational techniques are discussed in J. B. Hewson, *A History of the Practice of Navigation* (Glasgow 1951) and in an article by R. T. Gould, 'John Harrison and his Time-keepers', *Mariner's Mirror*, XXI (1935).

The Journals of Captain James Cook on His Voyages of Discovery are being published for the Hakluyt Society, splendidly edited by J. C. Beaglehole with introductions which are authoritative studies in their own right. Two volumes have been published to date: *The Voyage of the Endeavour 1768–1771* (Cambridge 1955) and *The Voyage of the Resolution and Adventure 1772–1775* (Cambridge 1961). The journals of other British Pacific explorers of the period which have been published for the Hakluyt Society include R. E. Gallagher (ed.), *Byron's Journal of his Circumnavigation 1764–1766* (Cambridge 1964) and Helen Wallis (ed.), *Carteret's Voyage round the World 1766–1769*, 2 vols. (Cambridge 1965). J. E. Martin-Allanic has written a monumental life of Bougainville which includes a detailed examination of French attitudes towards the discovery voyages after 1763, *Bougainville navigateur et les découvertes de son temps*, 2 vols. (Paris 1964). The Spanish expeditions to Tahiti have been dealt with in B. G. Corney (ed.), *The Quest and Occupation of Tahiti by Emissaries of Spain during the years 1772–1776* (Hakluyt Society. London 1913–19). Among a number of books dealing with the Spanish advance northward from New Spain a good general account is Charles E. Chapman, *A History of California: The Spanish Period* (New York 1923). Russian activities in the North Pacific are described by F. A. Golder, *Russian Expansion on the Pacific 1641–1850* (Cleveland 1914), and S. R. Tompkins and M. L. Moorhead, 'Russia's Approach to America. Part I: From Russian Sources 1741–61. Part II: From Spanish Sources 1761–75', *British Columbia Historical Quarterly*, XIII (1949). The diplomatic implications of the Nootka crisis have been investigated by W. R. Manning, *The Nootka Sound Controversy* (Annual Report of American Historical Association for 1904: Washington 1905). For this, as for many aspects of British imperial history in the late eighteenth century, Harlow, *op. cit.*, is essential reading. An account of the early settlements in New South Wales will be found in any standard history of Australia: a recent and highly individualistic one is C. M. H. Clark,

A History of Australia, Vol. I, *From the Earliest Times to the Age of Macquarie* (Cambridge 1962).

Chapter 8

The colonial implications of Anglo-Spanish and Franco-Spanish relations in the period after 1763 are examined in two excellent articles in the *Hispanic American Historical Review*: Vera Lee Brown, 'Anglo-Spanish Relations in America in the Closing Years of the Colonial Era', V (1922), and A. S. Aiton, 'Spanish Colonial Reorganization under the Family Compact', XII (1932). The dispute over the Falkland Islands is examined in Julius Goebel, *The Struggle for the Falkland Islands* (New Haven 1927); also in Martin-Allanic, *op. cit.*

The American Revolution and the War of Independence have given rise to a vast literature of which only the briefest selection can be given here. Two reliable studies of the causes of the Revolution are L. H. Gipson, *The Coming of the Revolution 1763–1775* (New York 1954) and J. C. Miller, *Origins of the American Revolution*, rev. edn (Stanford 1959). Esmond Wright, *Fabric of Freedom 1763–1800* (London 1965) is a thoughtful study covering a longer period. B. Knollenberg, *Origin of the American Revolution: 1759–1766* (New York 1960) is particularly useful because of the emphasis given to the years before 1763. Among books dealing with specific aspects of the Revolutionary period are: O. M. Dickerson, *The Navigation Acts and the American Revolution* (Philadelphia 1951); E. S. and H. M. Morgan, *The Stamp Act Crisis* (Chapel Hill 1953); J. M. Sosin, *Whitehall and the Wilderness: The Middle West in British Colonial Policy 1760–1775* (Lincoln, Nebraska 1961). Collections of speeches and documents bearing on the Revolution have been gathered together in compact form by S. E. Morison, *Sources and Documents illustrating the American Revolution 1764–1788 and the formation of the Federal Constitution*, 2nd edn (Oxford 1929) and Max Beloff, *The Debate on the American Revolution 1761–1783*, 2nd edn (London 1960). A straightforward account of the American War of Independence is J. R. Alden, *The American Revolution 1775–1783* (New York 1954). A brief, lucid account of Washington's leadership will be found in Esmond Wright, *Washington and the American Revolution* (London 1957). Piers Mackesy, *The War for America 1775–1783* (London 1964) is a masterly exposition of the war and its problems from the viewpoint of the British government. S. F. Bemis, *The Diplomacy of the American Revolution*, 2nd edn (Bloomington 1957) and Harlow, *op. cit.*, deal with the diplomacy of the war and with the peace negotiations. Harlow has an especially good section on Shelburne's policy during the negotiations.

An invaluable guide to works on the Spanish colonial empire for non-Spanish readers is R. A. Humphreys, *Latin American History: A Guide to the Literature in English* (London 1958). The eighteenth-century empire is set in perspective in a brief book by George Pendle, *A History of Latin America* (Harmondsworth 1963). Two longer general histories, with particularly good sections on the colonial period, are H. M. Bailey and A. P. Nasatir, *Latin America: The Development of its Civilization* (London 1960) and J. E. Fagg, *Latin America: A General History* (New York 1963). Among older studies still of service are Bernard Moses, *Spain's Declining Power in South America 1730–1806* (Berkeley 1919) and H. I. Priestley, *José de Gálvez, Visitor-General of New Spain 1765–1771* (Berkeley 1916). A recent study of an important administrative innovation in the empire is John Lynch, *Spanish Colonial Administration 1782–1810: The Intendant System in the Viceroyalty of the Río de la Plata* (London 1958). Brazil in the first half of the eighteenth century is described in C. R. Boxer, *The Golden Age of Brazil 1695–1750* (Berkeley and Los Angeles 1962), but there is no good companion-study in English for the second half of the century. Nor is there any adequate biography in English of Pombal – Marcus Cheke, *Dictator of Portugal: A Life of the Marquis of Pombal 1699–1782* (London 1938) has only a few pages on Pombal's colonial policy. Several of the essays in H. V. Livermore (ed.), *Portugal and Brazil* (Oxford 1953) have information on the eighteenth century; and general histories of Latin America (including those listed above) normally have sections on colonial Brazil.

On the rise of anti-colonial sentiments in France the standard work is C. L. Lokke, *France and the Colonial Question: A Study of Contemporary French Opinion 1763–1801* (New York 1932). An abridgement of the third edition of the Abbé Raynal's *Histoire philosophique des Deux Indes*, with notes and an introduction, will be found in Gabriel Esquer, *L'Anticolonialisme au* XVIIIe *siècle* (Paris 1951). The early anti-colonial movement in Britain is concisely described in the opening chapters of R. L. Schuyler, *The Fall of the Old Colonial System: A*

Study in British Free Trade 1770–1870 (London 1945). Adam Smith's *Wealth of Nations* is available in several modern editions, including a paperback reprint of the 1904 two-volume edition with introduction and notes by E. Cannan.

Chapter 9

Developments within the French colonial empire between 1793 and 1815 – with particular emphasis on events in Saint Domingue and Napoleon's objectives in Egypt and Louisiana – are described at length in J. F. Saintoyant, *La Colonisation française pendant la Révolution 1789–1799*, 2 vols. (Paris 1930) and *La Colonisation française pendant la période napoléonienne 1799–1815* (Paris 1931). Two books which illustrate the range of interpretation which Toussaint l'Ouverture's career has provoked are T. L. Stoddard's mainly unsympathetic study, *The French Revolution in San Domingo* (New York 1914) and Ralph Korngold's adulatory *Citizen Toussaint* (London 1945). A moderate and scholarly treatment of the slave revolt of 1791 will be found in the opening section of J. G. Leyburn, *The Haitian People* (New Haven 1941).

J. C. Herold has related the story of Napoleon's Egyptian adventure in *Bonaparte in Egypt* (London 1962). Napoleon's policy on Louisiana is thoroughly examined in E. Wilson Lyon, *Louisiana in French Diplomacy 1759–1804* (Norman 1934). The motives for Baudin's expedition to the Pacific are dealt with in the opening chapters of J.-P. Faivre, *L'Expansion française dans le Pacifique de 1800 à 1842* (Paris 1953). Overseas aspects of the wars between Britain and France are conveniently summarized in two chapters in *The Cambridge History of the British Empire*, II (Cambridge 1940) by J. Holland Rose: 'The Conflict with Revolutionary France, 1793–1802', and 'The Struggle with Napoleon, 1803–1815'.

R. A. Humphreys's bibliography should again be referred to for a selection of books in English on the revolt of the Spanish American colonies. The early chapters in Humphreys's own book, *The Evolution of Modern Latin America* (Oxford 1946), provide an excellent introduction to the subject. The authoritative biography of Miranda is by W. S. Robertson, *The Life of Miranda*, 2 vols. (Chapel Hill 1929). J. B. Trend has written a useful short study on *Bolívar and the Independence of Spanish America* (London 1946). The introduction in C. K. Webster (ed.), *Britain and the Independence of Latin America, 1812–1830*, 2 vols. (London 1938) traces the British role in the wars of independence. Britain's commercial influence in Brazil before and during the colony's move towards independence is examined in A. K. Manchester, *British Preëminence in Brazil: Its Rise and Decline* (Chapel Hill 1933).

P. E. Roberts, *India under Wellesley* (London 1929) is a careful and scholarly study of British expansion in India at the turn of the century. A different side of British activity is dealt with in Holden Furber, *John Company at Work: A Study of European Expansion in India in the late eighteenth century* (Cambridge, Mass. 1948), which examines in detail the Company's trade. C. N. Parkinson, *War in the Eastern Seas 1793–1815* (London 1954) sketches the hostilities of the period. The fullest biography of Raffles is C. E. Wurtzburg, *Raffles of the Eastern Isles* (London 1954). A monograph by John Bastin, *The Native Policies of Sir Stamford Raffles in Java and Sumatra* (Oxford 1957) draws on both English and Dutch sources.

A warmly sympathetic account of the abolitionist movement will be found in Reginald Coupland, *The British Anti-Slavery Movement*, 2nd edn, with introduction by J. D. Fage (London 1964). Coupland's approach is vigorously criticized in Eric Eustace Williams, *Capitalism and Slavery* (reprinted London 1964), where the relationship between changing economic factors and the acceptance of abolition is stressed. The best general study of the West Indian slave-owners' position remains L. J. Ragatz, *The Fall of the Planter Class in the British Caribbean 1763–1833* (New York 1928). Extracts from Mungo Park's journals are included in C. Howard and J. H. Plumb (ed.), *West African Explorers* (London 1951). The motives and achievements of the African Association are scrutinized in A. Adu Boahen, *Britain, the Sahara and the Western Sudan, 1788–1861* (Oxford 1964).

The standard work on British policy at the 1814–15 peace negotiations is C. K. Webster, *The Foreign Policy of Castlereagh 1812–1815* (London 1931). The most recent and authoritative guide through the complexities of trade statistics is Phyllis Deane and W. A. Cole, *British Economic Growth 1688–1959: Trends and Structure* (Cambridge 1962).

Index

The numbers in bold are the reference nos. of the illustrations